S0-CLI-260

D1520243

UNDERCURRENTS OF INFLUENCE IN ENGLISH ROMANTIC POETRY

UNDERCURRENTS

OF INFLUENCE IN ENGLISH ROMANTIC POETRY

BY

MARGARET SHERWOOD

PH.D. (YALE UNIVERSITY), L.H.D. (NEW YORK UNIVERSITY)
PROFESSOR EMERITUS, WELLESLEY COLLEGE

Essay Index Reprint Series

BOOKS FOR LIBRARIES PRESS
FREEPORT, NEW YORK

First published 1934
Reprinted 1968

PR 571
.S5
1968

LIBRARY OF CONGRESS CATALOG CARD NUMBER:
68-26474

PRINTED IN THE UNITED STATES OF AMERICA

[We] may not hope from outward forms to win
The passion and the life whose fountains are within.

Coleridge: *Ode to Dejection.*

FOREWORD

THESE essays, relating some of the imaginative interpretations of life in a few of the poets in the great period preceding our own to certain trends of thought, chiefly evolutionary, dominant in our own, and tracing, in informal fashion, the genesis of these ideas, as applied to aspects of intellectual and spiritual life, in the eighteenth century, are meant to be suggestive, not fully demonstrative. They in no way constitute a treatise, but are a series of appreciations, founded upon thought developed during work done for many years in a seminar in English Romanticism, and a course in nineteenth century English poetry in Wellesley College. No claim is made that the earlier writers were the first to state these ideas, only that they stated them well, and in a manner that became greatly influential. In suggesting the influence of an earlier author upon a poet's mind, no attempt is made to point out all the influences that may have affected him. If there is something of repetition, this is due to the fact that each essay was intended to stand by itself.

The word evolution and the word philosophy are used in their earlier, larger, not later and narrower meanings. Evolution, by its root meaning an *unfolding*, is as rightly applied to the inner life, to growth in matters intellectual and spiritual, as to the physical development of man and the universe. Philosophy, literally a love of wisdom, may well still be interpreted by us in the Greek sense, as an application of truth to life; fortunately not all wisdom is comprised in rationalized proof of abstract ideas.

Thanks are due to Mr. Jacks, Editor of *The Hibbert Journal*, for permission to reprint the essay here entitled: *Wordsworth; "The Imaginative Will."*

Deep gratitude is hereby expressed to my friend and colleague of many years, Professor Martha Hale Shackford, for unwearied patience in listening to these essays, encouraging criticism, and invaluable help in reading proof.

M. S.

WELLESLEY
June, 1934

CONTENTS

study Shelley

UNDERCURRENTS OF INFLUENCE IN ENGLISH ROMANTIC POETRY

I

A GREAT TRANSITION PERIOD

NO ONE can read the poetry of the late eighteenth and the early nineteenth century in England without being aware that it has a certain freshness and vitality, such as that in branches and twigs flushing with new life in early spring, when sap runs swiftly. There is a radiance in its beauty when the sense of new life meets perfect expression, as in the lyrics of Blake, and the best of Burns and of Wordsworth, but it shines out also through broken and imperfect forms. Something indeed like the quivering life of a wakening world thrilled through men's consciousness in this great creative period, manifesting itself in lyric, in dramatic, in narrative, and in reflective verse, in a greatly widened and deepened range of thought and of feeling. At that moment Mother Earth might well have spoken, as in *Prometheus Unbound*, of new energy, running down

> Even to the adamantine central gloom
> Along these marble nerves; 'tis life, 'tis joy,
> And through my withered, old, and icy frame
> The warmth of an immortal youth shoots down.

Under the flowering in the literature great forces were astir, manifesting themselves also in life and action; the vitality, emotional, intellectual, and spiritual that one finds in the poets draws from deep sources; it was a period of swift development in men's thought in the philosophic, the scientific, the political world.

The fact that the poets turned again to lyric forms, after a period when little need had been felt of this method of expression, is significant; the heroic couplet indeed proved inadequate to voice the fine shades of thought and of feeling which formed part of the new awakening. Equally significant is the extension of the lyric, the widening of the field of musical thought; many a thought, many an emotion hardly voiced before finds poignant expression; new themes, new insights appear, for the coming of the lyric means always fresh discovery of life; old forms come again to life to serve as modes of expression of fresh experience. The thrill of human life in Burns:

> And I will luve thee still, my dear,
> Till a' the seas gang dry;

the thrill of spirit life in Blake:

> I heard an Angel singing
> When the day was springing:
> "Mercy, Pity, Peace
> Is the world's release";

and the blending of the two in Wordsworth:

> Enough, if something from our hands have power
> To live, and act, and serve the future hour;
> And if, as toward the silent tomb we go,
> Through love, through hope, and faith's transcendent dower,
> We feel that we are greater than we know,

bring fresh feeling, fresh thought flowing in new and delicate music through old forms.

The note of the lyric, as of all other life at this significant period of the world's history is freedom, — here, freedom to express individual thought and feeling in one's own way. In much of it the language, in its simplicity and its expressiveness, seems as if newly created to voice the exquisite freshness of experience, and the lyric comes again to its own, in spontaneity such as that of primitive song, or of Elizabethan days, with breadth, originality, as in the latter, but with a difference. During the long reflective period of the eighteenth century man's mind had turned inward; the profound tragic experience of the French Revolution had left its mark on mind and spirit; if the lyric work of this period has much of joy, it has much of that keener life which is pain; in both, it bears the marks of man's deepening experience. It is, in Blake, Wordsworth, Shelley, and Keats, intellectual as well as emotional; for all its spontaneity of feeling it carries a burden of thought which is no longer a burden, as in some of the seventeenth century metaphysical lyrics, for here intense thought and intense feeling are one, and one with the music of the verse.

As the lyric brings its haunting suggestions of thought, emotion plays its quickening part in the reflective poetry. New and great philosophical, great social and political conceptions are presented in the form of verse, and the poet starts out to conquer new realms in the inner life of man:

> The intellectual power, through words and things,
> Went sounding on, a dim and perilous way!

A sense of the mystery and the greatness of existence seeks for expression; a new awareness is manifest in the verse of reality beyond the realm of sense, as if the separating veil were growing thin. Wordsworth, in *The Prelude*, *The Recluse*, *The Excursion*, pondering the inner problems of man's life and destiny, combines profound thought and feeling in dealing with the subjective aspects of man's life; Shelley, in the *Prometheus*, grappling with objective problems of man's life, social and political problems, under all the rainbow beauty of his imaginative presentation of myth, shows constant, untiring energy of thought, imbued with passionate feeling.

Coleridge, philosopher and theorist of the period in England, bequeathed to posterity but broken and imperfect expressions of searching thought that left untouched few aspects of life and of literature; of the destiny of man, here and hereafter; of the destiny of nations. Yet the air still holds something of the vibration of that wonderful mind which expressed itself most adequately in conversation, wherein, as in his broken verse and some of his prose, deep feeling and individual insight blend with deep thought.

Keats' depth of thought has but slowly won recognition, his readers having been so enthralled by the visible, tangible, audible beauty of his verse that they have failed to find their way to the heart and inner source of it. His endeavor, in *Endymion*, to think out the problem of the idealist poet; in *Hyperion*, to present the deepest of all problems, the tragedy and the hope of perpetual change, show a blending of intellectual and emotional ardor in great originality of insight.

So, in the graver verse of the time, thought, at its best, is touched to deeper penetrative power by emotion, emotion by thought, and a haunting phrase of Wordsworth suggests a new idea of mental power, different from that of an age that had enthroned reason alone:

> he whose soul hath risen
> Up to the height of feeling intellect.

The age which recognized and stated, in Wordsworth, conviction of emotion as a factor in finding truth, made a definite step forward in the science of mind, and in the art of living.

It is, perhaps, in a certain intensity, an ardor of thought, as well as in the searching out of profounder problems, that the reflective poetry of the period differs most from the typical reflective verse of the eighteenth century. This intensity in the questioning, in which emotion bears its part, stamps the impress of the thinker on the thought, reveals his individuality. The reflective verse is different from that of the eighteenth century, even when the same subjects are treated. There one finds amiable and leisurely contemplation of the universe from the outside; man, be he Pope,

Brooke, or Akenside, observer and thinker, is a thing apart; in Wordsworth, Shelley, Keats, man is involved in what he contemplates; he is thinking from the inside. The difference is in part due to the fact that life and thought have been molten, welded together in the furnace of the French Revolution; the tragedy, the suffering of those crucial years is still a central energy. In that eighteenth century reflective verse there is conscious intellectuality, playing about abstract themes, religious, philosophic, or other; here, there is a certain urgency, a sense of need to fathom the secret of existence, to understand,— as if man had more at stake in the universe. The poet does not go out, in the fashion of Blair or of Young, to urge thought by the mechanical act of looking at a grave, urging himself to melancholy meditation on life and death and the hereafter; thought presses in upon him; there is passion in his verse; the race, born into intenser life through suffering, faces the challenge of that restatement of the human problem brought by a great war. For illustration, compare the Solitary in Wordsworth's *Excursion*, with any one of the graveyard school of poets; in him the passion of pain and doubt and negation, set off against their mild skepticism or mild assurance, has the validity which experience gives to thought.

But the French Revolution with its aftermath was only one factor in the deepening life; new ways of thought contributed much to it. The interest in the human mind and its ways of working, the attempt at analysis, from Locke and Hume and Hartley, down to the master-philosopher, Kant; and the emotional melancholizing of the reflective graveyard school alike contributed to the "rediscovery of the inner life" that went on in the eighteenth century, as interest in the world of objects deepened into interest in the mind of man in its relation to those objects. An increasing realization of the significance of individual thought and feeling, a search for more complete self-possession, manifested itself, culminating, in England, in Wordsworth's *Prelude*, a study, such as had never before been made, of the growth of a poet's mind in the presence of nature and of human nature. And, as the exploration of the inner world continued, science, busy with interpretation of the outer world, was discovering new attitudes, new points of view, preluding a new manner of thought which was to change the basic conception of the nature of man and of the earth on which he lives. The change, the growing intensity in men's thought, drew from many sources.

Perhaps the most significant aspect of the quickening of all human powers at this period is in the re-awakening of the imagination; English poetry, after a period when this faculty had been in abeyance, coming to its own again in free play of imagination not known since Elizabethan days. The new recognition of its value appears, not only in creative work, but in theory in regard to its nature and its activity, in affirmation of the authority of individual insight. Wordsworth and Coleridge, and, in a later generation, Leigh Hunt, Keats, Shelley, in formal or informal fashion, discuss its operation. Wordsworth and Coleridge laid the foundation in England of the modern conception of the imagination as the supreme faculty of the human mind, the divining power, a power that is able to shape, to create in the light of its divining insight. Man's thought was moving, in new and conscious study of the inner life, toward critical recognition of the influence of one faculty on another, that unity of all human powers, ever manifest in all greatest literatures, but first in this period becoming matter for formulation.

As regards this divining power, it is evident that, in the poetry of this period, though much of it lacks the perfectness of form of the world's great masterpieces, the imagination, in its fulness and its freedom, is working nobly, creating great beauty of a distinctive kind, and that, in Wordsworth, at least, and in Keats, it is conquering new fields in interpreting the mind of man. Of a distinctive kind,— so that one would recognize always a certain type as a product of this era, which differs from other so-called romantic eras, in its power of probing the experience of the individual soul, piercing to the inner world. When has the penetrative imagination, which searches out and finds innermost meanings, been so fully enlisted in the service of human thought? In other kinds of reflective verse we find it working; thought about philosophical and social matters, as well as perception of values of inner experience, is presented in concrete terms, wrought by the imagination. As regards forms of verse, lyric and narrative are more successfully fashioned; the period is but falteringly creative in the matter of drama. Life proves too manysided, too complex in its inner working for the making of framework, of plot, to represent it; the perceptive powers waken so swiftly, on so many sides, that the "shaping power" of imagination can hardly keep the pace. If there is failure here, at times, in the balance and co-ordination that show in the greatest literature which survives the centuries, as in those enduring masterpieces, all the human powers of emotion, intellect, imagination, are working in co-operation. This quickening of all human powers, of emotion, intellect, imagination, results in verse in which we discover widening sympathies, the dignity of deep feeling, the weight of deep thought, and the beauty of divining imaginative insight and expression.

Of that power of penetrating far into the depths of experience in oneself or others; Wordsworth is the deepest exemplification. In the interpretation of man, the peasant, the vagrant, even in the interpretation of the lower orders of the living, of beast and bird, is a feeling as if the human being in some sense shared these different phases of experience; as if the quickened life in the individual had resulted from finding himself part of a larger whole. This apprehension of the larger whole is the basis of the nature poetry of the period; it is this which gave imagination at this time its greatest impetus. The poet, freshly sensitized, became conscious of life, of sympathies, contacts between himself and others of which he had hardly been aware, and his individual existence was expanded by every appreciation of life not his own. Whether he penetrates nature, ancient myth, primitive literature, drawing together present and past in new and conscious sense of relationship, his quickening imagination is reaching out, trying to grasp more of the vast whole, to understand. The result is an enlarging of the range of understanding, a widening and deepening sympathy, quicker perceptions in regard to aspects of experience beyond one's self. Phases of life which had hardly been touched by human emotion, were now, by imaginative insight, brought into the realm of human feeling. Much of the new vitality goes into the discerning of suffering, sympathy with pain:

> Can I see another's woe
> And not be in sorrow too?

Of this sensitiveness, awareness of life vastly shared, there are innumerable instances: in Blake and Wordsworth, the sympathy with suffering children; in Burns, Blake, and Wordsworth, with suffering animals; in Wordsworth, Keats, Shelley, the deep sympathy with suffering men and women. Led by the poets, man reaches out toward a new sense of responsibility for his fellow creatures. Throughout the period, human nature is feeling its way through imaginative insight, quickened by feeling, to a new comprehension of the significance of life. There was, Mr. Herford says, "An extraordinary development of imaginative sensibility. At countless points the universe of sense and thought acquired a new potency of response and appeal to man, a new capacity of ministering to and mingling with his richest and intensest life."

In literature, and sometimes in philosophy, the period is,

for better or worse, defined as the Romantic Period, though it is by no means the only period that could be so characterized. The term is inadequate, as are most terms which are used in critical definition of aspects of literature, but we have no other to express the characteristics of this literature which differs from that of the preceding pseudo-classic period, in free play of imagination, free expression of emotion, liberty or license in the matter of form. In considering the output of this new era we need to get beyond definitions, beyond partisanship for this or that type, into the springs of life and feeling manifest here; to perform that most difficult and delightful of tasks, to understand. In so doing we adopt a method of criticism which first came into being at this time, on a wave of deeper thought, that wide-spread effort to follow growth and development in all things, our aim being, not so much to sit in judgment as to interpret, to enter into the individual author's endeavor, to attempt to understand the way in which both he and the works in which he expresses himself came to be: a study in growth and process.

This is a literature in which manner and matter escape from a recognized pattern or norm into a freedom which often brings new and significant beauty, which at times works havoc with the laws of coherence and of probability. It has its weaknesses; what period has not? In spite of much in it that was attempted but not achieved, it was a great period, one of the greatest of all great literary periods. Perhaps none is fuller of intellectual and spiritual energy, of the very vibration of life. If there is weakness, there is greater strength, strength that comes from a realization of drawing life from deep springs, and that holds high promise for the future. We must not, because some of the followers of the banner of romanticism were guilty of excesses, fail to appreciate its profound significance for us who are inheritors of its discoveries in the world of thought and of feeling. The very excesses were proofs of the profound nature of the convulsion that was going on.

Of the informing spirit and the achievements of that great period of heightened life, the Renaissance, men speak in terms that have almost become a formula, repeated in textbooks, prefacing discussions of any one aspect of that life. The diverse manifestations are pointed out of a vast energy of life which showed itself in vigor of scholarship in the revival of learning, in wide adventure, in great art achievements, in the beginnings of modern science. For one other great period of heightened life, the late eighteenth and the early nineteenth century, a period full of creative activity in many lines, we have no such characterization, no such formula, that will enable the student to grasp something of the central force at work at the heart of this great epoch, and to follow it in its various manifestations in the world of thought, of creative art, of practical achievement. Nor do we hear much of interrelations of all these, of the drawing nearer of different peoples in sharing a common experience of intellectual and creative life even while fighting one another on sea and land. If the underlying characteristics of the period have not been crystallized, as in the case of the Renaissance, it is perhaps, in part, because we are too near, too much involved in the forces at work to clarify, to get the right perspective. The general statement that it was a period of political revolution is made; that it was the time of the romantic movement in literature, but here scholars walk with uncertain feet, few, if any, suggesting how close was the connection between the development in literature, the development in philosophy, and in the political world; how far-reaching, how profound was the revolutionary movement of the time, how deeply it affected all aspects of human thought.

The marvel of the Renaissance is the eager energy showing itself in many different ways; the marvel of the Revolutionary period is its unified character; the manifestations of the new energy are much more one than in the Renaissance. In the Renaissance physical, artistic, intellectual adventure, both humanistic and scientific, is a something centrifugal, speeding out in many directions; in the Revolutionary period, of political, spiritual, intellectual adventure, there is a centripetal tendency. Literature, philosophy, and the world of action are, at this later time, moved as by one mighty impulse,— centering in the thought of man, the study of his inner and his outer conditions vindicating his dignity, a development, preluded by one aspect of Renaissance life, its humanism. In all this there is one central vibration; in going back we get something of the same electric shock, whether we touch expressions of the political, philosophical, or literary life.

It was a period of fundamental upheaval in every department of life, political, social, and in the world of thought; its record is written on the map of Europe, of America, and in Kant's *Critique*; in the annals of history, of philosophy, of literature. This was the time of the birth of our modern world; of changing thought, political, social, philosophic; of changing forms of government; the depth and energy of the revolutionary movement springing from fresh apprehension of the rights, the powers, the possibilities of man, can hardly be overestimated. No one can tell the whole story of the vast revolution of the time; it was something, in the words of Josiah Royce, "as profound as it was universal, a primary thing."

Within few years there was swift development, such as some scientists tell us are revealed in the earth's surface, as if the mysterious inner forces ever at work felt a special urgency, a quickening of the pulse of nature, as, after a period of quiescence, came a time of rush and stir. Perhaps evolution uses revolution; earth's surface would seem to suggest this. It was, intellectually, one of the periods of deeper discovery, creative moments, that make one wonder if Nature has her own inspired times of lifting the curtain; as if, in the long development of humanity, as in that of individuals, there are periods more vital than others; moments of living insight, intellectual and spiritual; moments of insistent life that will not be denied. A period of vast changes; of a deepening sense of life and the values of life; a period of great suffering; a period of great hopes; on the one hand, the tragedy, the excesses of the French Revolution, the misgivings that rose therefrom; on the other, the creative mood of youth, revealed by Wordsworth:

> Bliss was it in that dawn to be alive: . . .
>
> Why should I not confess that Earth was then
> To me, what an inheritance, new-fallen
> Seems, when the first time visited, to one
> Who thither comes to find in it his home.

If there was joy, there were also throes of great agony, but it was the exultant agony of an era coming to birth.

Life upon earth is always full of contradictions; if one must think of this as a moment of swift and passionate change, one must think of it also as the outcome of slow forces, long at work, now moving in quickened *tempo*. Many influences from the past converged in this period of vast upheavals, of wakening hopes; dogma was shaken in matters of church, state, society, literature, by forces long preparing. Revolutionary influences came from France, from Rousseau, with his revolt against civilization, his plea to return to a state of nature, his glorification of emotion versus thought; his passionate denunciation of life as organized by man, his great affirmation of government as resting on the will of the governed; from Voltaire, with his pungent satire on insincerities and sham, his bitter attacks on religious dogma, especially that of the Roman Catholic Church, — Voltaire the humanist, who pleaded for liberty of thought and conduct, and protested against cruelties and wrongs; from the Encyclopedists led by Diderot with their attacks on the laws, as framed and administered, on the injustice of existing taxes, on the slave trade. A very wind of changing thought, swept away abuses; skepticism led to deeper inquiry; it was a tearing down before rebuilding; constructive theories, practical or not practical, were worked out, as that of Condorcet, whose dream was of perfectibility. England was not far behind: Thomas Paine, that "undaunted soldier in the war of the liberation of humanity," affirmed in his *Rights of Man* (1791) that these rights are God-given rights, that men are born free and equal. Paine for his *Age of Reason*, was, like Voltaire, branded as an atheist; though like him, he was a Deist,— as well as a humanitarian who pleaded for justice to man and beast. In the work of these two men, those theologians who had attempted to force religion to the littleness of mere reason, of formal logic, had their right retribution. Important in the period was William Godwin, who, following Rousseau, wished to abolish all institutions of church and of state, convinced that, if all that which had been,— which was all wrong,— could be swept away, all that which would come to be would be right.

One would but despair in attempting to point out all the intellectual forces operative in the eighteenth century, growing more potent toward its close; it is not ours to trace in detail the great political and social changes, the changing thought in religion and philosophy, but to follow some aspects of the gradual expansion of man's thought and feeling as manifested in the literature of the period, seeking to find the causes of this fresh realization of the significance of individual experience, this wakening faith in the validity of individual insight, imagination. There was a deepening sense of the meaning and the mystery of life; a deepening sense of its potential beauty. Of vast influence throughout the century was a poetic-philosophic idealism, that had stolen into seventeenth century thought through the Cambridge Platonists, and had been popularized by Shaftesbury, drawing from ancient sources, Platonic and Neo-Platonic, ideas concerning the soul's development. Plotinus' belief that there is a seed of the incorruptible divine in every creature, may well have contributed something to the growing consciousness of the inherent dignity of man.

The most important movement in thought was that in philosophy; there is, perhaps, no more significant moment in the whole history of philosophy. Greatest of the thinkers who represent the forces at work at the heart of the period was Kant, whose philosophy marks the deepest phase of the revolutionary impulse of the period, transferring the seat of authority for knowledge from the world without to the world within. Against the theory of innate ideas, curiously implanted in the human mind, mechanically working; against the contradictory doctrine of Hume, denying the existence of such ideas, affirming that we have only momentary shattered states of thought, Kant opposed his doctrine of the integrity and activity of the individual mind, of the power of the mind to weave together impressions, so giving unity and validity to thought. In his interpretation of space and time, not as objective realities, but as subjective modes of perception, the center of the universe changed from without to within. This quiet man of method, from whose daily walks the inhabitants of Königsberg set their watches, brought about, in the realm of thought, a world-wide revolution, turning the universe, not inside out but outside in. In this great philosophic idealism is expressed belief in the supremacy of the individual in the intellectual world, in the moral world. To Kant the mind of man is creative interpreter, in space and time forms, of the universe in which he lives by virtue of birth; the will of man, the moral sense of man, who owes allegiance not to outer rule but to his consciousness of inner responsibility, is creator of that spiritual world in which he lives by virtue of choice. It is a dynamic theory, bearing witness to the power of both the intellect and the will of man.

In the world of science, of natural philosophy, came an equally significant dawn of change. An idea, one of the most fortunate of all that have suggested themselves as solutions of the problem of human existence, was taking hold of the minds of a few advanced thinkers,— the idea of the constant change in all life, not as mere mutability, irrational, aimless, as in the conception of some of the ancients, but as growth, progress, based on law. The organic idea came slowly into being; the conception of the universe as one living whole; of the life of man in all its varied aspects as part of this great whole; with this, the idea of development; of inherent law, working out great results. If, in the political world, faiths were held and hopes were wakened which, later, somewhat failed and darkened in the reaction, through all this period the saving conception was coming into being of the slowness and surety of man's development, as slow as sure. Over-ardent hopes had skipped too eagerly to the goal, but the same period brought to saner, keener minds the sanity of corrective thought; and the age which had put its faith in revolution brought its own antidote in the birth of the idea of evolution, tempering the swiftness and impatience of belief in the efficacy of sudden change with some conception of the illimitable aeons required for human development:

Time, that aged nurse,
Rocked me to patience.

For the idea that was wakening was to change man's whole way of interpreting the earth and his life upon it. To the tentative evolutionary theories of the time both scientist and philosopher contributed, and shade by shade, the great conception gathered. Of great importance in this connection is the name of Johann Gottfried Herder, "a liberal prophet of the modern natural philosophy," who, conceiving all life as fundamentally one, gave, in his *Philosophy of History* (1784–1791), an interpretation of life from its first dawn as progress from lower to higher, an endless development, in which the later stages depended on the lower. So came a growing apprehension of a living oneness of nature; of a vital continuity in phenomena, and of unceasing progress as the inner law of life. That early thought of evolution was groping, tentative; there was lack of adherence on the part of some of the greatest scientists, but there was subtle suggestion, far-reaching influence of these ideas working in the minds of both scientists and natural philosophers, and, through the latter, in the case of Herder, upon the humanists. To Herder the physical universe was one vast, developing whole, informed by spirit, acting both within it and above. In the mind of this thinker, and it came to be the case with others, the physical conception went hand in hand with a spiritual conception, which supplements and completes that increasing tendency throughout a great part of the eighteenth century, manifest in the philosophy and in the poetry, to study and to express the inner life of man. While scientists were eagerly studying that which went on without, in the world of physical phenomena, to other thinkers, that which went on within was of increasing importance. In the great conception of Herder, of infinite spirit, working throughout all matter and through human consciousness, the two streams met, to flow later through the philosophy of Hegel, the poetry of Browning.

As the lyrics of the period bring a note of spring, so the wakening thought of the period recaptures something of the freshness of the early world. The early Greek physicist philosophers, who first taught the world to think, had an idea of the oneness and the growth of things; the new conception, as is the way within the world of thought, was an old idea, revived, developed, profounded. The race but repeats individual experience. As the thinker, by slow logical process, often reaches a point which he discovers to be the same truth as that of which he had caught a glimpse in a first swift intuition, so, it may be, the experienced, thought-weary world, went back to that early, intuitive grasp of truth, and began to develop it, with the intellectual skill and resource won from centuries of thinking. And the measure of growth from those primitive days to our own may be found in the spiritual conception which was the fine flower of this idea of the universe as one vast living whole.

Not only in science, in tentative evolutionary theories of the time, is man drawing near to earth in conscious recognition of relationship; poetry too shows human consciousness as deeply aware of man's relationship to earth, not as a mere walker on its surface, but as stirred by its winds and tides. Earth was bone of his bone, flesh of his flesh,— this had been known from old time, but hardly understood; now, new voices were beginning to say, spirit of his spirit. *Genesis* had told of physical relationship; now there was a wakening sense that the God who walked in the garden in the cool of the day spoke, not in a voice apart, but, mysteriously, in the very murmur of the leaves, in the breezes abroad in the grass, in the waving branches of the Tree of Life, in the rippling of the stream.

Of this stir of kindred consciousness in the whole visible, audible world, Wordsworth was the deepest exponent. One finds in his poetry expression of those mysterious sympathies extending as far as the farthest reach of human thought, and farther. Here is direct consciousness of unity of being; subtle response between the life within and the life without.

The prevailing spirit of a period may manifest itself, not only in conscious thought, expressed as critical or philosophical doctrine, but perhaps unconsciously, in mood, as revealed in lyric verse. Blake may have been unaware of the ideas which the natural philosophers were formulating, but the mind of man is often influenced, perhaps by means of vibrations in the ether as yet undetected, without the aid of spoken or written word, of what is in the minds of other men. Surely Blake's thought and feeling of intense energy, life, activity throughout the universe, expressed in the prophetic books, in all his interpretation of man, of animal, of flower, reveals imaginative perception in accord with the affirmation of creative impulse ceaselessly at work in all life. The idea of nothing as fully created, but of a constant act of creation going on, is suggested, in profound spiritual import in Blake's idea of Heaven, not as a place in which all sins are forgiven, but in which they are constantly being forgiven:

> And throughout all Eternity
> I forgive you, you forgive me.

In the deep stirring of men's minds at this period ideas were flashed out by poets and developed by philosophers which have widened and deepened for all time the current of intellectual and emotional life, and have become part of our enduring heritage, underlying our thought in all departments of human knowledge, both humanistic and scientific, determining our methods: the organic idea; the conception of the universe as one living whole; of the life of man, in all its varied aspects, as organic,— part of a great whole; the idea of a law of development operating throughout the universe, apparent not only in the physical but in the intellectual and spiritual being of man. Men were turning from the static conceptions of earlier centuries to a dynamic interpretation of the universe; from the conception of immutable laws, imposed from without, to a conception of an inner law of being, working within, through vital processes. There was not only a broadening and deepening, but a changing of the very texture of thought; rationalistic definition was giving way to alert curiosity. Humanity was on its way to a new synthesis, from a sense of man as created to a sense of man as coming to be. The change was indeed, in the period to come, to dominate not only man's mind but his imagination, bringing a new and different way of perceiving and interpreting existence. In Browning, Meredith, and others, evolutionary theories become the very stuff and substance of their imaginative rendering of life.

So we watch in this period the slow coming of a conception which was to revolutionize man's way of interpreting himself and his environment, in this universe of which he is discovering that he is an integral part; his way of interpreting, not only the earth under his feet, but history, religion, language, literature. The discovery of a law of growth in all aspects of man's intellectual and spiritual, as well as his physical life, was to transform thought and the ways of thought. The basis of our modern scholarship was laid in these days; in every department of knowledge, actual or potential, the object of the scholar is to find out how things came to be,—an idea so obvious, written so plainly on the face of the green earth in traces of all that had ever lived or moved there, that one wonders why men were so slow in grasping it, in working out its application to all human achievement. The very words, research, investigation, now constantly applied to all processes of humanistic, as well as of scientific study, suggest a wide difference from the dogmatic methods of earlier days.

Germany led the world's thought at this moment, developing the historical method of study, and the name of Herder is most important among the leaders of the period that was being ushered in, in the interpretation of life in all its aspects in terms of growth, which was to be the characteristic method of the nineteenth century. Gleams, hints of the ideas that made for change had appeared in England; the same complex forces were working there; but England was inarticulate as regards sustained formulation, while Germany developed a great philosophic literature, a great critical literature, great scholarship. Yet England, lacking, as usual, a philosophy, had, as usual, a conduct, and the forces becoming apparent in Germany in ideas, conceptions, manifested themselves here in imaginative literature,— all the richer, perhaps, because the critical sense halted behind the creative.

As, in the seventeenth century, government, science, philosophy, literature, derive from one principle, a conception of outer authoritative law, so now philosophy, science, literature, forsaking the rigidity of accepted dogma, go hand in hand, with an air of quest, in search of truth, truth of thought, truth of observation, truth of experience. If one could so far stretch one's imagination as to think of a Botticelli (or a Pollaiuolo?) of this day,— he could have pictured them hand in hand upon their quest, with garments fluttering in the heartening wind that had risen, stepping blithely to a music that their ears have caught, with a look of expectancy upon their faces, like that worn by the young Tobias and the angels, stepping out to follow life and the ways of life, growth and the ways of growth.

Most deeply, perhaps, in the profounder questions regarding the relations of man to man upon the earth, it was the time of the birth of our modern world. If it was a period of intense individualism; if the political world echoed and reechoed the slogan of liberty, equality, fraternity, with emphasis on liberty and equality, the rights of the individual man; if Adam Smith's *Wealth of Nations* (1776) based economic theory on the assertion that human welfare is best assured by leaving man free to carry on individual enterprise as he pleases, every man for himself; if Kant developed the idea of individualism to a point beyond which it could not go, in affirming that man, through action of his mind, is individual interpreter, in time and space forms, of the universe; through his will, creator of his moral world, yet a great truth was making itself manifest, which supplemented and corrected extreme individualism. The word *fraternity* was in that political slogan, and came last possibly because of some sub-conscious sense of its greater importance. It carries with it a suggestion of the bond between man and man, and influences were at work which were to change the conception of the bond, in social and political matters, from outer rule to recognition of inner relationship. As the feudal had slipped into the individualism of the revolutionary period, this was to slip into a sense of organic relationship between man and man,— a new note in human development, or, if not new, an extension into social and political spheres, of a feeling of relationship that had existed only in brotherhoods, or among them who shared a common faith. One of the most interesting aspects of the period is that, in this time of intense individualism,— so like the Elizabethan period in its energy of life, its sense of awakening to possibilities of fulfillment of individual life, so unlike it in its wakening sense of individual responsibility of man for man,— imperceptible forces were beginning to undermine faith in self-centered individualism, leading wiser minds to knowledge that, only in relation to a larger whole than the individual self could the individual reach his full development. It is true that Kant's theory of the mind is an individualistic one; the potent energy of the individual mind acts singly. Yet the "collectivist" idea is in his ethics[1]; man in exerting his will toward good must, of necessity, recognize the whole; must show in his choice the dignity of a law of the universe. If he is an extreme individualist as regards the intellect, in the world of moral endeavor, he is one of a great brotherhood.

In this crucial period of the world's history the increasing fulness of individual life showed, in part, in a widening sense of relationship, an entering into other lives, as if the fullest development of the individual involved also the fullest sharing, bringing more complete fulfilment of one's function in the larger body:

A paradox
That comforts while it mocks.

It is strange, perhaps, to mention, in the world of thought, the name of the young poet Keats soon after the great name of Kant, yet he, not so much through any suggestion of thought from others, as from his own deeply struggling experience —

For what a height my spirit is contending! —

found the solution which he expressed, imperfectly, it is true, in *Endymion* and in *The Fall of Hyperion*, that fulfillment of individuality can come only through entering into, losing the sense of your own life in the life of your fellows.

Many springs fed this growing recognition of the interdependence of all lives,— the poetry of Wordsworth playing its large part in it,— of the oneness, the underlying unity of humanity, which was to flower, in the nineteenth century, not only in theory, as in the philosophy of Carlyle and of Emerson, but in innumerable practical activities. Economists were slow in discovering the inner trend, were not, indeed, aware of it until poets led the way. Shelley anticipated and inspired much of later economic theory, exemplifying his own saying that "Poets are the unacknowledged legislators of the world." The many reforms of the thirties of the nineteenth century, the inexhaustible philanthropies of our day, derive, as from roots, from this period. Deeper roots there are in primitive Christianity, but, on the spiritual side, this idea of organic relationship was in truth, a restatement of the heart of Christianity in philosophic terms: "I am the vine; ye are the branches." The many dogmatists who, in later years, trembled at the word evolution, sure that it attacked the ground work of their faith, were unaware that the spiritual conception of human souls as one, which accompanied, in some minds of finer insight, the physical conception of the universe as one, but reinforced the central idea of Christianity,— that man is not only his brother's keeper, but is, in a fine, mystical sense, his brother.

It is sometimes permitted, by virtue of a power first satisfactorily characterized in this period with which we are dealing, the imagination, to creep back into the heart of another age, feel something of the thrill of life of the time, the forces by which it is animated, hope with its hopes, know something of the ideas which afforded it intellectual satisfaction, as of problems of life in part solved. To enter the world of philosophy, the world of poetry of the late eighteenth and the early nineteenth centuries is to enter a charmèd phase of human thought which it is well to know, for a certain refreshing quality in it, deriving from that central conception of "one life within us and abroad"; to share the great experience, intellectual and spiritual, of feeling oneself a living part of a living universe.

One might well envy the deeper thinkers of the time their joy in discovering that man is not, in reality, a pawn, moved hither and thither in life by irresistible external forces, manifest in outer law, working changelessly, eternally; or a bit of the handiwork of an arbitrary God, set to study, successfully or unsuccessfully, as the case might be, the whim of the Creator, but an active factor in his own destiny in a world of change, a world governed by an inner law of development, with which his concurring will may act in harmony in working out great ends. As men passed from the conception of a universe governed by laws dictated from the outside to a conception of laws working within, they felt a new interest, a deeper concern in life; to this, the nineteenth century, the Victorian Era in England, owes much of its resolute seriousness, which was based upon a conviction of the deep responsibility of the individual for the triumph of the good. Man's deeper thought of God was no longer an abstract conception demanding syllogism, argument, demonstration; he did not need to ask for proof of the existence of God, being part of God. In his will toward good, his insight into it, his struggle toward it, he was aware of a power within him, yet greater than he.

Those lines of Wordsworth, quoted at the outset, might seem potent enough to check the eighteenth century type of theological argument, of proof of truths too high for proof, in their suggestion of the fulness of life that must be lived if one is to find a solution of the problem of existence. It is good to recapture something of this intellectual and emotional apprehension of the fact that man's mind alone is too small for the potential life that is in him; that all faculties of the human being not only may, but must work together in the attainment of truth,— emotion, mind, and the flower of the two, imagination, as well as will: man, organic creature, must use all the powers of his organism to play his part in an organic universe. For, as the slow-coming evolutionary ideas showed that, in the physical world, every creature must call upon all that is in it to win its life, so, in the world of the inner life, man must call upon all that is in him to win. All the faculties of the human being must be brought to bear, in unity of working, upon the problems, temporal and eternal, of man's life, if they are to be solved.

This period, which saw much of the anguish and the tragedy of change in the political world, yet, digging deeper, began to divine the ceaseless change at the heart of things not as meaningless, but as potential progress, an idea that was, through intermediate stages of discovery of the law of growth, in all aspects of man's intellectual as well as his physical life, to develop into a conviction of possibilities of endless progress for mind and soul. An illimitable future opened before him, an infinity of growth. In these ideas which bring hope, and something of the quickening impulse of the march, lies the key to the future, to the deeper interpretations of life in the nineteenth century: Wordsworth, Coleridge, Keats, are touched by them; Shelley in part only; Byron not at all. The philosopher Hegel drew inspiration therefrom. They are the basis of much of Tennyson, of all of Browning, of Meredith.

In a time of disintegration and faltering, an age of analysis, waiting a new synthesis, we may well turn back to this period, with its wakening sense of great life, working in and through all being, fearful of letting go, in the labyrinth of this our life, of something that might prove a genuine clew. So doing, we may recover that assurance of endless progress, hope that lies in a conviction of continuity and progression, of underlying law working toward great ends.

II

SOME PHASES OF DEVELOPMENT OF THOUGHT IN THE WORLD OF LETTERS IN THE EIGHTEENTH CENTURY

I

THE great flowering of poetry in the so-called romantic period of the late eighteenth and the early nineteenth centuries in England was not a sudden portent; growth was swift, but not sudden. More and more the student turns back to the eighteenth century to study origins, trace influences, search out undercurrents of thought, that he may better understand that rich, complex, modern product. Throughout a great part of this century groping for fuller life is revealed in the form and in the content of the poetry that is written; wandering in that world of letters of the mid-eighteenth century is like wandering in the forest when spring draws near, when one hears a faint murmur and rustle of life, everywhere an air of expectancy, of awaiting. As the century goes on there is increasingly a reaching out for fuller existence, a release of human nature from the bonds of convention, a slow liberation of emotion, imagination, and the deeper powers of the human mind. Such conditions prevail only when great ideas are stirring beneath the surface, waiting to emerge.

Today our thought and our imaginative insight are dominated by evolutionary conceptions; our tendency is to interpret all aspects of man's life in terms of growth and development; to think of the past as indissolubly bound up with the present; we are constantly questioning, in every department of thinking, how things came to be. Our literature, our scholarship, our philosophy, our psychology reflect these habits of mind. It is of singular interest to turn back to a period when these ideas did not prevail, to try to trace, in the minds of a few thinkers, incipient stages of these tendencies, to follow the deepening life of the thought of man as his very vocabulary changes from abstract rationalistic terms to terms of growth; fascinating to question whether the tendency which developed into the historical method in the humanities, into the evolutionary conception in science, may not have manifested itself in minor forms, in subtler ways; to question literature here and there to see in how far it reveals the slow changing of the very texture of man's thought, as a consciousness of process, of life opening out endlessly, replaces the desire for abstract finalities of judgment. Back of all the varied apprehensions of growth, of life in things, lies the ground idea of our modern thought, of the oneness of the universe, which finds its spiritual counterpart in the idea of the close interrelatedness of all human lives, society as one; as the idea of physical development, evolution, finds its counterpart in the idea of spiritual evolution. In searching for glimmerings of these ideas in the period to which we turn, no claim is made that the writers in question were the first to suggest them. This is a dangerous assertion to make in regard to any idea, and especially in regard to evolutionary ideas, which go back to the very dawn of man's thought, in Greece.

In the early eighteenth century certain reactionary tendencies begin to appear against the prevailing modes of thought of the preceding century. We of the complex present have difficulty in finding our way back into the simplicity and objectivity of seventeenth century thought, in its dominant trend. One knew where one was in that period; law was law, and conformity was expected of the right-minded citizen. The dogmas of church and of state had the authority of long tradition; science was establishing its creed of unquestionable law throughout the physical universe; kings were upon their thrones, the critics upon theirs, and absolute power in carrying out decrees was as evident in the world of literature as in the political world. It was not, outwardly, a world of perplexity, of mystery; all was clear and aboveboard. Whatever your private reserves, your duty was not to thread your way through intricate mazes of speculation in regard to the ultimate realities, or in regard to matters of right and wrong. Reason was adequate to reach the truth of things; duty was conformity, at least of one's outer or official self, to an objective standard; one gave official consent to creeds established by law. Wandering back to that world of hard, definite mountain outlines and unshaded plains, we should feel as lost in it as did Sir Thomas Browne, with that questioning mind: "I love to lose myself in a mystery; to pursue my reason to an O Altitudo!" . . . "Where there is an obscurity too deep for our reason, 'tis good to sit down with a description, periphrasis, or adumbration."

His distinctive figure, standing in the market-place at Norwich, with a look of whimsical thoughtfulness upon his face, might well symbolize that human instinct that will not down, that is forever alert in periods of dogmatic certainties as in others, searching beyond the found. He was not alone in that seventeenth century in pursuing thought to an *O Altitudo!* but he and his like were not the dominant voices. The seventeenth century had its mystics; the outcast philosopher Spinoza had achieved that which would compel future generations to think more deeply; the thought of Plato and of Plotinus was creeping in through the influential Cambridge group, to become more and more potent in the minds of certain thinkers in later days,— the subtlest and the most pervasive influence helping bring about the romantic movement in literature and in philosophy.

But the dominant note was the note of outer authority. Periods of over-assurance are weather breeders; too clear a sky is a sure token of mysteriously dispersed clouds that gather quickly, and over-confident assertion is the mother of doubt. The coming of new moods, new mental attitudes, new inquiries that meant, in time, the breaking of the certainties, was but natural sequence; submerged currents of thought and feeling began to emerge; men reached out to new ways of conceiving and interpreting life; questioning of every kind of authority went hand in hand with search for deeper truth than any formula, political, scientific, philosophic had yet found. The slow approach of revolution in every department of thought ended, toward the close of the eighteenth century in a period that was revolution indeed. Contemplation of that outer world of illimitable spaces and certain movements that had been gloriously revealed by seventeenth century science was not enough; men became increasingly conscious of realities that the laws of physics did not reach. Reason was supreme, but, in the skepticism of Hume, reason began to doubt itself, inquiring into the nature of the instrument by which these outer facts were known. The trend of speculative thought turned from without to within. In philosophy came a curiosity and desire to probe the nature of the mind, a movement that, toward the end of the century, in the philosophy of Kant, transferred the seat of authority from outer law to the human mind itself. The drift of interest in the world of letters was from objective to subjective; many were filled with longing to explore their own inner experience and that of others, to make conquest of the world within. From that standard of impersonality in the pseudo-classic canon of literature, that endeavor to present, in rendering human experience, only the typical, that which is true of all men, men passed to a belief in the profound significance of the personal reaction to life, the interpretation of the world as individually possessed;

passed, too, from a conception of a law of form, imposed from without, to a conception of individual shaping power, working, imaginatively, from within. In science itself came a movement that, toward the end of the century, brought, not abandonment of the idea of universal law, but discovery that man must dig more deeply into the hidden nature of things to find reality of law; and the static conceptions of the seventeenth century began to give way to a tentative conception of the dynamic, of law at work within the universe, in incessant activity and change, the beginning of the modern idea of evolution. Dogmatic theology trembled, as it trembles still, at the thought of God, changing from that of a power, sitting apart in a long seventh day of rest, to that of a power still mysteriously working within.

Yet seventeenth century philosophy, seventeenth century science alike had their own awe-inspiring sublimities, which stimulated the minds and imaginations of men in ways which we have only partially divined. The vast oneness of all that is was a dominant seventeenth century affirmation; in metaphysics as in science, philosopher and scientist were groping toward the infinite along different trails. Spinoza in his *Ethic* (1677), affirmed the one absolutely infinite substance, God, as the only existence; while the scientific discoveries, the Copernican-Galilean revelation of the vastness of the universe, and of the laws that govern it, stretched the mind of man toward the infinite of the world of matter. To Galileo's proved vision of a vast system, one in its working, in which earth was only an atom, no longer the center of the universe, was added knowledge more significant still. Men's thought was different after Newton discovered the law of gravitation and, in his *Principia* (1687), revealed the interdependence of all that is, body answering body by virtue of an inner bond, reaching from inmost center to inmost center, known in its working but not in its ultimate nature, every atom affecting every other atom. No more important idea was ever launched; it deeply influenced thought, and not scientific thought alone.

Swiftly on the trail of the scientists' "what" followed, as usual, the speculation and affirmation of those who must know "why." Contemplation of the working of the laws of the universe revealed to certain thinkers that the old conception of God, inherited from the Hebrew people, was not great enough for the God manifest in the laws ruling through infinite space. These laws had been clearly demonstrated; the Deists, holding their reason adequate to solve all problems, imagined that they could demonstrate as clearly the God who made the law. Working back to the creator from the created, they claimed that no further revelation of him was necessary than that made manifest in his works. Out of questions regarding the nature of the universe, ruled, in both scientific and in theological thought, by power from outside, developed fierce debate. There was consternation in theological circles over the newly-discovered truths of science; in England the Deist controversy made up an important part of the thought of the late seventeenth and the early eighteenth centuries, centering in the question of a God revealed through nature, versus a God revealed through Scripture; natural law versus supernatural happenings. Hard blows were given and received; and, as in "battles long ago," "much slaughter was of people on both parties"; "and either smote other in middes of their shields." "Then they stood together and gave many sad strokes on divers places of their bodies, and the blood brast out on many sides and places." The theologians were rather the victors, but, as is usual in the irony of life, their victory was loss; in grasping the weapons of their opponents, in over-rationalizing the religion they were defending, they went far toward deadening the very springs of faith in the Church they served. Out of the perplexity and turmoil of these troubled times emerged thought and feeling which were to have vast consequences in the literature of a later period.

II. Shaftesbury

Of the liberating forces from the somewhat rigid type of thinking prevalent in much of the seventeenth century, with its tendency to stress outer law, Anthony Ashley Cooper, third Earl of Shaftesbury, was one of the most important. A humanist, a lover of philosophy in his own sense of the word, as an application of truth to life, he set forth in his informal essays, *An Inquiry Concerning Virtue or Merit* (1699), and *The Moralists* (1709), both published later in *Characteristics* (1711), his system of thought. Doubtless his mind and imagination had been stimulated by the recently vastly extended knowledge about the physical universe; with this blended much of ancient thought, in one who could read Greek at eleven, and who was much influenced by the Cambridge Platonists; he was influenced too, both in his conception of the spiritual infinite, and in his ethics, by Spinoza.[2] He came as peacemaker. In a time of conflicting views and troubled minds, he turned from speculation to conduct, trying to find a way out; his whole inquiry as to the nature of the universe and the soul of man might be summed up as a quest of the inner law. All his thought in regard to the ruling of the vast whole bears on man's power to find the law of right conduct, whereby his individual being can be brought to vibrate in harmony with the whole.

He affirmed that the universe is one, and is one vast good, a harmony, a beautifully wrought out work of art, made by a wise and benevolent creator; that the beauty and harmony are apparent in the whole order of nature, and that the Deity, in his perfectness, is made known in his perfect working through all life, his perfection manifest in nature, and potentially manifest in man; that man, by his instinctive moral sense, may achieve virtue by following the underlying law of his nature; that virtue consists in finding and fitting himself into the harmony.

Of deepest significance in Shaftesbury's thought is his stress on the unity of the vast whole; the life throughout the universe is one, drawing from one central source, God. The God of Shaftesbury's thought is at once transcendent and immanent, presiding over, ruling that which he has made, immanent, for nature is an expression of his mind and will. From phraseology which has led some of his critics to call him pantheist, using the word carelessly, his mind quickly adverts to a God of personality, omnipresent in his work indeed, but hardly in a pantheistic sense, rather as an artist's personality is present in picture or statue, so that one might say, in contemplating *Le Penseur*: "This is very Rodin!" The celebrated apostrophe in *The Moralists*: "O glorious Nature, supremely fair, and sovereignly good! . . . impowered creatress," goes on to invoke the "impowering Deity, supreme creator," a significant sequence, leading to "O sovereign Mind!" There is too strong an insistence on moral quality in Shaftesbury's idea of God for any real approach to pantheism, the doctrine that the forces apparent in nature make up the whole of God.

Shaftesbury's love of nature comes from his conviction that it is a direct revelation of the power and beauty of the Creator; perhaps his clerical opponents would have been less shocked if they had recalled similar views expressed in *Job* and in the *Psalms*. He is no nature mystic; it is reason's measured conclusions in regard to the characteristics of God manifest in his work that rouses Shaftesbury's enthusiasm, rather than joy in nature experience. There is not, as in Wordsworth, physical and spiritual rapture, transcending thought. In his idea of immanence he is stating in new form, with a minimum of speculation, something akin to Plotinus' idea of a world-soul, deriving from a transcendent deity.

Shaftesbury was one of the chief sources of that stream of Neo-Platonism which became an undercurrent in our deeper nature poetry and in idealistic thought in the late eighteenth and the early nineteenth centuries in England and in Germany. Scornful of metaphysics, unmindful of the steps by which Plotinus built up his theory of successive emanations from the One who is the source of all, through pure thought (*nous*), then, the world-soul, of which all souls are part, which,— forever turned on the one side toward pure mind or spirit, is turned on the other toward the world of sense, of nature,— he seized upon the central idea, so appealing to the idealistic mind, of ultimate reality as spirit, shaping all life from within.

"The beauty, order, and unity of the phenomenal universe are due to the world-soul, which harks back to God," says Mr. Thilly, in interpreting Plotinus. In Plotinus' theory, nature is filled with God, as the leaves of the beech tree, growing green in spring time, are filled with living light.

Back of this thought lies that of Plato; the influence of both is apparent in many of Shaftesbury's utterances, as in this statement: "Whatever in nature is beautiful or charming is only a faint shadow of that first beauty." Philocles in the *Moralists* is won by Theocles "never to admire the representative beauty except for the sake of the original," as the rational mind cannot be satisfied with that which comes from sense alone. Every real love depends on the mind. But the thought of Plotinus is of a oneness or unity which is not in Plato; in the latter, as set forth in the *Timaeus*, the creator-architect, from outside, weaves together mind and matter through the world soul; in Plotinus, from the One emanates pure thought, from which proceeds the world-soul, both manifestations of deity's very self.

The student of English nature poetry does well to try to trace this conception of oneness, of the inner working throughout the universe of the one power which is spirit.

Undoubtedly some of the puzzles attending the apparently diverging uses of the word "Nature" in this period and later might be solved by carrying the study farther back. Nature, as connoting the world of leaf and blossom; as connoting the instinctive, the spontaneous; or the Rousseau naturalness; or the feelings and actions of the "noble savage," — these are varied uses of the word, and there are others, difficult to reconcile with one another. Do they not, possibly, spring from a common source? That Neo-Platonic idea of the divine spirit forever informing the green world and the heart of man may have lent itself to many different uses; the divergences, which seem at first glance to be contradictions, are, perhaps, but rays, to use Plotinus' favorite figure, converging to the central source of divine light.

Work as he will, the student can hardly trace the central idea to its ultimate source. The conception goes far back of Plotinus into that oriental thought by which his thought was touched. It is said that Beethoven kept on his writing table this inscription, copied from one of the pyramids: "I am that which exists. I am all that is, was, that shall be. No mortal man has lifted my veil. He is one only, self-created, and to that Only One do all things owe their being." To the imaginative mind this brief statement is perhaps more convincing than is the idea when set forth in the system of Spinoza, with mathematical proof. Reaching far back into Greek thought, conceived at first as mere physical or material force, this thought of indwelling life has run through many phases, appearing in the mysticism of Boehme, in the philosophy of Bruno, gathering in later days a spirituality in part drawn from Neo-Platonism, which Shaftesbury helped transmute into modern terms of thought. Carlyle's *Sartor Resartus* is founded on the idea:

"O Nature! — Or what is Nature? Ha! why do I not name thee GOD? Art thou not the 'Living Garment of GOD'?"

"Who am I; what is this ME? A Voice, a Motion, an

Appearance; — some embodied, visualized Idea in the Eternal Mind? . . . Him, the Unslumbering, whose work both Dream and Dreamer are, we see not; except in rare half-waking moments, suspect not, . . . We are — we know not what; — light-sparkles floating in the aether of Deity." It is worthy of note that Carlyle borrows Plotinus' metaphor of the radiation of light as symbolizing the self-expression of deity.

Carlyle quotes the Earth-Spirit in *Faust* regarding Nature as the *living visible Garment* of *God*, a conception which Goethe is all-too-often regarded as having originated:

> In Being's floods, in Action's storm,
> I walk and work, above, beneath.
> Work and weave in endless motion!
> Birth and Death,
> An infinite ocean;
> A seizing and giving
> The fire of the living:
> 'Tis thus at the roaring loom of Time I ply,
> And weave for God the Garment thou seest Him by.

Wordsworth gives expression to the idea:

> A motion and a spirit, that impels
> All thinking things, all objects of all thought,
> And rolls through all things.

Shelley echoes it:

> While the one Spirit's plastic stress
> Sweeps through the dull dense world, compelling there
> All new successions to the forms they wear;
> Torturing th' unwilling dross that checks its flight
> To its own likeness, as each mass may bear;
> And bursting in its beauty and its might
> From trees and beasts and men into the Heaven's light.

As in the thought of Plotinus, in Shaftesbury, nature comes forth from God, but God is more than nature. The mistake in dubbing Shaftesbury pantheist comes from thinking that

that which is conceived as an emanation of the Deity is the whole of Deity. That Plotinus-inspired early nature interpretation had ever the idea of transcendent Deity, felt, in sense and in soul, through the emanation of his very self in nature, which was not the whole of that self. Back of Shaftesbury's conception, and that of the Deist poets who followed in his footsteps, lies a blending of Christian and Neo-Platonic thought. When Shaftesbury turns from Nature to the Deity, he is thinking of the God of Christian faith, conceived in terms of personality, as interpreted in the Gospels. The prepossession of long tradition of God lingers in this transition thought of Shaftesbury; the God of vengeance of many of the orthodox has given way to the God of benevolence, goodness, gentleness, still author, source, ruler, possessed of independent existence.

The individual soul was, in Shaftesbury's thought, as in that of Plotinus, part of the universal soul, and so, potentially at least, a part of the perfect harmony drawing from the central source:

"This self of mine . . . 'tis a real self, drawn out from and copied from another principal and original self (the Great One of the world.)"

The soul of man is, therefore, basically divine, and the dominant idea of Shaftesbury's ethics is that man's task on earth is the full development of his nature, in finding and following the inner law of his being. Shall such beauty and harmony as are apparent in the universe exist throughout nature, and not in man? Looking within, he finds an innate moral sense; the seed of perfection is in him. Let him develop this inmost individuality; fitting himself, with growing insight, into the vast, enveloping harmony of the universe, he becomes more and more a part of that harmony. Man's soul would seem to be the only unfinished thing in this universe of otherwise finished perfection; he may, if he will, complete the perfectness.

"Every creature has a private good and interest of his own, which Nature has compelled him to seek." Shaftesbury believes that there is a law of good for every creature, a law of choice for every creature capable of thought. It is for man to follow the higher impulse, obey the finer instinct, for instinctive taste will guide him; he should search out and follow the law of his highest possibility. Gradations of experience are recognized; the pleasures of mind and soul are higher than pleasures of sense; taste is reckoned an active factor in ethical as in aesthetic discriminations.

Shaftesbury's doctrine, so far as the inner life is concerned, but not as regards the outer, physical universe, is a doctrine of development; there is a note of spiritual progression in the thought of the possibilities of individual experience. The beauty and order of the Shaftesburian universe are, so far as regards man, a potential rather than an actual perfectness, an ideal toward which to strive, rather than an established fact; otherwise, why urge the pursuit of the beautiful, the good, the true? Man is endowed with, not virtue but the instinct for virtue; there is recognition of the fact that facing difficulty in choosing the good enhances the virtue; without effort, virtue would not exist. Is there not, in Shaftesbury's thought of man moving, if he can so direct his mind and will, toward perfectness, an anticipatory note of the idea of spiritual evolution, which played so large a part in nineteenth century poetry and philosophy? If it harks back to Plato, Shaftesbury gives it a stamp of his own; man has his chance; nature, through its divine origin, provides him with possibilities; he is urged, through constant searching out the of ways of beauty, constant refining of taste, constant fitting his thought and his conduct to the higher code, to help perfect this harmony which, because of him, is incomplete. There is an insistent note of "becoming" in this idea of refining and developing taste, progressive insight into virtue, and struggle to attain. Shaftesbury's is no negative doctrine; he affirms that the love of the good must be positive, springing, not from fear of consequence of evil, but from love of good for its own sake; virtue must rise, not from fear of punishment, but from love of God.

Significant in this age of rationalism, on the part of a professed rationalist, is the idea of the attainment of truth as, in part, a matter of ardor, of affection; of feeling, instinct, impulse as a help to the intellect in divining the deeper law of good in one's being. This idea of instinct, impulse drawing directly from the divine, and leading toward the good, the beautiful, the true, has within it a quickening power, as the wide influence of Shaftesbury's thought abundantly proved. Vast possibilities opened out with this freeing of man's nature, his inward response to that compelling Beauty, Goodness, Truth; belief that his moral activity is necessary to complete the harmony of the universe could but develop and deepen his individuality. So, in that seventeenth and eighteenth century thought, the Perfect Whole tugged at the whole of you, rousing every faculty, bringing the whole being into play. This was not the mystic's flight of the alone to the Alone, but the Whole appealing to the whole of man.

Shaftesbury's is a comprehensive ethic, including all aspects of man's life. So fair is this world of nature, written so clearly on her face the law of beauty, of harmony, it behooves man to get into his moral life, into his actions, his manners and into the products of his imagination,— his art, his literature,[3] this beauty and this harmony. Thought drifting down from the world of Greece underlies his idea that the right development of that which is latent in man's inmost nature is his task on earth, the fulfilment of the utmost possibilities of his being. The harmonious and rounded development of the individual, and of all that he produces, should shadow forth the perfectness at the heart of the universe.

The orthodox world looked askance upon this heartening

doctrine, shocked by this conception of goodness, benevolence, both in God and man, yet surely it represented a wholesome reaction in a world which had heard too much of evil. It was well to affirm a reign of benevolent law in a universe which had too often been interpreted theologically as ruled by divine caprice. To turn from the contemplation of sin to the contemplation of goodness would not seem a cardinal offence; Shaftesbury's critics might well have paused to reflect that he affirmed only that goodness is actual in the case of God, possible in man, a harmless and stimulating assertion, as the world later discovered. Adroit and charming is Shaftesbury's criticism of some aspects of established faith. He makes no attack, but gentlest and most well-bred of all earth's rebels, in speaking of the influences that will foster and encourage the tendency toward good, latent in every human being, he asks if belief in a capricious, angry, revengeful God must not be a great deterrent to virtue; if belief in a God of justice and benevolence is not an aid to well doing. The perfection and height of virtue, he says, must be owing to belief in such a God: sin-harried man might well turn to find stimulus and incentive in the idea of a world created and ruled by so gracious a deity.

Shaftesbury's philosophy has been pronounced superficial; he did not, certain critics say, deal adequately with the problem of evil. The retort courteous to this might be: Who has? In the *Inquiry* and elsewhere he shows himself perfectly aware of the existence, if not of the power of evil. Coming of gentlefolk, with, apparently, little first-hand knowledge of the harsher realities of life, he knew perhaps less than a moral philosopher should know of the need of moral struggle, but the case against him is overstated. Of treachery, ingratitude, cruelty, vice he was aware, but he was convinced that, in spite of evil, the major trend of things in human affairs is more right than wrong. He did not deliberately ignore the darker side of life, but seems to say:

"Let man, who has dwelt so much on sin and discord turn his attention to the other side for a bit." There is suffering in life; there are accidents, misadventures; the harmony, in some aspects of man's experience, seems broken. By virtue man can make this up to himself; "his merit is reward."

"Had goodness never met with opposition nor merit ever lain under a cloud; where had been the trial, victory, or crown of virtue? . . . Where patience, meekness, magnanimity? Whence have these their being? What merit except from hardship? What virtue without a conflict, and the encounter of such enemies as arise both from within and from abroad?"

If this optimistic philosophy did not meet the full challenge of the problem of evil in the world, at least, in emphasizing a truth that had been too much subordinated by too exclusive insistence on man's propensity to sin, it was a step on the way to a deeper conception of evil and of good. If the inner law of right is harder to find and to follow than he imagined, he yet enunciated a truth that greatly needed to be made known, the possibility of good in every creature. Perhaps the minimizing of evil came, in part, from the seventeenth century way of thinking in wholes, from confusing spatial with inner values, as is sometimes the way, notably in our own time, when science is to the fore. In a universe of illimitable vastness, showing such stupendous workmanship, perfectly functioning, slight interruptions, exceptions, were of small account. Spinoza's lofty strain of thought influenced many minds in this period and after; he held that, in the face of that infinity of goodness, which is God, evil shrinks to negligible proportions.

Shaftesbury's influence was perhaps in nothing more potent than in his emphasis on the social nature of virtue. That haunting idea of the whole underlies all his thought in regard to ethics, as in regard to the physical universe. The idea of unity is ever with him. "Now in this which we call the universe, whatever the perfection may be of any particular systems, or whatever single parts may have proportion, unity, or form within themselves, yet if they are not united . . . in one system, but are . . . as the driven sands, or clouds, or breaking waves, then there being no coherence in the whole, there can be inferred no order, no proportion, and consequently no project or design. . . . All things in this world are united." As in the world of matter, so in the social and moral world; whether or not there is here conscious reflection of Newton's theory of gravitation, there is a striking instance of the same idea appearing in widely different spheres of thought, the idea of cohesion in the affairs of men, as in the atoms of the universe. Throughout the whole *Inquiry concerning Virtue or Merit*, the interlinking of all human lives, that basic idea of modern sociology, is emphasized. "For whatsoever is the occasion or means of more affectionately uniting a rational creature to his part in society, and causes him to prosecute the public good or interest of his species with more zeal and affection than ordinary, is undoubtedly the cause of more than ordinary virtue in such a person."

It is by no means claimed that Shaftesbury was the initiator of the gospel of good will toward men; doubtless the initial stages of the doctrine of benevolence go far back of Christianity, back, even, of recorded history. But Shaftesbury, in his persuasive, unpolemical fashion, of setting forth the idea of an inner bond, uniting man with man, of a conviction that no man could be good unto himself alone, was vastly influential. It has been well said that the whole trend of ethical thought was different after his day; modern sociology owes him more than it realizes. For his social theory he drew, probably, from many sources; something of the best of Christianity goes into it; much of his early training. In all that he says about the social sense, in his ethics, based on the idea of man as a social being, you get the impress of his breeding. It is true that he thinks in terms of cultured society, of a comradeship in taste and in morals that hardly takes into account the common people, yet his insistence on the unity of mankind led to more catholic social creeds. Much of his ethical thought suggests the Greek idea of the perfection or health of the state coming through the striving toward perfection of the individual citizen.

In this idea of interrelatedness between man and man, the individual functioning rightly only in the larger body, is a foreshadowing, though he does not use the word, of the organic idea, which is the basis of our thought to-day in regard to humanity. And in the suggested interpretation of growth in the social affairs of men from the primitive, there is, as in his interpretation of the individual attempting to attain virtue, something of that idea of growth, of becoming, through which we of the modern world interpret life and its possibilities.

Shaftesbury's philosophy, more influential than if it had been more formally stated, had vast consequences in succeeding years. He left an enduring impress on life and thought, through suggestions that were later to develop into ethics, sociology, philosophy; in England and in Germany his thought permeated literature to an extent that has hardly been recognized. He greatly influenced, among others, Hamann, Herder, Goethe; and Kant's Categorical Imperative owes something to Shaftesbury's faith in the power of the individual to find and follow the law of right. French Deism derived much from him. Possibly he wrought as much by his limitations as by his gifts; he was incapable of writing a formal, systematic treatise, but his lack of argumentativeness, of aggressiveness was an asset, for his power of gentle insinuation, both of criticism and of his articles of faith, enabled him to steal into the minds of men before they were quite aware, and he became, in the eighteenth century, a pervasive influence. He seemed to touch the very springs of vitality in the human soul in his idea that man's moral activity is necessary to complete the perfection of an all-but-perfect universe. The problem of spiritual development proved indeed a knottier problem than he had thought; man had to learn that becoming a part of the eternal good is a difficult matter, to learn that a long, slow process of evolution lay ahead. But some strain of that Shaftesburian harmony lingered long throughout his century, and lingers still.

Shaftesbury's influence was obvious and great on certain poets of the so-called Deist school, who soon followed him: Thomson, in the *Seasons*; Henry Brooke, in *Universal Beauty*; Pope, in the *Essay on Man*; Akenside, in *Pleasures of the Imagination*, and others; but there was in him a subtlety of thought and perception that these early imitators did not have. The more gifted and individual poets of the mid-century, Gray and Collins, do not appear to have been touched by his thought, and it is noteworthy that the finer phases of his influence did not make their appearance until the full tide of romantic poetry came in. There was a long period of incubation of those ideas of the whole, which was gradually growing from mechanism into life, and of an inner law of harmony, which was to play so large a part in nineteenth century poetry, — ideas which came into their own in touching the minds of Wordsworth and of Coleridge. Does not the trail lead to Wordsworth's inspired lines:

> Dust as we are, the immortal spirit grows
> Like harmony in music?

In the lines in the *Ode to Duty*:

> Thou dost preserve the stars from wrong;
> And the most ancient heavens, through
> Thee, are fresh and strong,

there is something of the association of the outposts of space with the inner moral law which recalls Shaftesbury, as does Coleridge's line in *Religious Musings*:

There is one Mind, one omnipresent Mind,
Omnific.

Shaftesbury stresses repeatedly the "Governing Mind," the "Universal Mind." Keats' "Beauty is truth, truth beauty," contains the essence of that Platonic doctrine, in the teaching of which in England Shaftesbury was a pioneer.

In Shaftesbury's appealing optimism the conviction that, in spite of evil, the major trend of things is more right than wrong, was an influence that has been, and deserved to be, enduring. Even Carlyle, who speaks of him with contempt, was perhaps not untouched by it, though he had found, as others had found, evil rampant without and within. Something in Carlyle's doctrine that, in spite of all, the great soul of the world is right, echoes in thunder-tones the silvery accents of Shaftesbury. His definition of taste as "a sense to discern, and a heart to love and reverence, all beauty, order, goodness" sound suspiciously like the author of *Characteristics*, whom he denounced as meaningless. Carlyle himself discerns something of the great Harmony, and in praising Goethe for catching the "Music of the Universe" is unaware of the strain of influence of Shaftesbury through Hamann and Herder to Goethe's mind. Who can say whether Herr Teufelsdröckh's idea of the oneness, interrelatedness of human lives, symbolized by the phrase "organic filaments" may not owe something to the current of thought that had its source in Shaftesbury's affirmation of the social ties that bind man to man, his incompleteness without his fellows?

"Yes, truly, if Nature is one, and a living indivisible whole, much more is Mankind, the Image that reflects and creates Nature," says Carlyle, through his spokesman.

Of Browning, with his one central conception of all life as spiritual development what can one say, except that, directly or indirectly he must be indebted to that persuasive thinker who, in England, popularizing Platonism, set astir the idea of a spiritual, ethical development of the human soul, proceeding toward some unseen perfection? That note of becoming, touched by Shaftesbury, was to become the dominant note of thought in the spiritual world of a later day. Browning's *Abt Vogler* has surely caught something of the rhythm of Shaftesbury's thought; discords are but part of a fuller harmony to follow as life grows great; and all the poems in which he sets forth his idea of evil as a transitory instrument in effecting eternal good reveal that Shaftesburian belief that there can be no enduring evil in the universe.

III. Henry Brooke

To get the full value of Shaftesbury's thought it is well to compare him with some of his followers, who developed his ideas in different ways, emphasizing the aspect that seemed to each most important. Of these Deist poets, Henry Brooke, in his *Universal Beauty* (1728–1735), is perhaps the most interesting. Shaftesbury's philosophy of the beauty and harmony of the universe is presented, chiefly with reference to physical aspects, with confident boldness of assertion and a wealth of detail. He sets forth the vastness and the nice workmanship of the universe as a revelation of the skill and power of the Deity, pointing out

> How He who inaccessible remains
> Yet omnipresent through all nature reigns.

He accepts law; accepts God, and, accepting the adequacy of Reason, sets about interpreting him promising "to answer every doubt":

> Light, matter, motion, music, order, laws!
> And silent dark nonentity the cause?
> But chance, you'll say — I ask you chance of what
> If nothing was? 'Tis answer'd, chance of naught.

God is the "Sovereign Geometrician," "the Eternal Founder, working with the Eternal Finger, the Eternal

Architect supreme who has "Equip'd magnificent the house of God." From this conception he slips with no consciousness of difficulty to:

> While from th' Unchangeable, the One, the Wise
> Still changing endless emanations rise,

and the idea of immanence struggles in him with the anthropomorphic conception of God.

Over and over he stresses the unity of the whole:

> The system one, One Maker stands confess'd,
>
> . . . . . .
>
> The One in various forms of Unity express'd!

and he plays, in successive antitheses, upon the idea of Almighty Power, revealed alike in great and small:

> Who only could infinitude confine,
> And dwell *immense* within the minim shrine.
>
> . . . . . .
>
> The One grows sundry by creative power;
> The Eternal's found in each revolving hour;
> The Immense appears in every point of space;
> The Unchangeable in Nature's varying face:
> The Invisible conspicuous to our mind,
> And Deity in every atom shrin'd;

an idea transmuted into poetry in a later era by Blake:

> To see a World in a grain of sand,
> And a Heaven in a wild flower,
> Hold Infinity in the palm of your hand,
> And Eternity in an hour.

There is a lively reaction to life processes in all things throughout the vegetable and the animal world, with special stress on the physical and moral characteristics of insects, and tributes to the wonderful skill of the Eternal Finger that directs these activities of time, with skill apparent in all the innumerable forms of life, the physical frame of man, beast, bird, insect, in the sap and fibre of the vegetable world. Brooke's is no universe created and set spinning in space, free of the creator; his conception seems to vibrate between the two points, — past skill apparent in the making and in the perfect working of his creatures, and present activity of God throughout.

> And One Sole Hand the maz'd volution guides!

he summarizes at the end.

In view of later developments of thought, Brooke's insistence that these various forms of life are complete is of special significance:

> Each organ, apt to each precarious state,
> As for eternity design'd complete,

reflecting the static conception of the science of his age. Time has changed this into:

"We find that all animals, regarded as pieces of machinery, are imperfect; each represents an attempt, more or less successful, to adapt a pre-existent structure to some new use." [4]

It was in the later eighteenth century that the idea of the unalterable perfectness of species began to give way to a belief in incessant change, forever being wrought by forward-pushing nature.

In all his contemplation of the finished perfectness of least things and of great, Brooke is more than mere observer; there is heightened feeling, wonder in his attitude. Though the rationalist can expound all that he knows, and more than he knows, he admits one last barrier, inaccessible to reason. There is something of a sense of mystery in his approach to infinite power:

> No plexur'd mode, no aptitude refin'd
> Can yield one glimpse of all-informing mind,

for matter's eternal barriers are fixed. God is omnipresent, yet inaccessible.

Brooke is far less comprehensive and less sensitive to moral values than Shaftesbury; his quest is not the inner law of man's life, but close scrutiny of the work of the Eternal Architect. If he has any glimmering of Shaftesbury's idea of virtue as social, it appears more in his admiration of the superior social virtues of bees and ants than in any study of man. The alleged beauty and harmony of the universe break when it comes to man, "proud, insulting man," the one exception, in so far as he sins, to the totality of goodness and benevolence. He is king of reason, but slave to sense, "incurious, ignorant, profane":

> Ah, Nature! thou hads't scap'd thy only blot
> Could man but cease to be — or hitherto were not:
> Ay, there's the task, the labour of our song —
> To prove that all is right, though man be wrong.
> . . . .
> To man, even man becomes a mutual prey,
> No gain can satiate, and no limits stay.

The humanitarian note of the Deist school is not lacking; beast and bird are adjured to flee the savage hunter:

> Fly him, ye rangers of the rolling flood!
> Fly him, ye songsters of the warbling wood!

A feeling for mice, "innoxious cottagers," is manifest in his plea to them to remain safe from the tyrant in their subterranean homes.

The problem of evil is presented only in connection with man; it is not in nature; it is not in God, but in man alone, a knotty problem, which Brooke does not attempt to solve. There is no suggestion of the existence of suffering in nature; those carefully guarded Deist eyes take care not to look too closely into nature; benignant affirmations must not be questioned. The only break in the perfect system comes in the curiously anomalous position of man, who, in the thought of Brooke, is not quite inside nor quite outside the house of life; the Eternal Finger shaped his body, but, alas! his naughty mind! One wonders how it was that Omnipotence faltered when it came to the making of man. Brooke does not find Shaftesbury's way out, of overcoming evil impulses by development of the finer tendencies of the human soul, though he agrees with him in regard to the existence of instinct. There is in Brooke nothing of that inward response in man to the divine power calling to him through the beauty of the universe, that sense of something answering back, which Wordsworth characterized figuratively as a "correspondent breeze," wakening within. God is to Brooke a God of Love, his greatest attribute:

> Placid and Mild; All gracious! All Benign;
> Of boundless love the ever boundless source!

in a perfectly functioning universe,

> Where worlds in endless revolutions move
> And swim on the abyss of endless Love.

It remained for greater poets of a later day to carry the idea of universal love to a logical conclusion; in Shelley and Browning, man is not merely recipient but partaker of the great power of loving, in the presence of which evil falters and fails.

There is something of Platonism in Brooke, filtered down through his master, Shaftesbury:

> So when the mind to central beauty tends,

but Brooke's is a conception of beauty moulded by the scientific thought of his time; beauty in nature comes from perfect fulfilment of function, use. That beauty which is the truth or nature of things is revealed in the perfectness of nature processes, such as atmospheric action as observed on land and sea; the growth from seed of plant, leaf, blossom. Though Brooke says:

> Our transient optic o'er the surface plays,
> And Nature's superficial mien surveys;
> But rare with deeper inquisition pries,
> Where Beauty's wrapt, recluse from vulgar eyes,
> Essential, sits on Truth's eternal throne,
> And universal, reigns o'er worlds unknown,

yet he walks with strangely assured step, in regions where Plato went questing, alert, in both the outer, visible world and in the world of the inner life, for glimpses of elusive, swiftly vanishing beauty, giving its hint of the perfect. Beauty to Brooke is as demonstrable as a proposition in Euclid.

IV. Pope

Brooke's *Universal Beauty* is an effective presentation of the daring optimism of his time. It is indeed difficult to think coherently in successive couplets where rhyme is even more important than reason, if you must choose, but Brooke surmounted the difficulty better than did Pope in his *Essay on Man* (1732–1734); though his couplets are less polished, less pointed, he is a far more convinced and logical reasoner than Pope, partly because his scope is more limited. Leslie Stephen is wrong in saying that Pope's *Essay on Man* is a continuous comment on Shaftesbury; it is not a continuous anything. Pope's thought is broken, and at times contradictory, but of great interest because of its fragmentary reflections of scientific and philosophic theories of the period, and because of the flashes of independent thought among his versified borrowings. Much has been written of his indebtedness to Shaftesbury, Bolingbroke, and others; it is hardly necessary here to trace the individual staccato utterances to their sources, or to discuss all aspects of the thought presented in the famous essay; rather to ask whether the leading poet of the day carried further the idea of oneness in the universe, unity in the boundless variety; helped develop the idea of the relation of the human mind to the outer universe; grasped the idea of oneness in the affairs of men.

Pope's aim, as stated in *The Design*, was to form "a *temperate*, yet not *inconsistent*, and a *short*, yet not *imperfect* system of Ethics"; to accomplish his purpose, he considers man with respect to the universe, with respect to himself as an individual, with respect to society. The unity of all things is epigrammatically expressed in couplets, showing his acceptance of the idea of a vast plan carried out by a wise and benevolent Creator, the first Almighty Cause, acting not by partial but by general laws; he reveals, too, his awareness of scientific discovery in regard to the vastness of the universe, and the laws which govern it. Worlds on worlds compose our universe, he affirms; system runs into system; other planets circle other suns, and all is one:

> The gen'ral ORDER, since the world began
> Is kept in Nature, and is kept in Man,

as

> The great directing MIND of ALL ordains.

He emphasizes especially the recently discovered theory of gravitation, the wholeness or cohesion of the perfect mechanism:

> From Nature's chain, whatever link you strike,
> Tenth or ten thousandth, breaks the chain alike.
> . . . .
> Let Earth unbalanc'd from her orbit fly,
> Planets and Suns run lawless through the sky.
> . . . .
> See plastic Nature working to this end,
> The single atoms each to other tend. . . .

These binding forces operate in animate as in inanimate life:

> Nothing is foreign: Parts relate to whole;
> One all-extending, all preserving Soul
> Connects each being, greatest and the least;
> Made Beast in aid of Man, and Man of Beast.

No early and tentative expression of the oneness of the universe is more striking than Pope's:

> All are but parts of one stupendous whole
> Whose body Nature is, and God the soul;
> That, chang'd thro' all, and yet in all the same;
> Great in the earth, as in th' ethereal frame;
> Warms in the sun; refreshes in the breeze;
> Glows in the stars, and blossoms in the trees,
> Lives through all life, extends through all extent,
> Spreads undivided, operates unspent;
> Breathes in our soul, informs our mortal part,
> As full, as perfect, in a hair as heart:
> As full, as perfect, in vile Man that mourns
> As the rapt Seraph that adores and burns;
> To him no high, no low, no great, no small;
> He fills, he bounds, connects, and equals all.

This passage gathers up into succinct phrases much contemporary thought in regard to unity throughout the universe; it is derived, in part perhaps, from scientific speculation, in part from Shaftesburian affirmation. In reading Pope, however, one is struck by the wholly sporadic nature of his thought of the immanence of God. From whatever sources it drifted into Pope's mind it wrought no change there, wakened no inquiry as to the relation of the inner life of man to the power manifest in the world-order,— Shaftesbury's chief interest,— affected none of his interpretations of men. If he grasped it as a metaphysical idea, he did not grasp it as a living reality. It is not inwrought with his other thought in his presentation of life; he does not work it out in connection with the whole of human life, of animal life, of vegetable life, and seems to have had little imaginative or rationalistic grasp of its import. One is inclined to think that it was only one of those tempting bits of other men's thought which Pope so deftly caught and held in the swift-snapping jaws of the couplet. His repetition of the scientific and metaphysical conception, in no way brought into the realm of human experience, contributed nothing to the conception of living reality which was to be the dominant thought of the future, and still less to the idea of the relation of the human mind to the outer universe.

Shaftesbury's idea of unity is far deeper than Pope's, as it includes the self, or soul, of man, which, Shaftesbury affirms, is a part of the "original self, the Great One of the world." Though Pope uses the phrase, "breathes in our soul," he leaves us in doubt as to his idea of the meaning of the word soul. It seems to have here a physical rather than a spiritual connotation, for, if it is the Spirit of God that is manifesting itself in everything, including man's moral nature, how can that nature be, as he affirms, vile? A couplet in the manuscript of the *Essay on Man*, omitted in the printed text, says bluntly that all evil comes from man:

> Of ev'ry evil, since the world began,
> The real source is not in God, but Man,

a couplet that nicely suggests the limitation of his thought of oneness. Is man a part of this oneness? Is the "general order," which, he says, is kept, since the beginning of the world in both nature and man, kept only in man's body? In Pope's mind there is, apparently, no thought of philosophical difficulty here. His inability, shared by other Deists, to relate the abstract metaphysical conception of the unity of the whole to the facts of the inner life shows in glaring fashion in connection with the problem of evil. The dogmatic assertiveness, the antithetical affirmations of Pope's couplets bring out in high relief that curious exclusion of imperfect man from the perfect scheme, revealing the contradiction more clearly than is the case in Brooke, who is discussing not ethics, but the physical universe. Shaftesbury tries to prove that man, by reason of his moral nature, is, and, through conscious effort and refining insight, may become more fully a part of the divine whole. Pope sees nothing of this inwardness of relationship, and has no idea of the possibility of the inner growth of man, through his concurring will, whereby the individual soul becomes more deeply a part of the divine order. Those aspects of Shaftesbury's thought which were to become most influential escaped him. To Pope, morality is the fulfilling of an outward law; he asks of man only intellectual recognition of his fixed status in the general scheme, and submission thereto.

Again in Pope, as in Brooke, we have the shrinkage of the values of human personality in the face of the wonders of the physical universe. Pope and his like were thinking in wholes, in space terms; if infinite vastness could show order, could anything be wrong?

> Remember, Man, 'the Universal Cause
> Acts not by partial, but by gen'ral laws' . . .
> . . . .
> All Discord, Harmony not understood;
> All partial Evil, universal Good. . . .
> . . . .
> When the loose mountain trembles from on high,
> Shall gravitation cease, if you go by?

There is absurdity in expecting in the moral world a freedom from exceptions and accidents which is not in nature:

> If plagues or earthquakes break not Heav'n's design,
> Why then a Borgia, or a Catiline?

Man is apparently so small that he does not particularly

matter, a strange attitude in a treatise on ethics. "Whatever is, is right," is reiterated with shrill insistence:

> Respecting Man, whatever wrong we call,
> May, must be right, as relative to all.

This was to make and repeat an abstract formula, defying the facts to challenge it, in spite of recognition of their existence as facts. Faced with a world of many wrongs, Pope and his fellow optimists retired within a half scientific, half metaphysical concept. "The science of human nature, is, like all other sciences, reduced to a few clear points," Pope says in *The Design*.

If, reaching an idea of the physical oneness of the universe, Pope failed to find its spiritual counterpart, and to relate the outer order to the mind and soul of man, he did attain an idea of necessary connection between man and man, in recognition of common interests, common needs. In part he follows Shaftesbury, and an aspect of the Shaftesburian social sense drifts into epigram, but Pope lacks the former's sense of inner relationship between man and man. Recognition of the interrelatedness of human lives appears in scattered passages bearing witness to the wakening conscience of the time, expressing itself in both word and deed, in regard to man's responsibility toward man.

Single phrases express the idea felicitously:

> Till one Man's weakness grows the strength of all.
> . . . .
> On mutual Wants build mutual Happiness.
> . . . .
> [The] human soul
> Must rise from Individual to the Whole.

All happiness is social; one order serves another:

> Such is the World's great harmony, that springs
> From Order, Union, full Consent of things.

To Pope, true self-love and social are the same: "*nothing* [*is*] *made wholly for* itself, *nor yet wholly for* another," and the statement is a fair expression of the Deist idea of the adjustment of part to part in the universe, applied to social relations.

Though Pope grasps the idea of unity in connection with the physical world, and catches a glimpse of it with respect to the social order, there is no thought in his work of the idea of development. Man, he says, is not an imperfect being, but a being suited to his place and rank in creation, established in unalterable relations. The dominant impression gained is of man stationary in a stationary universe; physical laws hold planets and suns in their places; moral laws hold man in his. He should stay where he is put; happiness lies in acquiescence:

> Aspiring to be Angels, Men rebel:
> And who but wishes to invert the laws
> Of ORDER, sins against th' Eternal Cause.

His mind should not venture beyond the barriers set. "The pride of aiming at more knowledge and pretending to more perfection [is] the cause of man's error and misery":

> Then say not Man's imperfect, Heav'n in fault;
> Say rather, Man's as perfect as he ought:
> His knowledge measured to his state and place.

Speculation stops short in Pope; he asks no further questions. His rebuke to the wakening curiosity of the time is one of the most interesting aspects of his thought. We must not seek out God; we can judge only by our own system; wait the great teacher, Death:

> Say first, of God above, or Man below,
> What can we reason, but from what we know?

Through Pope one gets the best idea of the fixity of the system, physical and intellectual, whereby the life of man was interpreted by ruling thinkers in the seventeenth and early eighteenth centuries. It was a world of the static, the defined, the limited, before men discovered that, in the flowing nature of the time world, was destiny that opened out illimitably. Perhaps scientific contemplation of physical laws had brought him a conviction of an immobile universe in which there was perpetual action without creative change. All is complete, finished: the vast system of the universe, the varied species that make up life on earth, the political and social order, and man's soul finished in his intellectual acquiescence in the place assigned him in the "dread Order." "Tis fix'd as in a frost." Pope's affirmation about the poet's working is equally applicable to his idea of other phases of experience:

"Since none can compass more than they intend," might well stand as the motto of an era before the idea of physical and spiritual development dawned, well set off against an equally representative phrase, coming from another era of a different order of thought:

> Ah, but a man's reach should exceed his grasp.

Pope's dictum, that the pride of aiming at more knowledge and pretending to more perfection is the cause of man's error and misery would seem to close the case in regard to his thought, yet now and then comes a haunting phrase, which sets one's mind stirring, makes one wonder just how much he means:

> So Man, who here seems principal alone,
> Perhaps acts second to some sphere unknown,
> Touches some wheel, or verges to some goal;
> 'Tis but a part we see, and not the whole.

The gleams, flashes of loftier thought in Pope are interesting; no less interesting his refusal, or inability, to "follow the gleam."

V

This world of the nature Deists, in spite of the horror which they roused in some minds in finding Nature a sufficient revelation of God is, in many ways, a pleasant world in which to linger, because of their assurance that, behind all this astronomical and geometrical wonder was a benevolent Deity, who had worked out and executed the whole plan. There is, after all, a reverence in their thought which should have protected them from the sneers of the unduly orthodox. Touches of the sublime may be found in couplets that overreach themselves in trying to express the attributes of an omnipotent Deity in two iambic lines, to define the undefinable in an antithetical phrase. They thought in vastnesses, in wholes, stupendous conceptions that challenged the reason and beggared the imagination. No wonder that this far-reaching thought helped burst the narrow bounds of the couplet, strained by the attempt to confine within it ideas of such illimitable import.

They found little difficulty in passing from the idea of immanence to the idea of an anthropomorphic Deity, planning and fashioning from afar. Pope, a few lines after the famous passage quoted, beginning

> All are but parts of one stupendous whole,

affirms that

> All Nature is but Art, unknown to thee.

God is no longer the indwelling soul, but the Artificer; man, apart,

> . . . Looks thro' Nature up to Nature's God,
> Pursues the Chain which links th' immense design.

He apparently shares with other Deist poets of the time the belief that no inquiry is needed as to the relation of this indwelling spirit to God, outside architect and builder. They missed the link implied in the idea of emanation of the very self of God manifest in nature, and did not feel the need of achieving "the synthesis of transcendence and immanence," which, in the words of Windelband, is sought by Plotinus. One finds in this group aspects of new scientific thought, with perhaps a far-off drift of Neo-Platonism, engrafted upon traditional theological doctrine, rather than any fundamental philosophical question and affirmation. In spite of many intimations of immanence, the thought of the outside Creator is overwhelmingly uppermost in their minds.

The skill of God, artist and architect, they loved to play upon in antitheses of great and small, the vast universe, and the insect's wing. There is something courtly, polite, in their polished complimentary phrases, suggesting the atmosphere of an artist's exhibition, where onlookers praise the work of the artist's hand, amiably assuring him that he does as well on a canvas of heroic size as on the minutest, or of a scientists' meeting, full of graceful acknowledgments of God as the head of the scientists, the sovereign Geometrician.

Curiosity, but more of admiration, is apparent in contemplation of the working, observed or assumed, of the cunning Artificer, in the immensities and in the minutiae of life on the earth and throughout the universe. This was not the scientist's attitude of patient observation, but contemplation and reflection in the light of a preconceived idea, for the intellectual and moral satisfaction it gave to discover its many proofs. There was a certain complacency in all this, apparently no doubt about the adequacy of reason to pronounce upon the finished whole of creation. Questioning comes slowly in the eighteenth century; Shaftesbury and his followers, Pope, Brooke, Akenside, Cooper and others answer more than they ask in their affirmation of beauty, harmony, goodness apparent in the perfect functioning of a perfect universe. But perhaps their very insistence implies secret misgiving; man is prone to affirm and reiterate that about which he would like to be sure. This characterization of God from meditation on his handiwork was the climax of Reason, its *chef-d'œuvre* in the eighteenth century, but rationalism that could explain the whole could yet leave the mind hungry and unsatisfied. With the exception of Shaftesbury, and perhaps Akenside, they had no glimpse of the need of revelation, not only in plant and insect, but in the spirit of man. This waited for later poet interpreters, in the romantic period. The coming of doubt as to the adequacy of man's reason to find out God marked the beginning of new and deeper thought in regard to the nature of God, and the mind of man.

One can but wonder what they who approached nature thus rationalistically really experienced. Did they touch, smell, hear, apprehend through the senses the beauty and the harmony concerning which they theorized so abstractly? Did they reach any understanding of the organic relationship between the individual and the outside world, or of the organic nature of the entire universe? The most important question in regard to the Deists is whether the much stressed unity is a unity of a living organism, or of a work of art,—better still, of a cunningly devised mechanism. It is overwhelmingly the latter, with part deftly fitted to part by the great Artificer.

One must note in connection with Shaftesbury and the Deist poets the original and valuable work of Mr. C. A. Moore in his article on *The Return to Nature in English Poetry of the Eighteenth Century.*[5] He is perhaps right in his affirmation that their philosophy, in bringing about a realization of the unity of nature, "was actually the chief agent in eventually forcing the minute study and love of nature as a whole upon popular attention." But I think that he is wrong in his affirmation: "This Deistic verse, taken collectively, holds in solution the entire doctrine of the modern romantic school." The Deistic idea was of a complete and perfect design, shown both in the immensities and in the minutiae of the universe, in the courses of the stars, and in the species of the animal and the vegetable world. These are complete; eternally the same, whereas the world of the romantic poets is a world of life and change. "One constantly hears the creaking of the gigantic system," admits Mr. Moore, in regard to the Deists; and he speaks of the mechanism of Shaftesbury's universe. That was a static doctrine; the idea of development was not in it; God was the master-craftsman, who had made a perfect work; the beauty and harmony of the universe in its unfaltering working was his finished achievement. The idea of anything incomplete, imperfect, would have seemed as sacriligious as the idea that a pseudo-classic poet could write an unpolished poem.

When the theory of a wonderful universe, functioning perfectly in every part, burst into life, nature becoming not only a whole but a living whole, static turning into dynamic; when the conception of the beauty of the finished changed into a conception of the saving grace of the incomplete, a new era in men's thought had begun, our modern era, of belief in one life throughout the whole, and of ceaseless development, but the time was not yet. That incessant activity, of Deist conception, was not incessant growth, but the idea of God forever operating at infinite points the intricacy of the wonderful machine of his devising, or contemplating its perfect working in a long seventh day of rest, may well have helped prepare the way for the coming of the idea of evolution, of unceasing activity which is growth, working within.

This coming to life of the thought of man,— it is interesting to know where, in this eighteenth century, it began; interesting to know where thought, groping toward it, stopped, as in the Deists. Here philosophers led the scientists, and great names are cited among the pioneers of the theory of evolution: Descartes; Spinoza; Leibnitz; Kant. Very gradual in the later eighteenth and the early nineteenth centuries is the stealing in of an apprehension of the organic nature of the whole world order, a conception of an inner life and growth in all that is, an idea fraught with profound significance for the literature of the future. Slowly into romantic poetry filtered the idea of a living oneness of the universe, spiritual as well as physical, and with it the idea of growth, development, a spiritual principle, ever active.

VI. Thomson

If, in the universe of the scientist, and in the universe of Spinoza in the seventeenth century man had been rather crowded out; if, in Deist thought of the early eighteenth century he occupied a somewhat anomalous position, as part of a wonderful mechanism, yet left outside, hardly accounted for in the scheme, except physically, sole mischief maker in an otherwise perfect universe, though he might wonder and adore, in the poetry and in the philosophy of the eighteenth century he began to find his way into the picture, to come into his own, and the various ways in which he did this are of great interest. One was by the gift of temperament. He began to be aware of a relationship between his mind, soul, and senses, and that outer world that the Deists interpreted metaphysically as revealing the mind and soul of the Creator. It is often asserted that English literature is in nothing more distinguished than in its nature poetry; the importance of Thomson in this development it would be difficult to overestimate. It was he who, more than any other, started poetry on its later way of conscious personal reaction to earth happenings, and his verse is a rich, moist, succulent soil in which later poets dug assiduously with great gain, going, those in the nineteenth century, far deeper.

Thomson was a Scot, with a Scot's affection for the hills and meadows and streams of home. Reading the *Seasons*, against the background of rationalistic work such as *Universal Beauty*, one discovers a world concrete, picturesque, warm, rich in color, with its harvest fields and its blossoming hawthorne, its thick grass for the cropping sheep, its running water,— all revealed through personal response. Brooke finds beauty in the inner mechanism of plants and animals, the plan on which they work or by which they are worked, an abstract conception of a plan; Thomson finds it in the plants and animals themselves, wallflower, wild violets, heath and wild thyme, robin, lark, linnet, hare. To Brooke the world is a system; to Thomson an experience; the world of the nature Deists was an idea in the mind; Thomson touched this world, smelled it, listened to it, and was immediately aware both that it was there, and of his connection with it. He brought not only the gift of the senses, but of affection for the scenes which he describes, love of meadow and hill and tree, rather than the rationalist's admiration for a mechanism perfectly working.

Thomson's *Seasons* (1726–1730) arrested and held men's attention for many years, in England, Germany, and elsewhere, giving new interest to the scene around them. There is rich descriptive beauty in color and line of mountain, meadow, and stream, of cloud, and sheltering trees, of earth phenomena and sky phenomena,— sunrise and sunset; the descriptions are often much generalized, yet show close observation. The carefully differentiated storms in different seasons: the summer storm, with its prelude of stillness, when the forest leaf shakes without a breath; the winter storm, with action of sea fowl and rooks; the famous falling of the snow:

> Through the hush'd air the whitening shower descends;

the flight of the swallows in Autumn; the birds and their

nesting, and the flight of the young from the nest; the withered leaf, snatched in short eddies; the "dew-dropping coolness" of a summer morning, these, and numberless other touches show a wide range of observation and appreciation.

If one can forget the classification of Thomson as a descriptive poet, forget the phrase, "landscape school," or "descriptive school," and read him swiftly, continuously, one will be struck by the fact that he is not, primarily, a descriptive poet at all, if the term means, as it so often does, sketching landscapes. The criticism that has been made that he does not make a clear picture, from a single point of view, as a landscape painter does, is beside the point; he is not trying to. It is, for the most part, process, action, motion, that he is presenting; not so much that which is as that which happens. All is activity; he tells what man and nature are doing; what man, as affected by nature, is experiencing; it is a world alive. He delights in the action of storms, the sweep of the wind, the falling of rain, the influence of sun on the vegetable and the animal world, the teeming life of the swamp; the influence of the sun on the mineral world, disintegrating the stones, the minerals. Something of this appears in Brooke, but Brooke delights in the idea of process, Thomson in the process itself, as of something shared.

These and numberless other passages show not only close attention to nature phenomena, but a new self-consciousness in regard to nature. Here is one noting his impressions of the world about him as if they were important, an individual looking, listening, touching, and recording his individual reaction. Yet there is an impersonality in Thomson's personal response to nature; he is not directing attention to himself; it is nature that he is observing, and he is doing what he can to reveal it. The ego here is important, not for its own sake, but as a power translating and interpreting the encompassing world for others less versed in the language, so that they see with his eyes, hear with his ears, touch with his touch. Here is beauty, no longer an abstract conception of fitness of organism to its use, but a joy, brought home through the senses, which stir feeling and mild reflection. In this sense-apprehension of nature in the *Seasons*, the eye plays the greatest part; next, touch, with special love of the cool, the humid, the dewy; then the ear, especially as regards the sound of the wind, the bird notes; fragrances are noted, but not very frequently.

The reality of Thomson's nature experiences in this vividness of sensation is significant. One feels here recognition of the nearness of man to earth life; the effect on his body, his mood, to a certain extent on his mind, of the changing seasons. He is depressed or stimulated, mentally and physically, by the sting of winter; joyous in spring; the heat of summer days draws him to seek shade and coolness, perhaps for slow reflection. He speaks of joyous winter days; and "congenial horrors of winter" suggests inward reaction, the effect on the mind; these experiences exalt the soul. The spring mood brings him a sense of love abroad in all the world, and a feeling that he shares "the passion of the groves." The organic oneness of man and nature, instinctively reflected in lyric poetry, especially that of spring, in earlier eras, is coming nearer to conscious reflection. He tries to show how the cyclic process of the seasons becomes a part of man's experience, a matter of personal concern for himself and for his neighbors, and to make known not only how deeply, physically, man is a part of earth, but how close his sensations are to mood and mind. In the rising of sap, the growth of roots while "Spring greens the air," and "full swell the woods," man has some share, for cosmic process is working within him, and he is conscious of it. Realization comes to the poet that he is made of the dust of the earth, realization also of what it means to be made of the dust of the earth. As he shares the spring processes, the life of growing, juicy things, moist, bright, and green, in autumn he shares that sense of ripening with ripening fruits that gives Keats' *Ode to Autumn* its rich, distinctive, interpretative note,— far subtler than Thomson's. Nature, in Thomson, is alive with the life of the creating Deity; and it is the breath of life which God breathes into the whole that rouses in him this physical response, which leads to reflective emotion.

He gives, not only a wide range of observation of happenings on the earth and in the sky, but a reaching out for further life,— the swing of the planets (inhabited, he thinks) in the power of the sun; the year cycle, not only as known at home, but as imagined in far distant places, reflective imagination, stimulated by scientific discovery, playing about far distances and remote scenes. In all this there is much of the Deist's contemplation of the great whole, the idea of the Creator's power as manifest in the immensities of space, but there is far more of individual reaction. Undoubtedly Thomson found in the sweep of that thought elements that stimulated his imagination and helped quicken into life a groping sense of the vastness of the universe, but Thomson was a nature-lover before he was a Deist; his close contact with nature is such as is possible only to one who has known nature in boyhood and youth. He is not observing, in the light of an idea of a preconceived plan, for the intellectual pleasure it gives him to see it working. Neither the abstract thought of the immensities nor of the minutiae of nature is of chief importance to him; it was the earth, with its mountains, meadows, streams, with which he had something of personal relation, that drew him. Except for a few passages his work would probably not have been very different if the Deists had never set about interpreting the revelation of God through nature. There would still have been, for Thomson, the sheep in the pastures, the shepherd on the hill; flowers in humble gardens; the wind in the woods, and streams flowing. It was the warm tangible earth with the growths upon it that led Thomson to consider theories of its nature and origin, rather than interest in a cosmic theory that had to be proved by observation.

As significant as Thomson's sense of nearness to earth is his feeling of nearness to the humble people who live close to earth. Though he justifies his choice of rural themes by reference to antiquity, and his praise of simple life bears something of the stamp of Augustan moralizing, his sketches of rustic folk seem an expression of feeling natural because he has lived near them. There was courage in avowing at this period lowly associations, sympathy with humble lives and occupations. Of common man he was observer and concerned observer, with something of that sympathy that later was to swell into so deep a current, revealing mankind's deepening sense of unity with man. There are protests in his work against social injustice, against the contrasts between poverty and wealth, and pleas to the powerful to succor the weak, yet there is little that is tragic in his interpretation of human life under the course of the seasons. Man, happily gathering hay in the sunshine, not unhappily ploughing, or washing sheep, or joyously crushing grapes in autumn, in "busy, joy-resounding fields" is presented, for the most part, in a state of industrious content, though now and then a glimpse of suffering comes, as in the case of the shepherd, perishing in winter snow, while his little children peep out of the cottage, trying to spy their father coming home. The social sense in Thomson is instinctive, not a philosophic theory, rather the neighborhood friendliness of Scottish humble life; his contribution was to become part of a larger sense of human relationships, from so many sources did the later deep conviction of the organic oneness of humanity draw.

His peasants are not individualized; there is a tendency to generalize, to include all ploughmen with his ploughmen, all reapers with his reapers, though now and then a single figure stands out:

> Wilder'd, o'er the waste,
> The shepherd stalks gigantic,

through the autumn mists. His pictures of human life do not approach the clear distinctness of Wordsworthian portraiture; he has not that touch which transfigures man and his nature background, revealing both as expressions of the divine. Note Wordsworth's shepherd:

> As he stepped
> Beyond the boundary line of some hill-shadow,
> His form hath flashed upon me, glorified
> By the deep radiance of the setting sun:
> Or him have I descried in distant sky,
> A solitary object and sublime,
> Above all height.

Needless to say, there is no attempt in Thomson to interpret the inner life of those whom he delineates, and there is no inkling of the Wordsworthian conception of the spiritual oneness of humanity.

There is, in Thomson, a significant drawing near to the animal kingdom in sympathy and understanding, new and surprising in this period, and the Deist sense of a perfect mechanism, in these minor lives, operated by the "Eternal Finger," slips into an intuition of personality in them, an interest in their life experiences. If Wordsworth cannot "measure" the "thoughts" of the birds, Thomson can interpret the ardor and the appealing arts of the wooing time. The burst of bird in song in spring, somewhat muffled by Thomson's vocabulary, gives in his verse genuine melody, and telling phrase:

> The blackbird whistles from the thorny brake.

The bird courtships; the nest building; all their story, in their love and in their parental care, as in the teaching of the young to fly, and in the parent bird trying to draw away pursuit; the loss of the wildness of note of the caged bird; the growing friendliness of the hungry robin in winter,— all these passages and many others show Thomson's close observation, and his power of interpreting wild life as if from the inside. The horse, in his strength, his courage, his pride, springing the high fence, swimming the river, is rendered in terms of horse. The poet flees with the terrified hunted hare, with the hunted stag, and seems to know his inner experience, sure at first of his speed, soon sobbing with effort, becoming exhausted, fainting, dying, with dogs at his throat. . . . He who writes thus is no mere observer of hare and stag, but one who knows how to share primeval fear, and is drawing nearer than men had done to understanding the lower orders of life upon the globe, and to a sense of kinship with them. In Thomson's pity for animals, as in his attitude toward humble human kind, he establishes something of a spiritual relation; no words of praise can be too great for his protests against cruelty, helping waken the compunction of the world.

Thomson troubles himself little with the abstract question of evil in this beautifully planned and beautifully managed universe. Concrete instances of suffering disturb him; of cruelty in nature he has a glimpse, but he dismisses it with the reflection that the beast of prey deserves to perish, unlike the plain ox, slain though he has not offended. The villain spider is roundly rated for being what he is, an attitude unlike that of Shaftesbury who found harmony in the fact that spider and fly were so adapted to each other in the economy of nature; the existence of tiger, leopard, hyena, lion, and venomous serpents is admitted, with their power to hurt. With other Deist thinkers Thomson explains that it is chiefly man who is the cause of what is wrong with the world, but he does not concern himself with the metaphysics of evil, though he suffers personally in the suffering of humble men, of beasts that man makes suffer. No explanation of the ultimate source is suggested; evil, in Thomson, in connection with human lives or with animal lives, is an incident, not a problem; men who do these things would better stop!

Thomson, in his thought of nature, of man, of animals, does not reach the conception of a later age of all nature as one, and alive, but he breaks soil, helps prepare the way for it. There is perception of organic relationships in his very writing about the seasons, of process and change, of the development of life, animal and vegetable, throughout the year, yet it does not reach the idea of a living whole, as inwardly interpreted. Reaction to nature contacts, to the touch of sun and wind, reveal man as, physically, a part of nature; mind and feeling are stirred through these contacts, for the works of nature swell the soul with pleasing dread; nature has power to "Soothe every gust of passion into peace;" the "infusive force of spring" can "serene his soul"; but all this lacks much of that inner identity of the soul of man with the soul of nature of which Wordsworth at a later day became the revealer. For all the sensation, the emotion wakened in him,

> Man superior walks
> Amid the glad creation.

Thomson's thought in regard to the power manifest in nature is quite in accord with that of Shaftesbury. In moments of deeper feeling he expresses belief in the immanence of a divine spirit in the phenomena of nature, quickly springing back to the idea of a personal God, from whom it emanates:

> What is this mighty breath, ye curious, say,
> That in a powerful language, felt, not heard,
> Instructs the fowls of heaven, and through their breast
> These arts of love diffuses? What, but God?
> Inspiring God! who, boundless spirit all,
> And unremitting energy, pervades,
> Adjusts, sustains, and agitates the whole.

> He ceaseless works alone, and yet alone
> Seems not to work.

Immediately after, he speaks of the informing Author, who appears in his works, the smiling God, the poet's mind, as is almost invariably the case, turning from the idea of power working within to that of external power, fashioning from the outside:

> Hail, Source of Beings! Universal Soul
> Of heaven and earth! Essential Presence, hail!
> To thee I bend the knee; to thee my thoughts
> Continual, climb, who, with a master-hand,
> Hast the great whole into perfection touch'd.

All nature, in

> Its life, its laws, its progress, and its end,

bears witness to design, sprung from the "Eternal Mind" philosophy is alert

> To conceive
> Of the Sole Being right, who *spoke the word*
> And nature mov'd complete.
> . . . .
> Such the All-perfect Hand
> That pois'd, impels, and rules the steady whole!

The *Hymn* begins with a passage which might denote pantheism, were it not for abundant evidence, in this poem and in the *Seasons*, that Thomson's most oft-recurring thought of the Deity was of a power, possessed of personality, creating as an artist creates, following a great plan:

> These, as they change, Almighty Father, these
> Are but the varied God. The rolling year
> Is full of thee. Forth in the pleasing Spring
> Thy beauty walks,

but the God of Seasons is an anthropomorphic Deity, ruling from without as well as manifest within, compelling praise from all that lives; man and nature join in that praise:

Nature, attend! join, every living soul,

. . . .

In adoration join; and, ardent, raise
One general song! To him, ye vocal gales,
Breathe soft, whose spirit in your freshness breathes;
O! talk of him in solitary glooms,
Where, o'er the rock, the scarcely-waving pine
Fills the brown shade with a religious awe.

The *Hymn*, Thomson's most spiritual effort, in which all voices of earth and air and sea, human voices, and voices of wind and wave, join in praise of the mysterious power which is working in and through all things, as well as above all, is prelude to that deeper intuition of oneness, set forth in unforgettable phrase in Wordsworth's *Tintern Abbey* and elsewhere; in Coleridge's *Eolian Harp*. But the difference is vast. Here are the many, praising the One, not a perception of the One in the many. Thomson makes you aware that, physically, man is a part of living nature; Wordsworth that he is also, spiritually, a part of the living spirit of nature. Thomson, except for the emotion of love, thinks rather than feels that immanence in the phenomena of nature; he perceives, praises, adores the qualities of the Creator, but never reaches the mystic's sense of communion with the divine. Wordsworth feels a oneness with spirit; the immanence is in himself also; he is instinctively aware of it, is it, for the "spirit" which "rolls through all things" is "in the mind of man" also. In Thomson the immanence is in the phenomena of nature, but not in the mind of man. He recognizes the one life in the contemplated world, but it does not include the mind of the contemplator.

One significant affirmation of Thomson is reiterated in varied ways by later poets. To him, the God of boundless Power is the God of Love; all nature-phenomena, even the comet, exist but

To work the will of all-sustaining Love.

This cosmic passion, which runs through all nature, is God working within; it finds its culmination in human love; we feel the present Deity most keenly when spring serenes the soul, raising life to a higher level, bringing in its joy a deeper sense of the fundamental harmony in the universe. From what drift of philosophy or religion the conviction of love as the central power of the universe came to him we may not know; perhaps some gentler aspect of his Scotch religious training contributed. There are flashes of the idea in both Shaftesbury and Brooke, though the latter gives no suggestion of its inner working. Whatever the sources of the idea, it is Thomson's best, and in the ending of the *Hymn* he surpassed himself, giving a prophetic gleam of insight into the wisdom of a later age:

> I cannot go
> Where Universal Love not smiles around,
> Sustaining all yon orbs, and all their sons;
> From seeming evil still educing good,
> And better thence again, and better still
> In infinite progression,

a suggestion of spiritual development, anticipating Browning, and far outstripping Thomson's age. This note of development, possibly deriving from Shaftesbury, appears in other places:

> Enough for us to know that this dark state,
> In wayward passions lost, and vain pursuits,
> This infancy of being, can not prove
> The final issue of the works of God,
> By boundless Love and perfect Wisdom form'd,
> And ever rising with the rising mind.

One wonders how much is implied in his winter contemplation regarding nature's vast whole:

> Its life, its laws, its progress, and its end;

and regarding the moral world:

> Which, though to us it seems embroil'd, moves on
> In higher order;

and in his anticipation of those scenes:

> Where the mind
> In endless growth and infinite ascent,
> Rises from state to state, and world to world.

Thomson's poetic vocabulary, in a great part of the *Seasons*, is one of the ironies of literature. A Scot's plain love of the world of out-of-doors veils its genuineness of feeling all too often in "horrific" phrase, so that one is hardly aware of the directness and simplicity of his response to the touch of nature. It is as if, puzzled by the immediacy of pleasure, he attempted to intellectualize the senses, as became a dweller in the house of Reason, to translate into analytic phrase, defining a quality, that which was simply sense experience. There is much close and feeling observation, many an effective expression, felicitous epithet, apparent in passages already quoted and many others; in the "hawthorn whitens"; in the freshness that breathes through the dewy fields; in

> A fresher gale
> Begins to wave the wood, and stir the stream,
> Sweeping with shadowy gust the fields of corn;

but there is, alas! far more pedantic phraseology, a passion for Latin derivatives, chiefly adjectives, and a fatal ingenuity in contriving them: "turgent," "relucent stream," "fallow ground concoctive," "the fond sequacious [human] herd."

> Luculent along
> The purer rivers flow;

> A whitening shower of vegetable down
> Amusive floats.

So the "amusive arch" of the rainbow.

The phraseology of Thomson is more than a mere vocabulary; it is, in great part, an act of intellectual obeisance to the standards of the age, reason reproving the immediacy of pleasure. Perhaps he felt himself, in a world of silk and lace and wigs and ruffles, a bit too near the soil, shamefaced in his love of nature and the homely ways of homely people; ashamed, in a world that tended to generalize, to seek the abstract, of his interest in little concrete happenings, the way in which, in the cottage, while the matron spins,

> The wasted taper and the crackling flame
> Foretell the blast;

in house dog and greyhound in the "buzzing shade," sleeping, waking to snap at a wasp; and so made atonement in his "prelusive," "amusive," "sequacious," if but to show that he could Latinize with the best. Yet in this searching out and compounding of adjectives is often manifest a nice sense of values, an endeavor to state the exact shade of effect upon eye or ear or sense of touch of some nature happening.

Thomson's influence was more apparent in a later and greater period than the eighteenth century. The large view, the cosmic aspect of nature life, the sense of action and process, the rich sense perception, were not apparent in his immediate successors, but in Wordsworth, Keats, Shelley they reappear, glorified by individual genius, and put to fine symbolic uses.

VII. Akenside

Shaftesbury had been content with affirming the unity, beauty, harmony of the universe, and man's actual and potential share therein; Thomson, with accepting this philosophy, while he busied himself with noting the concrete things of earth, and their effect upon himself and other men;

Akenside was not willing to stop here, and, in his *Pleasures of Imagination* (1744) pursued an inquiry as to how these effects were produced in the mind; whence came "The resemblance of certain aspects of inanimate things to the sensations and properties of the mind?" Thomson had said: "The scarcely moving pine," in the solitary glooms,

> Fills the brown shade with a religious awe.

Akenside asks how this awe comes to be:

> Mark the sable woods
> That shade sublime yon mountain's nodding brow;
> With what religious awe the solemn scene
> Commands your steps!

He is evidently puzzled by the question, why? of which Shaftesbury was, apparently, serenely unconscious, as to what the connection might be between this outer order and the mind of man. The answer is one which only a disciple of Plato, or of Plotinus, or of both could have given. The universe is an Idea of God, made manifest to sense. Before the creation of sun, moon, mountains, streams:

> Then liv'd th' Almighty One: then, deep retir'd
> In his unfathom'd essence, view'd the forms,
> The forms eternal of created things: —
> . . . .
> What he admir'd and lov'd, his vital smile
> Unfolded into being. Hence the breath
> Of life informing each organic frame,
> Hence the green earth, and wild resounding waves.

It was the Deity who first experienced the *Pleasures of Imagination*; creation was the result of the Almighty One's imaginative vision and creative power.

Akenside accepts Shaftesbury's system, and, in framing his aesthetic theory, selects certain points for further development, conscious of the lost link in the thought of his predecessor. Nature is an emanation of God; the mind of man and Nature, coming from the same source, have hidden correspondences. Like two needles, drawing their mystic virtue from the same stone, they remember "the alliance of their birth." This emanation, the creative outflowing of the Deity, accounts for the intercourse between God and man through Nature, for "The ideas of the Divine Mind [are] the origin of every quality pleasing to the imagination," affirms the argument to Book I. This is surely reminiscent of the idea of Plotinus of the world-soul, of which all souls are part, turned on the one side toward the realm of pure idea, on the other toward Nature. Akenside says: "There are certain powers in human nature which seem to hold a middle place between the organs of bodily sense and the faculties of moral perception . . . the Powers of Imagination. Like the external senses they relate to matter and motion, and at the same time, give the mind ideas analogous to those of moral approbation and dislike."

As Memnon's image was touched to music by the sunbeams,

> Even so did Nature's hand
> To certain species of external things
> Attune the finer organs of the mind:
> So the glad impulse of congenial powers,
> Or of sweet sounds, or fair-proportioned form,
> The grace of motion, or the bloom of light,
> Thrills through Imagination's tender frame, —
> From nerve to nerve: all naked and alive,
> They catch the spreading rays: till now the soul
> At length discloses every tuneful spring,
> To that harmonious movement from without
> Responsive.

This explains the opening lines:

> With what attractive charms this goodly frame
> Of Nature touches the consenting hearts
> Of mortal men.

Did Wordsworth find suggestion here? In *The Recluse*, he says:

> While my voice proclaims
> How exquisitely the individual mind
> (And the progressive powers perhaps no less
> Of the whole species) to the external world
> Is fitted: — and how exquisitely, too —
> . . . .
> The external World is fitted to the Mind.

Not all human beings are alike gifted in reading the meaning of supreme beauty written on the face of nature. There are certain chosen souls, Akenside affirms, who penetrate the secret of divine significance:

> But some, to higher hopes
> Were destin'd; some within a finer mould
> She wrought, and temper'd with a purer flame.
> To these the Sire Omnipotent unfolds
> The world's harmonious volume, there to read
> The transcript of himself.

The poet invokes some being of finer insight to help him see and understand:

> Some heavenly genius, whose unclouded thoughts
> Attain that secret harmony which blends
> The ethereal spirit with its mould of clay;
> O! teach me to reveal the graceful charm
> That searchless Nature o'er the sense of man
> Diffuses, to behold, in lifeless things,
> The inexpressive semblance of himself,
> Of thought and passion.

The poem ends with:

> Thus the men
> Whom Nature's works can charm, with God himself
> Hold converse; grow familiar, day by day,
> With his conceptions, act upon his plan;
> And form to his, the relish of their souls.

Akenside combines much of Addison's theory of the imagination as presented in the *Spectator* papers, with this esoteric doctrine, which would have been far from Addison's thought. Following Addison in the classification of the pleasures: the Sublime, the Wonderful, the Beautiful, he greatly broadens the basis of the theory by admitting other senses as factors in these pleasures, not the eye alone, the most intellectual of the senses.

By his sense of the sublime man is drawn to the grander and more awful aspects of nature, which lead him nearest to essential Deity: "Alpine heights," "empires black with shade," the phenomena of the heavens, "the blue profound," the "unrelenting sway" of the sun over the planets;— looking above and beyond all this he shall see

> That uncreated beauty, which delights
> The mind supreme,

for the Sovereign Maker said that the soul should

> Through all the ascent of things enlarge her view
> Till every bound at length should disappear,
> And infinite perfection close the scene.

The treatment of the wonderful is far more significant than that of Addison, though the influence of the latter is seen in the anticlimax of the end, in which the village beldame, harping on superstitions, plays the major part. Akenside sets forth the quickening challenge of the unknown, of strangeness, which

> Wakes each active power
> To brisker measures. . . .

> The bounteous Providence of Heaven,
> In every breast implanting this desire
> Of objects new, and strange, to urge us on

> With unremitted labor to pursue
> Those sacred stores that wait the ripening soul
> In Truth's exhaustless bosom.

The daring youth explores strange climes; the pensive sage burns the midnight taper, seeking the intellectual strange and unknown; the virgin follows the enchanted tale, and in all this there is a suggestion of the quest, a prefatory hint of the charm of "beauty touched with strangeness."

In the treatment of Beauty Akenside follows Shaftesbury, who follows Plato, in the identification of beauty and truth. Beauty, especially beauty of nature, brings its quickening challenge; and with scenes of nature beauty are recalled old tales of beauty in the land of beauty, Greece. As in Brooke, beauty throughout the world of nature and of human beings is a manifestation of fitness of form to active use. Aspects of nature fertility,

> And every charm of animated things,
> Are only pledges of a state sincere,
> The integrity and order of their frame
> When all is well within, and every end
> Accomplish'd. Thus was Beauty sent from Heaven,
> The lovely ministress of truth and good
> In this dark world: for truth and good are one.

Akenside's rising scale of beauty is significant: the lowest is color; then comes line; then symmetry; higher still is vital beauty, where to

> The vital change of growth
> Life's holy flame and piercing sense are given.

He gives his own adaptation of that Platonic conception of the beauties of earth as steps by which man may mount "from fair forms to fair actions, and from fair actions to fair notions, until from fair notions he arrives at the notion of absolute beauty." Beauty is an attribute not only of existences in the physical world; it involves also the whole moral and intellectual being of man. Not even the exaltation which comes from the contemplation of the whole:

> The range
> Of planets, suns, and adamantine spheres,
> Wheeling unshaken through the void immense,

is the greatest exaltation. This Beauty, which is truth, finds its supreme expression, not in those things which are seen, but in those that are unseen. Beauty, sweeping through the universe, reveals itself most fully in the mind, heart, soul of man; in patriotism, loyal friendship, sympathy:

> The graceful tear that streams for others' woes;

in home affections, love. Nothing else in all the wonder of the universe is so wonderful as man's power to frame the sacred laws of action and of will. Between the supreme unseen and the answering powers of man's spirit, the Imagination acts as mediator, and Virtue, taking on beauty of form, draws the human heart her way.

Akenside's is on the whole a rationalistic rather than an aesthetic theory of the imagination, as working in connection with nature and the arts. He recognizes the sense element in the appreciation of beauty, but rationalizes the sense contribution to beauty; he does not see Beauty "shining in clearness through the clearest aperture of sense," as did Plato; thought must transmute it into an indication of the perfect working of a perfect system; all the pleasures of imagination, in the long run, are valued because they lead to clearer ideas of God. The sublime gives you the most exalted conceptions of the Deity; beauty shows the marvels of his adaptation of created forms to use. Akenside, in the end, takes the appeal of beauty out of the realm of immediate pleasure into the realm of pure thought. Those powers in human nature which "hold a middle place between the organs of bodily sense and the faculties of moral perception . . . give the mind ideas analogous to those of moral approbation and dislike." There is no suggestion, as in Wordsworth and other nature mystics, of heightened spiritual life, of the immediacy of the divine. Beauty is most conspicuous

> Even in outward shape,
> Where dawns the high expression of a mind:
> By steps conducting our enraptur'd search
> To that eternal origin, whose power, [is]
> Through all the unbounded symmetry of things,
> Like rays effulging from the parent Sun.
> . . . .
> Mind, mind alone, (bear witness Earth and Heaven),
> The living fountains in itself contains
> Of beauteous and sublime.

Akenside's house of thought is a half-way house to the realm of romantic poetry. Much in the thought, or in chance phrase, in the verse of Wordsworth and of Coleridge, shows his influence. Among the many notes foreshadowing the thought and feeling of a later age are his affirmation, when he is treating the sublime, that there is something in the human soul that demands the infinite, and the hint, already noted, of the appeal of strangeness in beauty. In discussing the wonderful, at the beginning, he seems to tread the borderland of the mystery of life, but one feels the tug of Addison's short-leashed thought in his speculative inquiry. The following passage is noteworthy, in its suggestion of the challenge of the unknown in calling forth latent power:

> Call now to mind what high capacious powers
> Lie folded up in man; how far beyond
> The praise of mortals may the eternal growth
> Of Nature to perfection half divine
> Expand the blooming soul?

In this transition thought we are well on our way to the idea of growth, development,— the underlying idea, in science and in philosophy, of the period in which romantic poetry came to be. In Akenside's own development, as he reveals in the fragmentary Book IV, written many years later, nature played a great part,— the dales of Tyne, the most ancient woodlands, the mossy falls of solitary Wensbeck's limpid stream, beloved of old. It is his idea that nature forms the poet, her perfectness shaping his genius:

> Nature's kindling breath
> Must fire the chosen genius; Nature's hand
> Must string his nerves.

The laws of poetic art, he says, have been much discussed by critics, but none has sung the deepest principle, for obedience to rule does not make poetry; genius comes from Heaven. Does he not mean that, as Nature is a manifestation of an idea in the divine mind, the poet, studying her inner order, her symmetry, draws directly from the divine? Already in Shaftesbury we find something of the idea of the inner harmony of the universe passing through the soul of the poet into a work of art. Akenside, in accepting this idea, and in stressing imagination as the most important factor in the creation of poetry, representing "the finest features of the mind," shows himself a forerunner, in the world of criticism, of a new era. Back of the conception of Wordsworth and of Coleridge of individual imagination, shaping a work of art from within, lies this eighteenth century idea of the perfect working of the vast universe, and to them this perfect working was apparent not only in the world of nature, but in the creative instinct of man. Doubtless they were indebted to their immediate predecessors, as well as to the fountainhead of these ideas in Greek thought. If Akenside seems knocking at a door that does not quite open; if, at times, he draws back from his finest intuitions into the realm of didactic reason, yet the *Pleasures of Imagination*, harking back to Plato and to Plotinus, and sowing prophetic seeds of suggestion for the future in regard to the supremacy of the imagination in poetic art, in regard to the intercourse between the soul of nature and the soul of man, in regard to the appeal of the strange, the wonderful, and to the potential development of the powers folded up in man, is a landmark in the development of thought in which romantic poetry finds its base.

VIII. Edward Young, of *Night Thoughts* (1742–1744)

A soliloquy,— for the imaginary listener Lorenzo never once invades the speaker's solitude,— in well-nigh ten thousand lines would seem to be carrying the instinct for self-expression beyond reasonable limits, yet Edward Young had many readers in his own day, and a popularity that lasted long. Possibly this is due to his power to voice epigrammatically the common thought, the common mood; in so doing he spoke for many in whom the urge for self-revelation exceeded the power of utterance. All too mistakenly praised for many years as a great poet, he has fallen into neglect and is usually dismissed as one who achieved little but endless and tiresome iteration of outworn dogma and of mood. In truth, to read the *Night Thoughts* through today is not an easy task; the humor of which its author is said to have been possessed, to the extent of outshining Voltaire in wit when they once met, naturally does not appear in so serious a work; yet to live for a time in the mind of Edward Young, as, under the sting of grief caused by successive deaths in his family, he attempts to interpret the universe, and human life both in this world and the next, is a not uninstructive experience. He was a thinker, and, through those argumentative lines of end-stopped blank verse where one feels all too often the insistent beat of the couplet, blow somewhat conflicting winds where past and future meet. With his general discussion of the rational basis of orthodoxy we need not concern ourselves, but it is interesting to ask how, midway down that century of deepening thought, the conception of the vast whole, of the unity of all, which science and the Deists had forced upon men's minds, affects a mind turning inward to self-scrutiny; whether the poet has an immediate sense of the immanence of the divine throughout the universe, and establishes a personal relation with the soul of all; whether he rests with his age upon the authority of reason, or feels the need of calling upon all his powers, in solving the problem that has come sharply home to him as a personal problem, death.

Young can hardly be called a nature poet, though he seems to feel most deeply and to think best in the presence of certain shadowy aspects of nature; night, darkness, and solitude evidently make him more intensely himself. "Night, sable goddess," upon her "ebon throne," presides over his meditation; as the bell strikes one, he invokes:

> Silence and Darkness! solemn sisters! twins
> From ancient Night, who nurse the tender thought
> To reason, and on reason build resolve,

to assist him. Darkness is an aid to thought:

> Thus, darkness aiding intellectual light,
> And sacred silence whispering truths divine.

For him, darkness has more divinity than daylight:

> It strikes thought inward; it drives back the soul
> To settle on herself, our point supreme!

Midnight and darkness hush the passions, set the spirit free, and reveal divinity:

> What awful joy! what mental liberty!
> . . . .
> Delightful gloom! the clust'ring thoughts around
> Spontaneous rise, and blossom in the shade,
> But droop by day, and sicken in the sun.
> . . . .

> This sacred shade and solitude, what is it?
> 'Tis the felt presence of the Deity.

He has apparently little awareness of the loveliness of the world in sunlight, but has admiration for the beauty of the moon, the beauty and significance of the stars:

> One sun by day, by night ten thousand shine
> And light us deep into the Deity.

The world of grass and tree and blossom hardly exists for him; he reveals little sense appreciation, and affirms:

> A languid leaden iteration reigns,
> And ever must, o'er those whose joys are joys
> Of sight, smell, taste.

The moonlight which he seeks is with him more an idea than an immediate delight; the stars all too often cease to be stars and drift into arguments:

> Weigh'd aright
> 'Tis nature's system of divinity,
> . . . .
> 'Tis elder Scripture, writ by God's own hand,

proving the existence of God, and man's immortality, for the boundless space through which they roam

> Suggests the sister thought
> Of boundless time.

They not only reveal Omnipotence, reveal eternity, but teach moral lessons:

> Wilt thou not feel the bias nature gave?
> Canst thou descend from converse with the skies
> And seize thy brother's throat? . . .
> . . . .
> . . . The planets cry 'Forbear'!

By their amiable interchange of rays they impress on man the need of subordination of self-interest to the whole. But, deeper than didactic teaching, is their effect on the inward man:

> O what a confluence of ethereal fires,
> From urns unnumber'd, down the steep of heav'n,
> Streams to a point and centers in my sight!
> Nor tarries there; I feel it at my heart.
> My heart, at once, it humbles and exalts;
> Lays it in dust, and calls it to the skies.
> Who sees it unexalted, or unawed?
> Who sees it, and can stop at what is seen?

The significance of the conscious, self-induced mood, the cultivated nature reaction is apparent. It is as if he said: my inner experiences, in some way half intentional, half unintentional, connect themselves with those outer things, sky, stars, and the power behind. I deliberately arrange matters so that aspects of nature will rouse certain feelings and start trains of thought in me; darkness and shadow appeal, because they somehow fit the shadow in my mind. I try to quicken those processes of thought and feeling which will make me believe what I want to believe, and thus seek out those aspects of nature which will stir most deeply that which is deepest in me. This approach to his inmost self, and therewith the approach through Nature to the supreme God, is deeply significant in this period of thought creeping inward. He does not consciously reach a sense of deep correspondence,— a sense "Of something far more deeply interfused," but he is on the way to it in experience, if not in thought.

The subjective nature of the work manifests itself from the beginning, in the conviction of the all-importance of this personal discussion of the after-fate of the individual; in the unrestrained expression of personal emotion; and in the emphasis placed on the service of individual instinct, feeling, in finding out truth. Young's *Night Thoughts* is an outpouring of half feeling, half thought, a mingling of the sincere in his expression of grief, and a half pleasurable sensation in his own sadness; a mingling of genuine faith, and of doubt stifled in insistent affirmation. There is a somewhat self-conscious revelation of self-induced emotion and reflection, sometimes genuine, sometimes spectacular:

> I keep my assignation with my woe!

but it is very human, and sometimes very wise in basing the interpretation of life, as did the philosophers of old time, in part upon experience. Sorrow is to him the best teacher; a later and greater than he divined, in the keen hurt of youthful years, the same truth: "Sorrow is wisdom," said Keats. In reaction from the despair of grief he cries:

> How wretched is the man who never mourn'd!

Swift-coming sorrows quicken his mind to deeper action in regard to the age-old problem; he finds that he who is uninstructed in death has never known life. His attitude toward death is far more personal than that of Blair, or of other members of the "graveyard school," or of Gray. Through his intense sense of what has happened to him and his, death becomes personified, a personal foe, and he became, one of his critics said, "undoubtedly the most patient and powerful limner death ever had." But he vibrates between terror at the physical aspects of decay, and praise of death as the gateway to greater life; and the eighteenth century love of antithesis lends itself admirably to presenting the contrast. The agonies of death, the horrors of the grave are dwelt upon, but death is eulogized as the "crown of life":

> Death, the great counsellor, who man inspires
> With every nobler thought, and fairer deed!
> Death, the deliverer, who rescues man!
> . . . .
> This king of terrors is the prince of peace.
> When shall I die to vanity, pain, death?

When shall I die? When shall I live forever?
Life is the triumph of our mould'ring clay,
Death of the spirit, infinite! divine!

Others, from old time, have harped upon the universality and the horror of death; it is not in this that the chief significance for us comes, but in the close rendering of personal reaction, his intense conviction of an individual future for himself and those whom he loved, his assurance of the deepening insight that comes to him through his sorrow. A feeling that, in the depth of his grief, he has come nearer than ever before to touching reality, may naturally have brought a longing to renew the sting, if only to reach through pain, nearer to truth.

The burden of *Night Thoughts* is the question of immortality. A shadowy influence of Hamlet's soliloquy runs through it, and at times one feels that the author fancied himself triumphantly answering Hamlet's questioning about death. This answer involves consideration of speculations of both scientist and philosopher of his own and the preceding period, mingling both with insistent affirmations concerning revealed religion, and emphasizes the importance of individual solution of this great problem. With the echo of Hamlet mingles an echo of Descartes, made to voice his central thesis, immortality:

What am I? and from whence? — I nothing know,
But that I am; and, since I am, conclude
Something eternal.

But he is more deeply concerned with the scientific affirmations of the preceding century in regard to the universe, and the Deistic interpretations of its nature. Of the idea of the vastness and the unity of the whole he is aware, and his imagination is touched by his knowledge; a sense of wonder and of mystery is mingled with his confident explanations:

In the vast ocean of unbounded space,
Behold an infinite of floating worlds

Divide the crystal waves of ether pure,
In endless voyage, without port!
. . . .
What involution! What extent! What swarms
Of worlds, that laugh at earth! Immensely great!
Immensely distant from each other's spheres!
What, then, the wondrous space through which they roll?
At once it quite ingulfs all human thought;
'Tis comprehension's absolute defeat.

He is aware of the reign of law:

What order, beauty, motion, distance, size!
. . . .
Apt means! great ends! consent to general good!

Though a stout defender of revealed religion he proclaims law more potent than miracle:

Say, which imports more plentitude of pow'r,
Or nature's laws to fix, or to repeal!
. . . .
The course of nature is the art of God.

The most interesting aspect of Young's reaction to immensity is, however, this, that the spatial whole is beggared by the potential greatness of man's mind, which can grasp the universe:

Those num'rous worlds that throng the firmament,
And ask more space in heav'n, can roll at large
In man's capacious thought, and still leave room
For ampler orbs, for new creations there.
. . . .
Though that immensely great, still greater he
Whose breast capacious, can embrace, and lodge
Unburden'd nature's universal scheme;
Can grasp creation with a single thought.

This vindication of the dignity and importance of the individual human mind, and the attempt to discriminate between quantitative measurements and intellectual and spiritual values is significant, and not unimportant in the history of thought of Young's time:

> And what yon boundless orbs to godlike man?

He teaches his all-too-patient listener, Lorenzo, when advising him to turn from St. Evremont, an infidel writer, that consideration of the vast whole is necessary for the attainment of truth; true free-thinking comes in sending the soul on curious travel, to make the tour of the universe, to become at home in each recess of space, and so

> To look on truth unbroken, and entire.

Lorenzo, he thinks, will surely learn God from immensity, from size; Young has much to say about vastness, but little about the Creator's handiwork in the minutiae of Creation. Boundless dimensions are to him a most convincing revelation of the Deity; contemplation of space stretches the mind. Truth lies in the system, the full orb; "who most examine, most believe."

> Parts, like half sentences, confound; the whole
> Conveys the sense, and God is understood.

So he urges Lorenzo to reach largeness of thought through contemplation of space, transcending time, and to "Give thy mind sea room" in the thought of eternity.

Young is quite in line with Brooke and other Deist poets in determination to understand and explain the Whole, but he takes a long step forward toward the ways of thought of a later day in his intense focusing on the individual soul, his emphasis on the all-importance of personal reaction.

The God who is understood by Young is the God of Christian tradition, though, as suggested, he adopts much of the Deist conception of a God revealed through nature. God is the "Stupendous Architect;" invisible, eternal Mind has wrought in Nature a work of perfect art:

> To read creation; read its mighty plan
> In the bare bosom of the Deity!
> The plan and execution to collate!

A touch of Neo-Platonism, probably derived from Shaftesbury or his followers, appears in anthropomorphic expression that could hardly be more unfortunate:

> When the Dread Sire, on emanation bent,
> And big with Nature, rising in his might,
> Call'd forth creation, (for then Time was born)
> By Godhead streaming through a thousand worlds.

Here, surely, is the working of the yeast of the thought of Plotinus which wrought, sometimes imperceptibly, through this and preceding centuries, bringing to many a mind glimmerings of an order of thought not wholly grasped. Something of this appears in the invocation:

> O thou, blest Spirit! Whether the supreme
> Great antemondane Father! in whose breast
> Embryo creation, unborn being, dwelt
> And all its various revolutions roll'd
> Present, though future; prior to themselves;
> Whose breath can blow it into nought again;
> Or, from his throne, some delegated pow'r,
> Who, studious of our peace, dost turn the thought
> From vain and vile, to solid and sublime!
> Unseen thou leads't me to delicious draughts
> Of inspiration, from a purer stream,
> And fuller of the God than that which burst
> From famed Castalia.

But the dominant influence in Young's thought of God is Biblical. One eloquent passage recalls the Deism of the Book of Job:

> Thou, apart,
> Above, beyond, O tell me, mighty Mind!
> Where art thou? shall I dive into the deep?

Call to the sun? or ask the roaring winds
For their Creator? Shall I question loud
The thunder, if in that th' Almighty dwells?
Or holds HE furious storms in straite'n'd reins
And bids fierce whirlwinds wheel his rapid car?

He is not without a sense of mystery. An eloquent address to the Deity speaks of him as revealed in the great, in the small, and yet unfathom'd, a common source of all. But again:

Mysterious Power;
Reveal'd yet unreveal'd! darkness in light!
Number in unity! our joy! our dread!

To Young, natural and supernatural revelation harmonize, and supplement each other. The fullest revelation is that which is embodied in Christian theology. Nature is also revelation, but not the chief; or not, as to the Deists, sufficient:

Read Nature; Nature is a friend to truth;
Nature is Christian; preaches to mankind,
And bids dead matter aid us in our creed.

An interesting bit of anthropomorphic speculation comes in the inquiry as to at what point of space Jehovah stood to say that creation was closed: "local is his throne":

Say at what point of space Jehovah dropp'd
His slacken'd line, and laid his balance by;
Weigh'd worlds, and measured infinite no more.
. . . .
I stand, the plan's proud period; I pronounce
The work accomplish'd; the creation closed.

For he carries in his mind that idea of the finished whole, on which foundation in Genesis, theology rested; an idea which the Deist poets, stimulated to new thought by science, had developed with such insistence and wealth of detail; an idea, too, which some of the greatest of the scientists, notably Linnaeus, held firmly, even when the conception of endless development in nature was creeping into other minds.

Of change in nature Young is aware, but not of progressive change:

> Nature, thy daughter, ever-changing birth
> Of thee the great Immutable, to man
> Speaks wisdom.

All in nature is revolution, as seen in the unending swing round the circle, the cycle of the seasons, the rising and setting of the stars, emblems of man, who passes, not expires:

> With this minute distinction, emblems just,
> Nature revolves, but man advances; both
> Eternal; that a circle, this a line;
> That gravitates, this soars. Th' aspiring soul,
> Ardent and tremulous, like flame ascends.

Here is a suggestive, forward-looking thought, if not of the development of the soul, at least of the soul as not wholly caught in the circle of physical nature happenings, but escaping, flame-like, at the last, to the divine.

Nature, the revealer, fails in one important point, the most important point of all; she teaches death, but gives not immortality. Here the supernatural revelation completes the natural; in this, God is shown, not only as the God of Power, but the God of love:

> For — Love almighty! Love almighty! (sing,
> Exult, creation!) Love almighty reigns!

The supreme expression of the God of love comes in this, that he is

> *Father of immortality to man!*

Of an inner relationship of man to God Young has little to say; man, God's handiwork, should worship and adore, should try to understand the Deity as revealed in his other handiwork, nature, and in the Christian religion, and should try to lift his moral being toward the highest he can conceive of God. His attitude is Hebraic, external; there is little of the old Greek thought of the interpenetration of nature by the divine, or of later, mystical thought, in which Greek and Christian blend, of being one with God. He does not harp on the unity of all as much as do Shaftesbury, Brooke, and Pope, but the same gap is apparent in his thought as appears in the conception of the two last named; he has no idea of a unity that would include man's soul. Yet one or two passages puzzle, as suggesting glimmerings of that Neo-Platonic way of thinking which surprise us now and then in this period, gleaming out in a system of very different ideas:

> He, the great Father! kindled at one flame
> The world of rationals; one spirit pour'd
> From spirit's awful fountain; pour'd himself
> Through all their souls, but not an equal stream;
> . . . And, when past
> Their various trials, in their various spheres,
> If they continue rational, as made,
> Resorbs them all into himself again,
> His throne their centre, and his smile their crown.

These are the utterances of one who had need to think, but no need to think the questions through. Such ultimate fate would seem to contradict Young's fierce contention in regard to personal immortality. If absorbed, why individual crowns? Again, this curious combination of two orders of thought appears in a bit of discussion of the relationship of man to God:

> Praise I a distant Deity! He tunes
> My voice (if tuned): the nerve that writes, sustains:
> But though past all diffused, without a shore
> His essence, local is his throne.

As in much religious thought of our own time as well as of earlier days, his is a deity triumphant over time, but not over space. In this, as in a passage already quoted, and in that in which he says:

> Our senses, as our reason, are divine,

he seems to be suggesting something of that idea of Plotinus, of emanation, of the divine revealed through the whole of being, but he does not elaborate, or explain, or wholly grasp it, and does not try to relate these bits to his traditional theological way of thinking.

It would seem that Young shared the orthodox conviction of man as the child of sin, and the Deist idea of the evil nature of man, as marring the perfect working of the universe:

> Man, hard of heart to man, of horrid things
> Most horrid! mid stupendous, highly strange!
> . . . .
> Man is to man the sorest, surest ill.

But Hamlet lifts his spirit, and the conflict in his mind, torn between the thought of man's greatness and his baseness, is expressed in antitheses, after the fashion of his day. He grows eloquent:

> Distinguish'd link in being's endless chain!
> Midway from nothing to the Deity!
> A beam ethereal, sullied and absorpt!
> Though sullied and dishonour'd, still divine!
> Dim miniature of greatness absolute!
> An heir of glory: a frail child of dust!
> Helpless immortal! insect infinite!
> A worm! a God! — I tremble at myself,
> And in myself am lost.
> . . . .
> A glorious partner with the Deity
> In that high attribute, immortal life?

Man's supreme claim to greatness lies in his hope, nay, his assurance of immortality. This, the central thesis and instigating idea of *Night Thoughts*, is discussed at length, with varied kinds of proof. As to the basis of his conviction, in regard to this and his other articles of faith, Young affirms that all his faith rests on reason; supernatural revelation is as reasonable as the laws of nature. He argues interminably about its various aspects. Reason bids Lorenzo believe:

> All sacred Reason! source and soul of all
> Demanding praise on earth, or earth above!
> My heart is thine. . . .
> No; Reason re-baptized me when adult;
> Weigh'd true and false in her impartial scale;
> My heart became the convert of my head. . . .
> Reason pursued is faith.

Though this dependence on logic would seem to contradict what he says of the use of other powers in reaching truth:

> If man sleeps on, untaught by what he sees
> Can he prove infidel to what he feels?
> . . . .
> And to believe, Lorenzo, is to feel,

one likes him better for his contradictions. They break that insistent and irritating repetition of belief that can come only from one who doubts what he is affirming. Perhaps it is wrong to call this contradiction; he finds that reason and instinct reach the same conclusions, but in different *tempo*:

> Reason progressive; instinct is complete;
> Swift instinct leaps; slow reason feebly climbs.

In his conviction that mind and feeling fuse in discovering truth he gives suggestion of larger thought, not unimportant in a rationalistic age bent on limitation of man's interpretative power to intellect alone.

If we inquire: What questions did Young ask, and what answer in regard to this supreme problem of future life, the most fundamental are: Why the creation of the fulness of powers in man, if they lead to nothing? Why hope, if it means but frustration? Why life, if it leads to death which is extinction? He emphasizes the unreasonableness of supposing that Nature's God, whose laws are so wise, so invariable, should do anything so capricious as to cut off short what He had begun. The Eternal Mind could not be so illogical as to permit the inconsequence of annihilation of its finest creation, man, full of promise of immortal things:

> Why was he wise to know, and warm to praise,
> And strenuous to transcribe in human life
> The Mind Almighty? Could it be that fate,
> Just when the lineaments began to shine,
> And dawn, the Deity should snatch the draught,
> With night eternal blot it out? . . .
> . . . .
> Shall we this moment gaze on God in man
> And next lose man forever in the dust?

The argument, which is most fully presented in Book VII, vibrates between the supposedly known nature of the Deity and the prophetic constitution of man's being. Man has instincts, hopes, abilities, passions, ambitions; reason tells us that these were not called into existence for nothing. All gain is loss unless man surmounts the grave:

> 'Tis immortality your nature solves;
> 'Tis immortality deciphers man,
> And opens all the myst'ries of his make.
> Without it, half his instincts are a riddle,
> Without it, all his virtues are a dream.
> His very crimes attest his dignity;
> His sateless thirst of pleasure, gold, and fame
> Declares him born for blessings infinite:
> What less than infinite makes unabsurd
> Passions, which all on earth but more inflames?
> Fierce passions, so mismeasured to this scene,
> Stretch'd out, like eagle's wings beyond our nest,
> Far, far beyond the worth of all below,

> For earth too large, presage a nobler flight,
> And evidence our title to the skies. . . .
> . . . .
> Think not our passions from corruption sprung,
> Though to corruption now they lend their wings.
> That is their mistress, not their mother. . . .
> . . . . I see,
> I feel a grandeur in the passions too
> Which speaks their high descent; and glorious end;
> Which speaks them rays of an eternal fire.

Even discontent argues for further life:

> His grief is but his grandeur in disguise,
> And discontent is immortality.

Valid is the testimony of all powers of man's mind and soul to the fact of continued existence:

> Our heads, our hearts, our passions, and our pow'rs
> Speak the same language; call us to the skies.

Because in the great future lies buried deep all that man should pursue with ardor, the fact

> Of restless hope, forever on the wing

holds promise:

> His immortality alone can solve
> That darkest of enigmas, human hope —
> . . . .
> Possession, why more tasteless than pursuit?

Boundless development lies ahead of man through the use of his whole being, the assurance of all his powers. Were he to live coeval with the sun, he would be learning still, and, dying, leave his lesson half unlearned.

In this emphasis on the logic of continuity, in arguing immortality for the fulfilment of the incomplete, in his belief in the inherent significance and promise of the passions, in resting on the evidence of faith and hope, he foreshadows Robert Browning; and he believes with him in the supremacy of love above all other powers. Humanity is

> A race
> Most wretched, but from streams of mutual love,
> And uncreated, but for love divine.

Students and lovers of Browning, reading *Night VII*, will find there, in the work of a poet of far lesser endowment, both intellectual and imaginative, much that, in sketchy fashion, suggests both in thought and feeling the life-long utterances of the later poet:

> Why life, a moment? infinite, desire?
> Our wish, eternity? Our home, the grave?
> Heaven's promise dormant lies in human hope;
> Who wishes life immortal, proves it too.

Very extended here is that feigned argumentativeness over a foregone conclusion that one sometimes finds in Browning; at times the phraseology, and the cadence of the lines, as well as the content anticipate the great Victorian:

> 'The famed Athenian porch
> (And who for wisdom so renown'd as they?)
> Denied this immortality to man.'
> I grant it, but affirm they proved it too.
> A riddle, this? — Have patience; I'll explain.

Startling in its foreshadowing of the central theme of Browning's work is:

> To love, and know, in man
> Is boundless appetite, and boundless pow'r;
> And these demonstrate boundless objects too.

As Young demands of life more than it can give, he demands of his gift more than it can achieve. Through the dogmatic assertion and argument there is an intermittent urge of feeling, trying to force his imagination to perform more than it can perform. Sublimity calls; the will gallantly responds; but the attempt to penetrate the infinite, to bring home to human sense and soul the wonder of sky-sublimities and of the fashioning deity is more than mortal may achieve, and he falls back on exposition. Brooke, Akenside, and other Deists were content to explain and expound, to appeal to reason, perhaps to rouse feeling also through the appeal: Brooke to describe the vastness and the nice working of the universe, Akenside to discuss the faculty of imagination whereby man inly possesses it. Young tries to do more, to picture forth in concrete terms the nature of his possession, but he lacks the poet's gift of evoking by word or phrase more than is actually said, and all too often has to take refuge in superlatives and exclamation points. Milton, by a magic of words, can make you aware of illimitable distances; Young, straining at the leash of his limitations, can for the most part, though he leans hard on Milton, but cry out over the vastness he is trying to present; few of his concrete touches have that subtle suggestiveness that sets the reader's imagination stirring. His efforts to rouse imagination by argument and outcry, as if by lashing he could whip up the god within to action, remind one of those pagans who lacerate their images of deity, in determined effort to secure affirmative answers to their prayers. Lacking great poetic gift, he tries to prod imagination by dogmatic assertion, as he at times tries to stimulate grief by iteration of his sorrow. The result is the unpardonable sin of the creative artist; he often expresses, or tries to express, more than he really sees, feels, knows. But his attempt to call imagination to his service; his groping in the presence of the night sky for greater intensity of thought and feeling; his delving into his inmost self for a deeper source of power than he can quite find, reveal his significance in a transition time. He well represents an age passing from exalting reason to one exalting imagination;

passing from content in contemplation of outer law, to a new curiosity and desire to understand the inner life of man.

So, in the mind of this argumentative gentleman some seeds were quickening that held promise for a later age; this shows in his critical as well as in his creative work. His *Conjectures on Original Composition* (1759), written in a letter to the author of Sir Charles Grandison, had vast influence, both in England and abroad. He protests against the prevailing imitation of the ancients as smothering originality and checking growth. He pleads for freedom of genius, and his idea of genius is based on the rightness of individual instinct, of Nature expressing her inmost significance in the gifts of man. The *Conjectures*, startling and original in an age of formalism, is full of a vivid sense of the creative power of genius, as springing, with instinct transcending the authority of outer rule, from some deep well of being. Nature's design is the development of individuality; the writer should dig deeply into the secret depths of his own self if he is to achieve anything of worth. Genius draws something from the heart of nature that no other can draw: "By a spirit of imitation we counteract Nature, and thwart her design. She brings us into the world all originals: no two faces, no two minds are just alike; but all bear Nature's evident mark of separation on them. Born originals, how comes it to pass that we die copies?"

The classics should indeed be read, but for inspiration, not for pattern; the poet should try to pierce to the spirit and life in them, in order to quicken the spirit and life within him, not smother it by trying to repeat.

"A genius implies the rays of the mind concentred, and determined to some particular point." Its instinct is unique, not to be duplicated. It works by some power beyond the reach of rule; "For unprescribed beauties, and unexampled excellence, which are characteristics of genius, lie without the pale of learning's authorities and laws." Its nature and its working are beyond the realm of "prose-reason," of understanding; "hence genius has ever been supposed to partake of something divine." He advises, as Carlyle later advised: "*Know thyself. Reverence thyself.*" . . . "Dive deep into thy bosom; learn the depth, extent, bias, and full fort of thy mind; contract full intimacy with the stranger within thee; excite and cherish every spark of intellectual light and heat, . . . however . . . scattered through the dull, dark mass of common thoughts." "Who hath fathomed the mind of man? Its bounds are as unknown as those of the creation; since the birth of which, perhaps, not one has so far exerted, as not to leave his possibilities beyond his attainments, his powers beyond his exploits." Unsuspected abilities may rise in man, evoked by sudden call, or striking emergency; the whole passage is full of a sense of the vitality and the mystery of the human mind, which brings to the arts, through understanding, imagination, passion, a power and a secret of growth that must not be checked by mere rule.

Because of this, there are, in races as in individuals, great possibilities of development, if they will be themselves and not hamper their growth by restrictions. Young is filled with enthusiasm at the thought of potential progress in knowledge, in the arts, of development in the all-encompassing life of the world, and he divines a secret promise at the heart of things of unpredictable growth: "Why should it seem altogether impossible that heaven's latest editions of the human mind may be the most correct and fair?"

Why may not the future produce, through the development of individual genius, drawing through its mystery from the mystery of nature itself, greater things than the past has known?

That authority of individuality, of personality, had its roots in a profounder philosophy than Young consciously knew. Back of this lies a liberating order of thought of which he had had glimpses, but which he had not made his own. One would search in vain, here, or in *Night Thoughts*, for any real grasp of the Shaftesburian idea of the beauty and harmony of the universe, God immanent, revealing itself in the soul of man, or of the Neo-Platonic thought which lies back of this, of an emanation of deity manifesting itself alike in nature and in man, or of the later Wordsworthian idea of the reaction of the individual soul to that immanent God, the "correspondent breeze." Yet the whole idea of genius in *Conjectures* would seem to imply that the soul of man draws from a central source, that genius has a divine origin. He is aware of those mysteries which "render mere prose men infidels to their divinity." And his thought is more comprehensive and more catholic than the ancient idea of the isolating visitation of the God, setting the poet in his divine madness off from his fellows, for there is in this suggestion of potential development of man and of races something of that broader and later Greek thought, perhaps one may say of the Neo-Platonic rather than the Platonic, of a common relationship of humanity in the divine. Certainly a sporadic passage in *Night Thoughts*, already quoted, gives a hint of this idea:

> He the great Father! kindled at one flame
> The world of rationals: one spirit pour'd
> From spirit's awful fountain; pour'd himself
> Through all their souls, but not an equal stream.

These glimmerings of a poetic philosophy which Young can not wholly grasp or utter keep the reader of *Night Thoughts* on the alert in ploughing through the long moralizing. The poet has glimpses of the deeper meaning, but he does not think the matter through; he falls back on Nature, but makes no inquiry as to what Nature is, failing to reach the new-old thought of her interpenetration by the divine.

One of Young's critics says that he was original in an imitative age, and looked upon Nature with his own mind and eye. It might be said that he so looked upon genius, divining its secret to be the truth of individual insight, drawing from depths unknown. In so doing he helped prepare the way for the conception of the imagination held by the greater critics of the romantic period, as man's highest gift, enabling him to penetrate by means of the truth of his own vision to the very truth of things. There was throughout some stubborn energy or vehemence of life in him, which, urging him to creation beyond his own powers, made him capable of such vigorous interpretation of the vital force of genius. His critical intuition far outstripped his creative gift. Only an extraordinary intellectual vitality could have enabled him at his advanced age to write *Conjectures*, with its freshness alike of thought and of phraseology, its affirmation of belief in a living well of power in chosen souls.

Young's *Conjectures* had a great, and, in some ways, unfortunate influence upon the youth of Germany in the *Storm and Stress* period. That idea of the secret power of genius, sprang from deeper sources than many of its adherents were aware. Young's idea of genius drew upon unexplored and unexplained Nature, a power undefined but illimitable, transcending the individual. Implicit in it, recognized or not, lay the old conception of the macrocosm reflected in the microscosm, the universal in the particular. But the *Conjectures*, though innocent in intent of its consequences in the Germany of the seventies, did much to foster the genius movement there, wherein the insolence of individuality was manifested, the authority of the petty ego in itself. Here was a fatal gap, a vital connection gone. Losing that reverence inherent in the idea in its Neo-Platonic source, of the infinitesimal, which in some divinely incomprehensible way, reflects the universal, the microcosm mistook itself for the macrocosm, and gave itself over to the isolation of personal caprice, ignoring the binding laws and binding obligations of its great origin.

It is difficult to connect the author of *Conjectures* with the author of *Night Thoughts* without making a closer study of the latter than even the most patient reader willingly undertakes. The *Conjectures* shows him, still in old age, full of vigor of mind, still growing at the age of seventy-six. Whoever will search *Night Thoughts* will find there the same personality, eager, demanding, full of a sense of something greater within him than had ever reached fulfilment. It is a revelation of a nature self-willed, of one who had perhaps found self-subdual necessary, and difficult,— that reported wildness of his college days never fully outlived. That dual temperament, alternately melancholy and gay, brought him many a problem. There was in him to the end an unconquerable urge of life, which enhanced the horrors of death, which made him lay hold on immortality as an inalienable right of his nature. It shows in his grief; it shows in his way of storming eternity. That impetuous insistence on immortality,— was it not a part of the welling up of life within him, the longing to achieve, which revealed itself in many varied and ineffective attempts at writing, and, less worthily, in that life-long yearning for earthly preferment? The world and his own gift had failed to bring him that of which he felt capable; like Andrea del Sarto, but more vehemently, he wants "one more chance."

There was something passionate, unreasonable in his way of reasoning about immortal life as an inalienable right of his nature; he will have it so. There is no suggestion of acquiescence in divine law if it should rule otherwise, of "*nella sua volontade è nostra pace*," if that will should not be his will. Near the end of his long poem he says that he has proved man immortal; he has not proved that which no man can prove, but in his presentation of the logic of continuity; in his conviction of the potential largeness of man's nature, the promise inherent in his passions and his powers, considered in connection with divine law operative throughout the visible universe, he has advanced ideas which man of any order of thought, mystic or scientific, idealist or realist, may well pause to consider. Withal there are fine enduring elements in him: intellectuality, moral purpose, loyalty of faith in the divine origin and guidance of the universe, belief in righteousness.

Night Thoughts, throughout, shows that the author had a sense of something greater within him than had ever found expression; he is always attempting to make Lorenzo think and feel more than he can. In reality, all that he pours out in addressing Lorenzo is self-betrayal; this alleged listener is but a projection of Young's own mind, that *alter-ego*, prone to doubt, over-ambitious, with a tendency to worldly-mindedness, and a nature open to temptation. The long harangues lose some of their tediousness if regarded, not as addressed to an exhausted hearer, but as being efforts at self-conquest of a divided nature. It is part of himself that he is addressing as he walks in the churchyard, or sits on a tombstone at midnight, a part of himself that must be subdued to ways of righteousness and of orthodox thought, that has to be constantly reminded of the littleness of the earthly life as compared with the heavenly. He speaks to his worldly self, fancifully outfitted with wife and child, questionable habits, and great worldly ambitions. "Thy bosom burns for power," he says reprovingly. Lorenzo is what Young feels he was in danger of being, would, perhaps, have been in different circumstances. Such onslaught of attack, salutary in self-castigation, could hardly be permitted in another.

To Young, incorrigibly alive at eighty-two, came Death, whose horrors and whose hopes he had set forth with vehemence that outran the reason he so proudly claimed. We find this personality, torn between longing for preferment on earth and for greater opportunity in Heaven, a mass of contradictions: melancholy and gay; posing and sincere; capable of passion of grief, yet deliberately inducing the mood of sorrow, finding grief, at times, not unpleasurable; witty, yet intolerably didactic; clinging to traditional dogmatic theology, yet, because of some vulnerable spot in his theological armor, forced to admit glimmerings of a far different order of thought; one moment admitting the service of instinct, of feeling, in finding truth, and affirming the insufficiency of reason; the next, affirming that reason is supreme.

In passages in *Night Thoughts*, as in *Conjectures*, Young seems, at times, to be drawing near the confines of a land of intellectual promise. Through all his over-insistent affirmations runs a thread of speculation and inquiry, but as, in his blank verse, in the all too eager forward march you feel the tug back of the couplet, you feel in his thought the backward tug of dogmatic theology. Orthodox in thinking man a child of sin, he yet finds in his nature, even in the sinful aspects of his nature, as in his genius, bewildering promise of greater things. In regard to both man and nature, his mind is touched by drift of thought that is passing, by drift of thought to come. Akin to those Deist poets who had been inspired by scientific discovery and affirmation, he dwells insistently on the wonder of the vast outer whole, and his contemplation comes back to rationalized proof of the greatness of God, demonstrated by the material greatness of nature. He does not win to a perception of the immanence of the divine, or affirm a relation between the individual soul and the soul of all. The creature stands off and adores the Creator, but is not an inherent part of the divine life. Young's thought of unity is the unity of the outer universe, not including the soul of man, though his idea of man who

> Can grasp creation with a single thought,

gives promise of a deeper conception that was soon to come. A growing inwardness of thought is reflected in his conviction that there is a greatness in man's mind that is greater than the vastness of space, and immensity is pressed into the service of intensity of feeling and thought. His introspectiveness, a reaction from the conception of the whole that left man's inner self outside, his self-scrutiny in the light of the facts of science and of human life, his study of the effect on self of the boundless system of the universe, are highly significant, and symptomatic of an age beginning to grope for an understanding of man's mind.

Equally significant is his recognition of the validity of his individual experience in arriving at conclusions about life and death. He summons to his aid more than reason in his interpretation of the universe in the light of self, of self in the light of the universe. One discerns an effort to conform to the intellectual standards of his age, and yet reconcile these with the assurances brought by the consciousness of life within him, that sense of inner greatness but outvalues the outer greatness of the universe. He feels the need of more than his troubled mind in laying hold on truth; feeling, instinct urge their authority upon him. In the wakening of his deeper self through the shock of grief, he gropes toward a realization that the witness of man's whole being is necessary for the solution of the riddle of existence, and this manner of thought, later to reach greater clearness and authority, represents a significant stage in the "rediscovery of the inner life." But the different elements of his personality are not fused; he turns anxiously from one to another, lacking the full accord of feeling, reason, imaginative intuition that the great poet, the great mystic reaches. Mood, intellect, observing eye take their turn, with an awkwardness of transition, as if the various faculties did not coalesce; there is no profound, central insight. He lacked that harmony and concert of the powers which actuates the penetrative imagination in divining truth. But he was a forerunner, and, to a certain extent, a pathfinder for poets of a later day, not only read but still reverenced in the years when both the first and the second generation of romantic poets were growing up, even if he fell short of their deepening wisdom; that, for instance, of a Wordsworth, whose insight, revealed in *Peele Castle*, growing clairvoyant through grief, attains that unity with self which is unity with God.

III

HERDER AND HIS BACKGROUND: AN APPRECIATION[6]

THERE is pleasure always in watching the human mind escape from the type of dogma that checks development into freedom where it may draw nearer essential truth. Perhaps no period of history in any country brings deeper satisfaction of this kind than that of eighteenth century Germany, winning her way to emancipation in matters of literature, philosophy, art, and building, in constructive thought, a basis for future thought for all countries. The last quarter of the eighteenth century was Germany's great hour.

On no other people did the domination of pseudo-classic law in the world of letters, French-engendered, press more heavily than on the Germans in the early part of this century; in no other country was this teaching carried to such an extreme; they showed their customary thoroughness in affixing the self-imposed yoke. Royal authority upheld these standards, for Frederick the Great, whose native predilection for French, fostered by governess and tutor in babyhood and boyhood, had received its crown and seal from cruel punishment administered by his father because of French tendencies, showed such fanatical devotion to French ideas as could be shown only by one who had suffered persecution for holding them. Conditions in the world of thought have a way of presenting themselves most arrestingly, so deep is our prepossession in favor of the concrete, the tangible, in the faces and forms of individual thinkers,—thought in this way acquiring something of personality,—

and the literary taste, the literary principles of the first decades of this century in Germany take on the face and form of Gottsched, literary dictator enthroned at Leipzig, who, a believer, as became the disciple of Wolff, in the dogma of the sufficiency of reason, applied the doctrine to literature, strong in the faith that there is no beauty that cannot be demonstrated, explained, produced by rule. His pictured face wears, with a touch of defiance, an air of proud possession, the satisfied look of one for whom life and art hold no secrets. The belief that clear thinking, correct ideas about poetry will produce great poetry needs no refutation except the results; Gottsched's *Cato* speaks all too eloquently, though unconsciously, in disproof of ideas expressed in Gottsched's *Kritische Dichtkunst* (1730). The principles of classic art, needless to say, do not necessarily lead, but pseudo-classic emphasis on the non-essentials of those principles did lead, and not in Germany alone, to an atrophy of imagination, a checking of individual creative power at its very source. Perhaps, too, in Germany the supremacy of dogma pressed more readily and more heavily because of an intellectual and spiritual impoverishment of the people following the Thirty Years War. To recognize the importance of form over matter; to be clear, reasonable, unimpassioned, impersonal; to be moderate; to remember order, proportion, unity of tone, harmony, common sense,— repeating over and over the pseudo-classic formula in full confidence in its saving efficacy might well have checked genius even if it had existed. Here, as in other countries at this period, is apparent failure to recognize the imagination as the supreme factor in creative work, a lack of perception of the unexplained forces that really move men, of the dynamic quality of genius.

In no way did the formula operate more tyrannically than in the matter of the exclusion of *das Wunderbare*, the marvellous, the very breath of being of the Germany we knew best: nothing must be introduced that could not be rationally explained. Happily, the rebels of the future are nurtured on the strictures of the present, and rebels must begin by using the weapons of their oppressors. The retort courteous to dogma is dogma. "No marvels," said Gottsched; "Nature, marvels, freedom!" cried Bodmer, the Swiss, in his *Treatise on the Marvellous* (1740). "Corneille!" affirmed Gottsched; "Shakespeare!" cried Bodmer. "Racine!" thundered Gottsched. "Milton!" shouted Bodmer and Breitinger together.

So the battle raged, and the rival hosts encamped. Thus was achieved a canon of the marvellous, which the romanticists later in their creative work, put both to good and to most extravagant uses; thus, too, in the naming of English poets a chink was made in imprisoning walls through which many a German was to find his way to freedom.

In the German reaction from pseudo-classicism it is hard to separate the inflowing streams from foreign, especially English literature, and from Rousseau, from those which mysteriously welled up on German soil after that long drought of pseudo-classic rule under Gottsched. It is a fascinating story, of inflowing and outflowing influences; of great personalities; there are so many sides to the reaction that it is impossible to follow more than a few in tracing the slow coming of those agencies that reclaimed the lost tracts of man's intellectual and spiritual life. Little by little, here and there, came the wakening of those powers which had become atrophied from lack of use.

Germany of the eighteenth century found in English literature many quickening influences, much that, in form and in matter, helped break through the soil which, under Gottsched and French rule, had grown arid and dry; in the philosophers, a bolder manner of thought, Locke, with his probing of the human mind; Hume, with his skeptical analysis of mental process, his reduction of reality to idea, with denial of connection between ideas,— analysis that led the way to a great philosophical faith, a great synthesis, in Kant; Shaftesbury with his winning and human semi-philosophic idealism: man must achieve beauty of feeling, thought, and conduct, and thus make himself part of the beauty and harmony of the universe. In poetry they found a bolder imagination; in the novelists, Richardson, Sterne, an outpouring of feeling, sentiment, which, joining that of Rousseau and of Macpherson's *Ossian*, became as powerful and as mischievous as a spring freshet, making them realize how alien to the Teutonic genius was the repression of feeling demanded by French convention. Even the delightful naturalism of the *Vicar of Wakefield*, which, one would think, belonged to no camp of theorists, became a liberating force. The very contact with the undisciplined English genius, instinctive, creative, not deigning to explain itself or to rationalize its conduct into concepts, acted as an inspiring energy. English literature, with its touch of wildness, reawakened, in the over-schooled Germans, something of the primitive; they found here the stirring of their own deeper instincts, which had become inarticulate. Shakespeare freed their spirits, the ballad wrought on their imaginations, and, with Ossian, ministered richly to the reawakening taste for the supernatural. Deeply significant was the recognition, coming earlier in England than in Germany, of the values of folk poetry; Ramsay, in the heart of the pseudo-classic period had been a pioneer in this matter; the publication of Percy's *Reliques* (1765) wakened old echoes, stirred forgotten feelings; the music of the ballad and of early song set nerves a-quiver that had long been bidden lie still. Through the ballad the very genius of the German people was touched again to life:

> For there was shed
> On spirits that had long been dead,
> Spirits dried up and closely furl'd,
> The freshness of the early world.

If we find in England in the Romantic Period literature of greater power, imaginative insight, and charm, with wholeness of appeal,— emotion, intellect, imagination going into its creation,— it is to Germany that we must look for interpretation of the tendencies of the time, for philosophic and critical investigation and exposition of the forces at work upon the minds of men, leading to new ways of thinking, new interpretations of human life, guiding the mind and imagination along new paths. English critics had not been behindhand in detecting and suggesting new influences; Dennis, had expressed belief in freedom of the imagination; Shaftesbury, his faith in a work of art developing in accordance with an inner law of beauty; Joseph Warton, in his *Essay on Pope* (1756), had protested against the poetry of reason and rule, and had shown, both in his verse and in his critical work, belief in passion, imagination, individuality in poetry; Edward Young, in his *Conjectures on Original Composition* (1759), had made an eloquent plea for the divine rights of genius. These and others had made utterances preluding the new order, but it was left for Germany to work out profound and philosophic statement of the new principles coming into being. Germany, a royal debtor, gave, in constructive criticism, a rich return for all the influences that had come to her from England, wakening her to new life. We observe here the strange phenomenon of a great critical literature ushering in a period of great creative literature, a contradiction, one would think, of the laws of life.

It is in connection with drama that these fundamental principles reach their fullest and deepest expression. That form of art which, more than any other, represents the depth and complexity of life, was the one which had suffered most under the *régime* of external rule. It was but natural that, when the reaction came, it should manifest itself most strongly here. Most potent of all the influences drawing the people of this race to leave convention and find the reality that is truth in art was that of Shakespeare. The young Keats, in one of those delightful early letters, written when his genius was striving into creative life, spoke of having an idea that the spirit of Shakespeare was presiding over him, guiding the development of his poetic instinct. One might well imagine that it was the spirit of Shakespeare that watched over eighteenth century Germany, wakening poetic sense to the need of seeking that truth that lies at the heart of human experience.

The first authoritative note of change comes from Lessing, all the more authoritative in its promise for the future because it rests upon a firm foundation of the best in the old. It is given to many to revolt, but given only to genius to find in the past the seed wherein lies waiting the growth of the days to come. Germany was indeed fortunate, in the stir of new influences in this transition time, in finding as spokesman a man of power, too great to belong to any school, a humanist, unwearied in the quest for truth. Learned, balanced, fair-minded, he lays a firm, unassailable foundation for criticism in the new era in his recognition of the authority in literature of life itself; in his power to select what was vital in past theory in regard to drama and to make it serve, not as a drag on new thought but as a quickening influence. He had great insight, great originality, that originality that discovers the greatness of the simple, the real, the natural. "Nothing is great that is not true." "We cannot have the sublime without the real."

Through the informal discussions of this or that play, in *Dramatic Notes* (*Hamburgische Dramaturgie*, 1767–1769), wherein he establishes the basis of modern dramatic cricitism, one is ever conscious of the penetration of his thought, his grasp of the central situation, his genius of critical insight into the essential, the real. No artifices, no clever, irrelevant touches of wit, or moral maxims, no externalities of any kind, should, in a play, interfere with the central action in its entirety; "True genius, inventing, will work out, in character and action, the most natural and common course of events." "Genius loves simplicity; wit, complications."

He finds this oneness of central struggle, presented through linked action, in inevitable sequence, in the simplicity of Greek tragedy; he finds it at the heart of the variety, the complexity, of Shakespeare; he does not find it in French tragedy, which has a way of mistaking the accidental for the essential, of missing the inner unity of action by introducing external complicating circumstances, which have no connection with the main action except in happening at the same time.

The court in which he tries Corneille, Racine, Voltaire, is the court of life itself, presided over in the world of drama by two great figures, side by side, Shakespeare and Aristotle, creator and critic. Aristotle, rightly interpreted, affirms the basic principles underlying great tragedy; Shakespeare is a touchstone for truth in the presentation of character, and the natural issue of character into action. Lessing pleads for the presentation of life in its reality, its depth, its passion; for wholeness of insight into the heart of human experience; for synthesis, not analysis. The mainspring of each character must be detected: "Not to describe the characters, but to put them into action under the eyes of the spectator," is the dramatist's task. His emphasis on the central simplicity of the struggle in any great tragedy, and the oneness of character and plot as character inevitably manifests itself in action, anticipates, though he does not quite reach, the vital conception of tragedy worked out by those who followed him.

Something of this same organic sense of things appears in his recognition of the fact that genuine drama must have its roots in the soil of the country that produces it, and cannot be transplanted; that Greek tragedy cannot grow on French soil; that a true masterpiece fills us so entirely with itself that we do not regard it as the work of a single being but as the work of nature. Many marks of the wakening thought of a new era are found in him. Eager for truth, versus dogma, for reality, versus conventional artifice; not discarding rooted universal principles that can stand the test of time, but keen of insight to discern the difference between such principles and sectarian dogma, his brief sayings about concrete examples betray great principles, and independent thought. Wherein he accepted Aristotle it was not because he was Aristotle, but because he was right.

Lessing, as Lowell rightly says, gave a new starting point to modern criticism; he was a great emancipator in the world of letters. Himself no romanticist, he yet paves the way for reaction from the pseudo-classic era, and also for the later reaction from romanticism that came with the more profound interpretation of the classics. A reasoner, something of a rationalist, in the battle of wits with the French he could meet and worst them on their own ground, striking a heavier blow. (Grimm, in his life of Goethe, speaking of the deadly rapier thrust of Lessing, said: "He took no prisoners.") The turning point was, recognition of the authority of life, versus dogma; first-hand observation, not imitation; search for truth, not the ultimate formulation of truth, the modern attitude.

His was a great personality, a great intellectual attitude. The eager vitality of his pictured face reveals the vigor of life in him, the steady, abounding energy for the quest. There was something heroic in Lessing, both in his life and in his thought. Unwearied in his search for truth, he finds no error of the search harmful, except sectarian error. In him the pulse of new life was already beating; among the many notes that prelude a later day,— his love of folk poetry; his interest in connecting the stage with popular legend; his democratic conviction that the sorrows of a king or prince are no more important for presentation on the stage than those of the common people; his protest against the critic's regarding himself as lawgiver,— nothing is more significant than his saying that if God were to hold all truth shut in his right hand, and in his left nothing but the ever-restless instinct for truth, he would choose the left. Here sounds the modern note, of life as spiritual adventure, spiritual quest.

On from Lessings's reasoned appreciation of Shakespeare as a great follower of fundamental dramatic law to the young Goethe's whirlwind rapture in regard to Shakespeare, as the emancipator of his spirit, who brought him a sense of enhanced vitality, making him for the first time 'feel that he had hands and feet,' through translations, appreciations, disputes runs the great story of Shakespeare's leadership in eighteenth century Germany. In all this, nothing is more arresting than the youthful Herder's significant interpretation in *On German Art and Style* (*Von deutscher Art und Kunst*, 1773). Shakespeare, he says, from life more complex than the simple life of the Greeks, whence grew the simplicity of their drama, has created tragedy, more complex, many-sided, but equally unified, a wonder-whole. In *Lear*, manifold aspects of nature and of human life are presented in all their bewildering complexity, in central tragic unity. One gains from the young author's enthusiastic presentation a feeling of unusual insight into the dynamic forces at work in life and in great tragedy, personality involved with personality in tragic clash of suffering and making suffer. Shakespeare has gone to the quick, has presented very life, life caught in the act. In the greater stress on the variety, the complexity in the oneness than is found in Lessing, and in the electric shock of Herder's enthusiasm, comes a more vivid sense of that living reality which is great tragedy, as if it indeed had a life of its own. It was in connection with tragedy that the new and vital conception of interpreting a work of art as an organic entity came into being,— an idea that became the core of the German interpretation of drama, and, later, of that of Coleridge.

It is no accident that growth from a narrower to a broader standard, from a devitalized theory to a vital one, was based on study of drama, for drama, wherein all sides of personality, thought, feeling, will are drawn into action, is the form of art which comes nearest to representing human experience in its entirety. One wonders how far a study of Shakespeare became, for certain thinkers of the period, a part of their philosophy of life, life in its *Einheit* and its *Vielheit*, its complexity, its tumult, its deep central significance. In the creative power at the heart of a Shakespearian drama Herder and his followers divined an agency at work akin to the creative power at the heart of the universe, and the work of Shakespeare, interpreter of the complex unity of individual life, in its moments of deepest struggle, helped them to an apprehension of some core of unity in the infinite variety of life on the earth, and became a key helping unlock the central door of the mystery of the whole.

Diverse aspects of thought in this period teeming with new ideas seem to approach, to lend one another something toward the solution of the special problem on hand. In philosophy, the disciples of Spinoza were pursuing the thought of the One; the disciples of Leibnitz were busy with the thought of the developing Many; the disciples of both, Herder among them, were pursuing the thought of the developing Many in the One; and, slowly dawning in science, was a conception of an inner oneness in the manifold manifestations of physical life,— a new manner of thinking that was to transform much scientific thought, and not scientific thought alone. Between these different aspects of thought, and that which related to the profound interpretation of man's life, in its unity and its complexity, which is tragedy, there were subtle interrelations, one wind of the spirit astir within them all.

There is exhilaration in tracing even a few of the ideas of Herder; it would be a brave person who would think that he could grasp or expound even a major part of the ideas that grew so swiftly in that teeming brain. No other name in the history of the German reaction in thought is more significant than his. There is cause for wonder that no one has, for English readers at least, put into brief form such an interpretation of Johann Gottlieb Herder as would make after generations conscious of their deep indebtedness to him. For that indebtedness of the whole of the nineteenth century, and, one would gladly add, the twentieth also, can hardly be overestimated. A bold and original thinker, already in his precocious youth, at twenty-two, in his *Fragments on the New German Literature*, (*Fragmente*, 1766–1767), he set forth ideas that were to revolutionize the study of language and literature, and other aspects of the intellectual and spiritual life of man, not only in Germany but in other lands. "Within ten years, one might almost say within five years after Herder had first spoken, the whole aspect of German literature had changed, and the whole land was ringing with immortal songs."

To Herder, more than to any other single thinker we owe those conceptions whereby the life of man, in its intellectual, its spiritual, its creative aspects, as expressing itself in language, in literature, in myth, in religion, is interpreted, not through rationalistic conceptions, in terms of the abstract, defined, limited, but in terms of life, of growth, development,— a conception which has since, increasingly, dominated the mind and imagination of the modern world, determined the methods of its scholarship. His first important utterances, made in *Fragmente*, affirm that the same law of change which operates in the physical life of individuals and of races, operates also in the intellectual and spiritual life of mankind. Art, science, language "grow, blossom, ripen, and decay." It was a new and significant idea, sounding the deepest note in that many-voiced cry of "Return to Nature" that resounded through the greater part of the eighteenth century. In the ceaseless working of nature as we observe it in leaf and flower we discern the very laws that govern the productive powers of man; there, not in man-made formulas shall one discover the shaping forces that produce literature and the arts. Here is the key to Herder's whole life work; all his thought is dominated by the imaginative conception of birth, growth, decay, and growth again in all things; it was by the wide application of this vivifying idea that Herder proved his genius, wakened his generation. First apprehended in connection with language, with literature, it was later to become a part of his conception of evolution in the whole world order.

In turning over the pages of the *Fragmente* one wonders at first, so familiar now are the ideas, why, as Hillebrand says, they ran through Germany like a train of gunpowder, why the effect was so great. The work is fragmentary indeed, discursive, suggestive, no reasoned philosophical treatise with demonstration of a single theme. It touches on many topics and many writers; it is full of interpretations, and of thought-provoking assertions,— protests against the imitation, on the part of his countrymen, of the language and literature of the French; against the educational tyranny whereby a dead language, Latin, is made to crush living German speech. It is the work of a young man, groping his way toward those living conceptions of truth most ably presented years later in his *Outlines of a Philosophy of the History of Man* (*Ideen zur Philosophie der Geschichte der Menschheit*).

The topic in which his distinctive trend of thought is most apparent is language. Language, it seems,— he was not the first to suggest this,— is a natural growth from the days when men and beasts shared a common speech, being as yet *Thiermenschen*, animal men,— a rude word to hurl into the polite society of the eighteenth century! "The hypothesis of

Süssmilch that speech was a direct gift of the Deity is contrary to all analogy, and destroys the wonderful unity of Nature; for everything grows or developes, and nothing is made perfect at once." It is later, in his prize essay on language, that he traces further stages of development, through "reflexion," man's consciousness of his aims and of himself. Already in the *Fragmente* he presents his idea that the individual life of each special race becomes articulate in its speech, and can never become articulate in any other. Language is indigenous, and can never be lent nor borrowed; hence the folly of borrowing a dead language, Latin, to express living experience, or an alien tongue, French, to express German experience. Speech and thought are as inseparable as skin and body; it is impossible for any man to reveal the inmost in himself in any language but his own. The philosopher should write in his mother tongue, with all the associations he sucked in with his mother's milk, for philosophy must be made our own, and part of our life, and our life is where our roots are.

Poetry, like language, is a natural growth of the country which produces it; early human speech being itself poetry, full of pictures and images. "Yet our poets, instead of singing like the poets of old, in the natural speech of mankind, go about searching for dead expressions and quaint artifices, for they have forgotten that in poetry expression and thought must be in closer unity than two lovers embraced, . . . being related as the body and the soul in Plato." Noteworthy in connection with this desire to find in contemporary verse the natural speech of man, is Herder's idea, later to become in England part of a great controversy in regard to poetry, of the "natural directness," the "naive beauty of the conversation of common men and unlearned women."

The idea that early human speech was a song, or poetry, springing from feeling, and that poetry is the common possession of all peoples, is the moving force in all Herder's interpretation of poetry, his special note in the eighteenth century cry of a return to nature. A lover of the poetry of the Bible, of primitive song,— in this influenced in youth by his friend, the prophet and sage Hamann, and by Percy's *Reliques* (1765), which made great stir in Germany, he set forth in his contribution to *Von deutscher Art and Kunst*, already noted, his plea for the beauty of primitive poetry, unstudied, irregular, emotional, unselfconscious. "Primal and universal feelings are the life blood of poetry." Here is presented the idea, representing much of Herder's greatest service, of the worth, the significance of primitive song, which springs from the life, the whole life, of simple people, and from all the powers, not disintegrated by thought, reflection. In such poetry, life in its simplicity and its fulness is presented, with reality not found in the work of the present day,— wherein verses are polished and repolished which represent no genuine passion, thought, or imagining. "We work according to rules that no genius will recognize as rules of nature; we make verses on subjects about which we cannot think, still less feel, still less imagine; we polish up passions which we have not got, and imitate strength of soul which we never possessed, and in the end all is falsehood, weakness, artifice." In Herder's thought, each individual race must keep through all phases of its development, something of its native genius, if poetry is to be poetry indeed.

It is true that he mistakes Macpherson's *Ossian* for pure, primitive poetry, but, if his example is wrong, his principle is right. Even Macpherson's *Ossian* did not deserve to be translated into German hexameters! One gains the impression that, for him, the music, the sound was the very self of folk song, an identity of form and content in indissoluble melody. He was always a lover of music and something of a musician. Perhaps the hymns sung in his childhood in his humble home at Mohrungen, and in the church close to that home may, in the emotion of their rendering, have wakened in him the love of primitive melody.

In his remarkable translations in *Von Deutscher Art und Kunst* of Scotch and English ballads and of Shakespeare songs, and later in his great collection of songs of all people, *Volkslieder* (1778–1779), Herder shows a skill that almost belies his creed as to the untranslateableness of poetry. For this he had a special gift; in feeling, diction, cadence these translations give charm for charm of the original. But there is irony in the fact that his original verse is stiff, didactic; it is only in translations that he can exemplify his theory of poetry, of simplicity, melody, outpouring of emotion in words that are feeling and combinations of words that are music, so far in him did the critical, and appreciative faculty outstrip the creative.

Working throughout Herder's early critical writings, curiously unifying remarks which have a tendency to become discursive, is his perception of vital process in all aspects of the life of humanity. He gives us not only new thought, but a new manner of thought; a new way of interpreting; it is as if his very mind breathed. Birth, growth, decay in all that pertains to the life of man,— this is one of those truths as obvious as breathing, so obvious that it takes genius to discover it! From first to last, through all his manifold studies of language, primitive poetry, literature, myth, his thought was tending in one direction, his mind, through intuitions, imaginative insight, reasoned opinions, was working one way. He could have said throughout his life what the young Keats said in his youth:

> There ever rolls
> A vast idea before me, and I glean
> Therefrom my liberty.

It was the idea of evolution.

When it began, the thought of change as progression, as

growth, and not as mere meaningless flux is a question that perhaps none can answer, but evolution, the doctrine of becoming, is an idea, which, in one fragmentary form or another, seems seldom to have been long absent from the mind of man, contributions to this or that aspect being made by philosopher, mystic, scientist. It represents man's most gallant intellectual and spiritual adventure, and a certain splendor attaches to the mere reading about the development of man's idea of development, even in Mr. P. C. Mitchell's article in the *Encyclopaedia Britannica*, or Professor Henry Fairfield Osborn's brief treatise, *From the Greeks to Darwin*, verifying where one may one's knowledge of this or that thinker. Few could verify all. The early Greek physicists,— Thales, with his idea of water as the mother of all life; Anaximander, with his theory of the metamorphosis of fish, or 'aquatic men' into 'land men'; Heraclitus, with his idea of perpetual cosmic movement as the universal law, Empedocles, with his conception of inner forces forever at work, attraction and repulsion, love and hate, and of the gradual appearance of higher forms of life, first plants, then animals; great Aristotle, to whom "the whole of nature is instinct with a vital impulse toward some higher manifestation" through the action of "an internal perfecting principle originally implanted by the Divine Intelligence"; Augustine, who read *Genesis* "in the light of primary causation and the gradual development from the imperfect to the perfect of Aristotle"; Nicolaus of Cusa, who sometimes says "evolutio" in making clear the relation between God and the world, *Einheit* and *Vielheit*, those individual existences which can not be understood except in unity with the whole, each working on each to highest purpose[7]; Paracelsus, who affirms that the world is an organism, full of life, which from its origin (*Entstehung*) to its ending (*Untergang*) runs through all shapes of existence which we find in the individual[8]; Bruno, who outlined "a theory of cosmic evolution conceived as essentially a vital process," the endless changes interpreted as the outward expression of an indwelling soul; Spinoza, with his "view of all finite individual things as the infinite variety to which the unlimited productive power of the universal substance gives birth, man differing from the rest of nature in the degree only and not in the kind of his powers"; Leibnitz, with his conception of clearly defined individual existences, forever developing, for to him the one substance of Spinoza's thought was living activity; Robinet, his disciple, who denied all distinction between the inorganic and the organic, and, applying the ideas of continuity and of ordered development to nature, expressed belief in an *echelle des êtres*, a rising scale of being, and affirmed that each type grows toward perfection; the great scientist, Buffon, who held a conviction of the Deity as having a single central idea in creating types, and who studied the mutability of species under the influence of environment; Linnaeus, who held firmly the idea of special creation, but grew to admit something of mutability of species,— a fascinating juxtaposition of names, to which many others could be added, standing for different orders of thought, denoting many avenues of approach, metaphysical as well as physical, to what has proved the dominant idea of modern thought, an idea which, on the physical side reached its culmination in Darwin; on the spiritual side, in the philosophy of Hegel and in the poetry of Browning and of Meredith. Most interesting in connection with the spiritual side is the comment in the *Encyclopaedia* on Boehme, the mystic, "who prepared the way for later German theories of the origin of the world as the self-differentiation and self-externalization of the absolute spirit."

Herder has his deserved place among scientists in working out the ruling idea of our modern thought, evolution, a still higher place among critics and philosophers, as the conception evidently first came to him through study of the achievements of man's mind and spirit, and he makes it the basis of a theory of spiritual evolution, forever operative through and beyond the physical. Influenced both by Spinoza and by Leibnitz, by that conception of Spinoza of the all-inclusive One, and of Leibnitz, of the unfolding Many, by Shaftesbury, also, in his thought of the unity and harmony of Nature, he held the conviction of one life throughout the universe, and of continuous development of the individuals who make up the one. "All things are full of organically operating omnipotence," apparent in internal vitality wherever life displays itself. On our earth "a star among stars," the one life manifests itself as an ascending series, climbing higher and higher, in the vegetable world, in the animal world, in all aspects, physical and mental, of the life of man, and the lower stages are conceived as conditions of the higher,— an important point.

Herder's ideas are most fully presented in his *Outlines of a Philosophy of the History of Man* (*Ideen zur Philosophie der Geschichte der Menschheit*), begun in 1783, the first part published in 1784, the second and third by 1787, the fourth in 1791. In Book V, entitled: "A Series of Ascending Forms and Powers prevails in our Earthly Creation," he says: "From stones to crystals, from crystals to metals, from these to plants, from plants to brutes, from brutes to man, we have seen the organization ascend." "The general Composition of Powers and Forms is neither retrograde, nor stationary, but progressive." "Nothing in Nature stands still; everything exerts itself, and pushes on."

In this vast oneness, with its variety of manifestations, the law of growth is from the simple to the complex. "Nature pursues her grand course, and produces the greatest variety from an infinitely progressive simplicity." "Unity pervades this inconceivable variety." Different species are formed; organs for special ends are developed from special needs, as the brain from the spinal marrow: "the progress of nature produced a more and more refined brain, slowly developing from spinal marrow, until it arrived at man"; after the law of species, each creature follows its own family organization, but "nature has only one prototype," and one organization prevails throughout the whole animated creation: "The nearer they approach [to] man, all creatures bear more or less resemblance to him in their grand outline; Nature, amid the infinite variety she loves, seems to have fashioned all the living creatures on the earth after one grand model of organization."

The crown and triumph of the long process of evolution is man. As the physical development culminates in man, man's development culminates in his intellectual and spiritual powers. He is a being profoundly modified in body, mind, imagination, by the physical characteristics of the land in which he lives; different peoples, living under different conditions, develop in many diverse ways, and the soul of a race grows as an individual soul grows, the different phases of its growth being clearly shown in its language and its literature. Tracing this diversity of development of language and of literature was Herder's greatest joy in much of his other work, and he had a special genius for detecting and expressing fine shades of racial individuality, one of his best interpretations being that of Hebrew poetry.

But man is not only a child of earth, tempered by wind and wave and sweep of plain. "The Sphere of human Organization is a System of spiritual Powers." This ascending series of powers involves in Herder's thought growth that has no ending. "This much is certain, that there dwells an infinity in each of his powers, which cannot be developed here." "Earth is the field where thou hast sported as a child of immortality."

Book V of Herder's *Ideen* contains a fine plea for belief in immortality, as a necessary consequence of the logic of growth. No power can perish; there is no instance of it in nature. It is impossible that a living, acting somewhat, in which the Creator himself is present, in which, by energies divine, he manifests his presence, should be converted into nothing." "What the all-vivifying calls into life, lives; whatever acts, acts eternally, in his eternal whole."

Herder was fully abreast with the most advanced scientific thought of his time, and contributed to it. His treatise may seem in many ways antiquated, but one finds there an interpretation of evolution that makes one feel the sweep of the one life through all the varied forms, in their inexhaustible fertile variety and individuality, their unceasing development. If scientists owe him a debt, poet and philosopher owe him a greater, for his deeper understanding of the import of the facts involved, his imaginative insight into their potential meaning. Significant on the physical side, the outstanding import of his work is spiritual. His conception of one life throughout the universe, animated by indwelling spirit, is in striking contrast to Holbach's view in his *System of Nature* (1770), that nothing exists save matter and motion, that man and the activities of man are but matter and motion, and it comes nearer the latest conjectures of the most modern scientist. In his suggestion of the trial and error method apparent in the development of both body and soul; in his idea that all destructive powers must yield in time to maintaining powers, and be ultimately subservient to the consummation of the whole; in his affirmation that "all the errors of man are mists of truth," ideas are expressed that have left their impress on philosopher and poet. Among those who present the idea of spiritual progress, Hegel, Browning, Tennyson, Meredith, Browning is nearest to Herder. That thought which carries us beyond the reach of thought, of an infinity in man's powers which can be developed only through immortality, has haunted our deeper poetry from Wordsworth to the *Testament of Beauty*.

In reading the *Ideen* one has that freshness of intellectual experience that comes from following the steps of a pathfinder, and this delight, which is ever great, is never deeper than in watching the changing phases of thought of this period, as man passed from a conception of himself as fixed, stationary, in a stationary universe, governed by inflexible, mechanical law, to an interpretation of himself as inextricably involved in the whole inner scheme of things, his fibres inwrought with the fibres of the universe, an organic part of a vast living, developing whole.

Herder makes a great, original and distinctive contribution to this conception, his greatest originality lying in his application of the idea of organic development to the intellectual, the spiritual, the creative life of man, and his influence is paramount in passing from static to dynamic conceptions in the interpretation of these aspects of human achievement. It is impossible to estimate accurately, perhaps impossible to overestimate, the work of Herder. When Hillebrand says that in his work "all the new ideas which have animated the intellectual world during fifty years are in germ"; and: "No one, Kant perhaps alone excepted, has contributed more to the stock of German thought, or has ever exercised a greater or more lasting influence over an age, a nation, or the world at large," adding that the *Ideen* has been the father to all the histories of poetry, religion, language, and law of our century, he probably does not exaggerate. If, earlier, Montesquieu had suggested the influence of environment in the development of human characteristics; if Winckelmann, and in slighter degree, Lessing, had employed something of the historical method; it remained for Herder to develop it, to relate it to a central conception of the organic nature of all life, and to broadcast this idea in manifold new applications. The historical method, the tracing of development,— what limit has there been to the application of these ideas? First came the achievements of the disciples of Herder, the scholars of the so-called

Romantic School of Germany, who laid the foundation for all scholarship that would trace growth, development, in all aspects of the intellectual, the spiritual, the creative life of man: the work in philology, in the study of language and of literature in their many aspects; of myth; of history; of religion. The Grimms created the science of philology; the Schlegels interpreted the poetry and the growth of poetry of many races; Wilhelm Grimm and Otfried Müller discovered that myth is a natural outgrowth of primitive imagination. The philosophers, Schelling and Hegel, who stand in close relation to the movement, carried the dynamic idea into metaphysics, both "conceiving reality as a living, developing process."

The "ideas" of Herder became philosophy, metaphysic, philology, history, comparative mythology, flashing, quicksilver-like, through all the world of thought. It was under the influence of the idea of organic evolution that the humanities came to life, and this idea has profoundly and permanently changed the way of interpreting man's life and man's thought. It is hardly possible to take up a treatise on any aspect of human existence or human activities without finding it permeated with these ideas of cohesion in the affairs of men, of organic development in their inner lives and their achievements, as throughout the universe.

Students of literature, in particular, owe Herder a greater debt than most of them realize. That belief in poetry as a natural growth among all races, the outcome of instincts common to all, has had far-reaching consequences in the regeneration of poetic theory in many lands, and in the inspiration of new poets. Equally potent has been his idea of the indissoluble nature of content and form in lyric verse, the soul of each race finding expression in its own peculiar rhythm of thought, feeling, and sound. Again, the idea of drama as having an inherent, living unity, grounded in nature, its form shaped by the imaginative insight of genius into the heart of great struggle, while it owed something to Lessing, contributed more to Schlegel and to Coleridge, and became the foundation of our later theory of drama. Schlegel, in his *Dramatic Art*, through patient study of the drama of various lands, in tracing the development from early times, among different peoples, in interpreting the indigenous nature of drama, in emphasizing the inner, vital unity of a great tragedy, and the power of the shaping imagination of genius to body this forth, was but carrying out exhaustively, with painstaking application, the principles of Herder.

Among the effects of Herder's ideas were some less enduring. Undoubtedly his protests against convention, his pleas for freedom, for spontaneity of expression, operated with those of Rousseau and of Young's *Conjectures* in instigating the *Storm and Stress* movement which swept Germany in the early seventies from north to south, from east to west, represented among many others, by Bürger, whose life was as wild a ride toward death as that of his own *Lenore*; by young Goethe, with his mind in intense rebellion, trying in *Götz von Berlichingen* to see if he could not shatter the dramatic unities of time, place, and action, as interpreted by the French pseudo-classicists, into such small bits that they could never be put together again; by the *Hainbund*, whose members took solemn oath of eternal fealty to nature and to genius. It was a ferment in the mind of youth, which contributed little in the way of constructive idea, being a rebellion against the fixed and determined, a revolt against what is established in thought or in the form in which thought is expressed, and was largely negative. It drew inspiration more from the destructive thought of Rousseau than from the constructive thought of Herder. What whirlwind was reaped from that wild sowing all students of German literature know. It is not strange that Herder's ideas, as expressed in the *Fragmente*, working on minds less philosophic, less deeply religious than his, should have produced effects quite incalculable by him. His wild followers, from whom he soon parted company, missed the deeper aspect of Herder's thought, that idea of continuity, of development, which was in his mind from the first. The self-styled geniuses, who, in their self-glorification, recognized no law in literature or in life above their own erratic, tangential impulses and whims, were far from recognizing the depth of Herder's thought of genius as the supreme human expression of the divine creative energy forever working at the heart of life, toward higher development.

If the first phase of the romantic reaction in Germany meant revolt against what is established, later phases meant, here as in other countries, a reaching out for beauty not yet attained, for fuller life, for freedom of the imagination. Among the many manifestations, Herder's is the chief inspiration for that aspect which appeared in quest for freshness, simplicity that would recall the day-break of thought and feeling of the human race; for that which sought in mediaeval life and literature elements of beauty and of significance lacking in the present; for freedom of individual and racial imagination to interpret the world which it knows. Whatever the sins and excesses of some of the followers of the banner of romanticism, the forces stirring at this time set free the imagination, and revived the spirit of wonder, the sense of the potential greatness and the mystery of life. This freedom of the imagination worked more fortunately in the romantic period in the creative literature of England than in that of Germany, as the names of Wordsworth and Coleridge, Shelley and Keats bear witness. If, in Germany, some aspects of the endeavor to recapture the charm of the primitive are less fortunate than others, in the intentional spontaneity and formulated *naïveté* of story-writers and versifiers who show a new manifestation of the old, pseudo-classic faith that the recipe, faithfully followed, will produce the desired result, some aspects of great beauty appear, the flower of the new inspiration making itself manifest in the lyrics of Heine, where simplicity of form and phrase veils and expresses the bitter-sweet irony of complex life.

The name of Goethe suggests one of the most important phases of Herder's influence. The meeting of these two young Germans, Herder the elder by five years, under the shadow of Strassburg Cathedral; the walks of Coleridge and Wordsworth on the Quantock Hills,— these are high moments in human experience, about which the imagination delights to play. Under the leadership of Herder, the discussions, covering, as in the way of youth, the nature of all things, reached far into the past and into the future; one might well think that, at this moment, Germany's great hour had struck from the old bell in the cathedral, which once bore the inscription:

> Das Bös hinaus, das Gut herein
> Zu lauten soll ihr Arbeit sein.

Nevinson says that, in influencing Goethe, Herder did his greatest work,— an opinion that might be challenged, though the work was great. It would be difficult to define the limits, if there are limits, of the influence of Herder on the young Goethe; a passage in Goethe's autobiography, *Dichtung und Wahrheit*, may suggest the extent. He says that through Herder's essay on language he first got the idea, in connection with speech, of the way in which human powers develop; he had been too much involved in the midst of things to have thought about their beginning and end. No day of their intercourse passed that was not, "in the most fruitful manner, instructive to me. . . . The more eager I was in receiving, the more liberal was he in giving. . . . As to the fulness of those few weeks during which we lived together, I can well say, that all which Herder has gradually produced since was then announced in the germ," and he adds that, in their conversations, he learned to attach to something higher all that he had hitherto acquired. That idea of development, of variety in unity, which is the key to Goethe's work; of the need of rounding out individuality, using all human powers, and fulfilling them to the utmost,— students and lovers of Goethe will best understand how far-reaching was the influence of these ideas of Herder on the young Goethe. It was the very touch of life on a nature as yet bound in the meshes of dogma and convention, and distracted by multitudinous interests; in the quickening and the centralizing of his powers it was more than an influence; it was a rebirth.

Herder was not alone among the predecessors of Goethe in a conviction of man's need of employing and developing all his powers; the idea had been growing that man, in his earthly pilgrimage, had been leaning too heavily upon a slender staff, that of reason alone. The story of the recovery of the banished powers of man in the eighteenth century is a long story. Rousseau would substitute feeling, emotion as the guide of life; the excesses of this reaction are written in novel, drama, essay of the period; Europe wept that it had thought overlong. A wiser leadership than that of Rousseau came from the seer of the North; Goethe, in *Dichtung und Wahrheit* says: "The principle to which all Hamann's expressions may be referred is this: 'All that man undertakes to perform, whether by deed, by word, or otherwise, must proceed from all his powers united: everything isolated is worthless. . . . He felt, imagined, and thought in unity."

This faith Herder embraced with his whole heart, and passed on to Goethe, and so to the world at large. Against the limitation of mere reasoning, the destructive process of constant analysis, Herder lifted up his voice in plea for the use by man of his entire self,— feeling, imagination, as well as judgment, and especially for recognition of the validity of that greatest gift which comes from a coöperation of all the faculties, intuition. This idea of the totality of the individual has not only an aesthetic but an ethical import, and means in both cases a reaching out for greater fulness of life. In the physical struggle for existence, in meeting the vast challenge of nature, man had to encourage, develop, every possibility within him to secure continuance of life, had to summon all his forces to act as one in answer to the need, the creative need, that wakened them.

How then, one might ask, reading between the lines of the *Ideen*, how then shall that finer part of him, the inmost essence of his being, the soul, reach her growth, unless all inner powers are developed to the utmost,— feeling, reason, imagination, reaching out to intuition of truth? A vital faith, whose "echoes roll from soul to soul" all down the nineteenth century.

One would be false to Herder's principles if one failed to suggest some of the influences that determined his development. Of the many impressions in regard to this boy of eager mind who walked the streets of his native village, knocking at the door of any house in whose window he saw a book and asking to read it, two are outstanding: his long hours of reading in the cherry tree in his father's garden, outside the village wall, strapped to the trunk for fear of falling, in forgetfulness; his bursting into tears "on finding Homer's comparison between the vanishing generations of men and the leaves before the wind." Doubtless from cherry tree and simile alike he learned already in childhood of life, growth, decay; the opening of the petals became insight, reinforced by who knows what of nature happenings, in sandy Mohrungen, with its lake, its Gothic church, its great wood, whose singing birds may have taught him much of the origin of primitive song. Even so the mew of some stray cat, the whimper of a half starved dog, may have become for him the expression of his own insistent hunger, and have suggested the relationship between human and animal speech.

Other pictures, clearly etched, through the medium of

sketch and biography, come down to us, more suggestive even than Goethe's description of him in *Dichtung und Wahrheit*, such as that of his poring over Trescho's books at night, by a faint light, the oil for which was purchased by saving the pitifully small allowance which was made for his breakfast; and again, the picture of him listening, in Königsberg to Immanuel Kant: to that early morning lecture on Time and Eternity; to those lectures on astronomy, physics, geography, on natural philosophy, on the history of man and of nations, a wide range of human speculation and knowledge. Nothing in life, it is said, was indifferent to Kant, and proof that this has a human as well as an intellectual bearing may be found in his invitation, poor *privat-docent* as he then was, to the penniless student from Mohrungen to listen to his lectures, free of charge. This was a young Kant, Herder later said, witty, ironic, destructive, a Kant, still a critic, not yet a constructive philosopher, destroying the rationalistic dogmatism of Wolff by bringing the skepticism of Hume to bear upon it. Kant taught him, "not philosophy, but how to philosophize"; how to observe, and how to think for himself, urging him on to the study of Nature: "Behold the height of the stars; how high they are!" — and to critical study of man and of systems of philosophy.

One catches a glimpse, too, of the youthful Herder listening to the explosive utterances of Hamann, mystic, seer, with an ancient prophet's sense of the divine in life, on the Bible, on folk poetry as the real poetry, common to all, on "the inner meaning and unity of nature." Both Kant and Hamann taught him of the universal, of vastness,— Kant, of the infinity, the vastness of the outer universe; Hamann, of the infinity within. The eager contemplation of his youthful pictured face, suggests, in its look of wonder, the hope of finding out.

Kant and Hamann opened to him a wide range of reading; Plato, Bacon, Leibnitz were read in connection with Kant's lectures; English dramatists and poets; Hume, Rousseau, and Montaigne were urged upon him by Hamann, and both introduced him to the philosophy of the English Shaftesbury, whose gracious answer to the age-old question of the nature of the universe and man's place therein enthralled so many of the better minds of the eighteenth century, and not in England alone. With charming persuasiveness he had set forth in the *Moralists* his conception of the universe as one, a harmony, a totality, in which all parts are fitted together in nice adjustment. This idea became a quickening force in Herder, an inspiration, not of thought alone, but of intuition, imagination.

One envies genius, not when, in the ripeness of its powers, it is concluding great work, and listening to the shouting and applause, but in its intellectual spring-time, when the mind quickens under the stimulus of great ideas,— these are moments of very life. One may indeed envy this lad, who had intellectually almost starved, and who had great hunger, drinking in the thought and the knowledge offered him at Königsberg, the world wakening to life with Hamann, to logical order with Kant, to the beauty of inner harmony with Shaftesbury.

Afterward, at Riga, by the northern sea, these influences proved more potent because not too long continued by direct contact, upon an imaginative mind the force of suggestion often working with more enduring effect than that of continued demonstration, because it stirs creative energy in the mind that receives. That idea of growth, development, so distinctively, at this period, his own, whence did it come? Some perception of dynamic force may have come from Hamann, but not of continuity; possibly from no one came the idea of inherent life in things, progressing from the simple to the complex. It came rather from Nature herself than from the teaching of his masters; he had been a nature-lover from the first. One wonders what life of little things or of great, growth of corn flower or of pine tree, what flow of river, what beat of waves upon the shore in constant change that still denotes indwelling law, what observation of the course of the stars, blending with his thoughts, helped in the great conception of evolution slowly forming in his mind at this time. That man's reaction to his physical environment is part of his development as a thinker, that mountain, plain, and ocean help shape the human mind and imagination,— this organic idea was one of Herder's contributions to the thought of the time, and doubtless its truth was proved in his own experience.

No matter what we read in him or about him we shall never know what hints, suggestions from nature quickened his thought as his whole cosmic philosophy developed in his mind, the idea of the universe and of man's place in the universe, the idea of evolution: "the Unity of Nature in her infinite development, the Continuity of Phenomena, or the necessary self-existence of God, not so much revealed in his works as indwelling under the form of the universe."

Back of it, as already suggested, lies something of Spinoza, of Kant, of Leibnitz, of Shaftesbury. Certain interpreters of Herder, in setting forth the influence of Shaftesbury, hold that there is little difference in their views of the world order, yet difference there is; it is through Herder's thought that the idea of a beauty, a harmony throughout the universe quickens into life. In Shaftesbury is presented the oneness, unity, of a finished structure, fashioned from the outside: one part fits into and completes another; "so much are the very leaves, the seeds, and the fruits of these trees fitted to the various animals." Here is no idea of change as growth, but of the activity of a benevolent, arbitrary power, full of lovely thoughts and amiable intents, fashioning with the finger of an artist. Architecture; development; in the juxtaposition of the two words one finds the difference, the suggestion of Herder's step forward from Shaftesbury's undoubted influence on his thought. To Herder the universe is no cunning mechanism, fashioned by an artificer of consummate skill, but a living organism, working out, in endless development, a complex yet centered life from within, animated by an indwelling spirit, "organically operating omnipotence." The glory of creation is attributed, not to the external shaping of the divine finger, but to the internal working of the divine spirit. Shaftesbury has an idea of succession, one form following another, but no idea of inherent development of one form from another. In him the idea of the necessary sacrifice of one form to another is a part of the harmony, the beauty, wrought by the master artist. As Shaftesbury's idea of harmony throughout the universe undoubtedly influenced Herder, perhaps also his idea of art drawing its deeper beauty and significance from this inmost harmony.

Of the personality of Herder one gains from the written accounts a clear idea; a sensitiveness that became, at times, nervous irritability, both helped and hampered him in his life work. He was high-minded, idealistic; intellectual,—this is the dominant note, but it is not a cold, dispassionate, merely reasoning intellectuality, rather an eager, intuitive, imaginative, all-absorbing intellectuality. Throughout his life he kept youth's passion to know all, the hunger for the infinite. "Gleams like the flashing of a shield" summoned him; "vast ideas" stretched out before him, but his "reach" too far exceeded his "grasp." His was youth's feeling of power before the work is attempted, of dismay after it is done, so great is the gap between infinite aspiration and limited result. Where there is human life there is irony; there was something ironic,— or was it tragic? — in Herder's very personality, in his temperament, an overbalance of penetrative power, and lack of creative power, in spite of life-long, incessant work, to put into architecturally firm form that which his divining imagination had found as truth. Something of sadness, of melancholy was in him; how shall a man of such vast and far-reaching ideas be satisfied with anything that he has achieved? Unsatisfied with the form of what he had wrought, his spirit wrestled with his teeming ideas as the Spirit wrestled with Chaos in the morning of the world, but he never saw that the result was good. He shrank from what he had done, and could not read his books, once they were printed, the contrast was too great between what he had planned, and what he had succeeded in executing; aware of the truth of much that he could not prove, he had, perhaps, a feeling that he had failed his own insight. Reading about him, one seems to be reading the characteristics of his whole period, in that deep realization of irony, of the gap between infinite aspiration, unlimited insight, and limited power.

But whatever discouragement he had was personal; in his thought of the future of the race there was boundless optimism, boundless hope. He kept throughout his life the reverent earnestness of youth; his mind was never touched by the cynicism that too often comes with middle age. Evidently, in that long life of incessant toil, and ardent thought, and strenuous moral endeavor, he had not even the relief and saving help of humor. If his was, as has been said, perpetual youth, this fact, which implies limitation, brings also something of gain; he kept the freshness, physical and mental, of young life unsullied, retaining until the last the ardor of those early moments of pure aspiration, intellectual and spiritual. There was a steadfastness, fine, right, healthy, in his controlled life and development, contrasting with the passionate, diseased excesses of Rousseau, and with the wild moral vagaries of some of the followers of the *Storm and Stress* banner. Herder was almost the only one, Nevinson says, who held to high ethical standards in that Weimar community, wherein he spent many of his later years, and Crabb Robinson pictures him moving with a certain gravity, dignity, in that gay Weimar world, in it but not of it.

There is youth in the vitality, the vigor, the continual springing up of fresh ideas in Herder's mind, as in the pushing of green shoots through the earth, under the falling of spring rain. His feeling of life, growth,— his very temperament is an inherent part of the thought which was to work so potently in the intellectual revolution. His was a new and subtle consciousness of the inner working of nature in language, in literature, in all aspects of the intellectual and spiritual life of humanity; it is as if nature herself, finding a voice wherewith to express herself, were revealing her very mind and imagination, her secret, inner processes. *The life in things*: in apprehending this lies the originality of the man who was the leader of the leaders in the critics', the scholars' revolution. In whatever he touches, language, folk-song, the whole development of the human race, he puts his finger on the very pulse of life there, gets to the very springs of being; this is his peculiar genius.

In that world of dry rationalism, of dualism, of the eighteenth century, with little conception of the relation of mind to body, Herder's thought is marvel. Who else had in theory so enwrought the body and the mind of man with earth processes, holding stoutly all the time to the conviction of spirit operating through all organic action and change, so that alike the inmost working of an individual mind and soul, and the life within a grain of sand, are part of the whole cosmic order, one with the stars in their courses? There was oneness in it all, the stirring within the human mind one with that which goes on in the farthest outposts of space; such was his faith in the infinite progression of life, Spirit obedient to its inner law of development.

Like most geniuses, he had but one thing, one great thing to say, and many ways of saying it. His life work was the application of this idea in different fields: the laws of literary development, of the development of language, of myth, of religion, and, in his greatest work, the *Ideen*, the laws, physical, intellectual, spiritual, of all that is. In all this he was a suggestor, rather than a demonstrator; his manner was gentle, his voice was not strong, and his pen was unable to do justice to the fulness of his thought. Perhaps, in the long run, the suggestors have counted for as much in human history as those who fully demonstrate and prove,— so much of final proof of this or that idea has been swept away. For completed demonstrations and proofs all too often, in the course of years, reveal themselves to have been but tentative conjectures in the long search for truth, not yet found. Suggestions start the mind of the reader or listener to working, quicken the creative instinct, start fresh investigation, whereas complete demonstration usually rouses the critic, and intellectual and spiritual strength are wasted in controversy, which might have been expended in independent search for truth.

Herder, "in whose work all the new ideas which have animated the intellectual world during fifty years are in germ," who scattered the seed of his thought with royal prodigality, is all but forgotten. Yet he is worthy to have Shelley's lines in the *Ode to the West Wind* quoted about him; higher tribute would be hard to find:

> Drive my dead thoughts over the universe
> Like withered leaves to quicken a new birth!
> And, by the incantation of this verse,
> Scatter, as from an unextinguished hearth,
> Ashes and sparks, my words among mankind!
> Be through my lips, to unawakened earth
> The trumpet of a prophecy! O, wind,
> If Winter comes, can Spring be far behind?

What greater hope could man have than to disappear thus in the sown seeds of suggestion, quickening ideas for the future?

Such sowing is fulfilment.

IV

WORDSWORTH: "THE UNITY OF ALL"

I

THE poet who, in *An Evening Walk* (1793), slips from visual impression to visual impression, gathering, after the fashion of his day, many concrete details into generalized description of various outer aspects of nature beauty, speaks, in *Lyrical Ballads* (1798), in a wholly different manner, giving, with strange directness and simplicity, an inner reaction. Deep experience has welded together the varied attributes of his personality into singleness of insight; the roving eye is at rest. In *Lines Written in Early Spring*, the experience of an individual consciousness, on a special moment of a special day is given, in a special spot, and the moment's insight carries with it an infinity of significance. Full of a sense of inflowing wisdom, inflowing of the divine, he knows that he shares one life, one consciousness with all the life around him:

> To her fair works did Nature link
> The human soul that through me ran;

he has faith that every flower, every budding twig, and every bird feels joy as he feels it. This world, whose beauty he has watched as a spectator, at a distance, now comes to him with a sense of inner relationship; he is part of it, with all that lives and moves upon it. It is no longer a world of fragments, in which he, like the rest, is a fragment, but is a living whole. The *Lines to my Sister*, recording another moment of revelation, affirm a belief that the one life breathing through all things is Love, a universal birth, and make an explicit statement of faith that the senses are avenues through which the individual soul may become aware of the all-enfolding soul:

> Our minds shall drink at every pore
> The spirit of the season.

Again, in *Expostulation and Reply*, he writes:

> The eye — it cannot choose but see;
> We cannot bid the ear be still.

Through these pathways of approach mysterious powers feed the mind that waits in a wise passiveness.

This affirmation of a oneness of experience through all created life, of the senses as a medium of communication between the individual and the all-encompassing, represent belief in an organic conception of life, and not of physical life alone, for the one life is that also of the soul within, and bring a lyric note different from that of the nature lyrics of any preceding century. Many later expressions of this faith appear in Wordsworth's verse, none more beautiful than the suggestion of the shaping power of the nature soul in *Three Years She Grew in Sun and Shower*:

> The floating clouds their state shall lend
> To her; . . .
>
> . . . and she shall lean her ear
> In many a secret place
> Where rivulets dance their wayward round,
> And beauty born of murmuring sound
> Shall pass into her face.

The organic relationship of mother and child with each other, and with the universe, is suggested in a passage in the *Prelude*, which is full of deep significance:

> For feeling has to him imparted power
> That through the growing faculties of sense
> Doth like the agent of the one great Mind
> Create, Creator and receiver both.

The consummate expression of Wordsworth's divine nature faith is in *Tintern Abbey*:

> A sense sublime
> Of something far more deeply interfused,
> Whose dwelling is the light of setting suns,
> And the round ocean and the living air,
> And the blue sky, and in the mind of man;
> A motion and a spirit, that impels
> All thinking things, all objects of all thought,
> And rolls through all things."

Again, in *The Excursion*, of the hills and mountains:

> Even in their fixed and steady lineaments
> He traced an ebbing and a flowing mind.

In this inspired presentation of the close interknitting of man, body and soul, with his environment, there is no dualism, but a perception of wholeness, of oneness. This power,

> A soul divine which we participate,

is not represented as wielding nature aspects from the outside, making them influential in human lives, but as inherent in nature, immanent in all phenomena, physical as well as intellectual, acting within the mind of man, impelling subject and object of thought into correspondence. In this interpretation, man is no longer body and mind, but a living unit,— the mind not a receptacle of innate ideas, mysteriously placed there, like jewels in a casket, but a central activity, receiving, even through that subtle organism, the body,

> Authentic tidings of invisible things.

Fuller, more thoughtful, less lyric expressions than those in the spring lyrics of the *Lyrical Ballads*, of the way in which "sense helps soul," becomes the instrument of soul, as sense touches emotion, emotion quickens thought, are to be found in various parts of Wordsworth's work. He speaks of the moment

When the light of sense
Goes out, but with a flash that has revealed
The invisible world.

Again, he says of the seers:

In a world of life they live,
By sensible impressions not enthralled,
But by their quickening impulse made more prompt
To hold fit converse with the spiritual world.

Keeping

The glorious habit by which sense is made
Subservient still to moral purposes,
Auxiliar to divine. . . .
— So build we up the Being that we are
Thus deeply drinking in the soul of things,
We shall be wise perforce.

In *Tintern* he says that he has owed to nature's beautiful forms sweet sensations, that have touched feeling, and so have passed "into my purer mind," have quickened love for his fellow creatures:

Nor less, I trust,
To them I may have owed another gift,
Of aspect more sublime; that blessed mood
In which the burthen of the mystery,
In which the heavy and the weary weight
Of all this unintelligible world,
Is lightened: — that serene and blessed mood,
In which the affections gently lead us on, —
Until, the breath of this corporeal frame
And even the motion of our human blood
Almost suspended, we are laid asleep
In body, and become a living soul:
While with an eye made quiet by the power
Of harmony, and the deep power of joy,
We see into the life of things.

If there is much of Platonism, instinctive or acquired, in "that peculiar conception of his that an entrance into the world of abstract thought may be won by the help of material objects," and in the suggestion of the affections as a power drawing toward the beautiful, there is also much of the modern wakening thought of the close interknitting of man and all the faculties of man with the earth of which he is a part, that organic relationship which was only then beginning to be understood.

Another rapt moment of insight into the ultimate, taking its impetus from earth, is presented in *The Excursion*:

> He beheld the sun
> Rise up and bathe the world in light! He looked —
> Ocean and earth, the solid frame of earth
> And ocean's liquid mass, in gladness lay
> Beneath him: — . . . . his spirit drank
> The spectacle: sensation, soul, and form,
> All melted into him; they swallowed up
> His animal being; in them did he live,
> And by them did he live; they were his life.
> In such access of mind, in such high hour
> Of visitation from the living God,
> Thought was not; in enjoyment it expired.

These passages have led to Wordsworth's being called both pantheist and mystic; man could hardly be both. If the pantheist is one who believes "that there is no God but the combined forces and laws which are manifested in the existing universe," Wordsworth is no pantheist. The consciousness in *Tintern* of the immanence of the divine, "A motion and a spirit" that "rolls through all things" is no denial of transcendence, no affirmation that spirit is matter-bound, as in the pantheist's thought, but suggests a more quick and vital way of drawing near the power impelling all things. Those who claim that Wordsworth was a pantheist forget that the spirit which "rolls through all things" has its dwelling place in setting suns, in the living air, and in the mind of man, but is not bounded by them. No one is coincident with his dwelling place.

Belief in the personality of this immanent and transcendent power was, from first to last, a fundamental part of Wordsworth's faith. Though in these early lyrics he does not use the name God, he later, in the *Prelude* and elsewhere, slips imperceptibly into the use of the term for the same conception, perhaps as his feeling of personality deepens with deepening experience. The God of his fathers is not absent from his thought of the "spirit" that "rolls through all things," in *Tintern*, or from the passage in the *Prelude*, identical with this in meaning:

> I felt the sentiment of Being spread
> O'er all that moves and all that seemeth still;
> O'er all that, lost beyond the reach of thought
> And human knowledge, to the human eye
> Invisible, yet liveth to the heart;
> O'er all that leaps and runs, and shouts and sings,
> Or beats the gladsome air; o'er all that glides
> Beneath the wave, yea, in the wave itself,
> And mighty depth of waters. . . .
> . . . .
> One song they sang, and it was audible,
> Most audible, then, when the fleshly ear,
> O'ercome by humblest prelude of that strain,
> Forgot her functions, and slept undisturbed.

In *Hart-Leap Well*, written early, in 1800, he says of the hunted stag:

> His death was mourned by sympathy divine,

and adds:

> The Being that is in the clouds and air,
> That is in the green leaves among the groves,
> Maintains a deep and reverential care
> For the unoffending creatures whom he loves.

None could intelligently deny the affirmation of personality here, in "sympathy," "reverential," "whom he loves," or fail to relate the use of the word "Being" to that just quoted:

> I felt the sentiment of Being spread;

also to the uses of the term in *The Excursion*, the first passage written early:

> So build we up the Being that we are;
> Thus deeply drinking-in the soul of things,
> We shall be wise perforce;

the other, written late, a declaration of faith in

> A Being
> Of infinite benevolence and power;
> Whose everlasting purposes embrace
> All accidents, converting them to good.

The combination of Biblical and poetic phraseology in

> It is a beauteous evening, calm and free,

shows the thought of God blending with the thought of the spirit of nature, speaking at that moment through the sound of the sea:

> Listen! the mighty Being is awake.

No man of Wordsworth's tradition and training could conceive of infinite spirit as having less than personality.

Wordsworth was indeed a mystic, but the type of his mysticism needs careful definition. Mysticism has taken many forms, and is perhaps an element in all deep religious experience; in all it implies belief in immediate communication with the divine. In Wordsworth's feeling of oneness with the divine, as manifested in the passages quoted, there is none of the longing, characteristic of the extreme mystics of India, of mediaeval Europe, for loss of identity, absorption of the individual into the infinite, rather an intensification of individuality. From his moments of profoundest realization of the infinite in his communion with nature he withdrew with deepening powers, for each stirring of the divine within him meant a quickening of his unique imaginative insight, that quintessence of his personality. Here he found a deeper self-realization, drawing the infinite into the finite:

> Of genius, power,
> Creation and divinity itself
> I have been speaking, for my theme has been
> What has passed with me.

That thought which earlier poets had delighted to present in antitheses, of the power of the Almighty as manifested equally in the boundless and in the infinitesimal, the macrocosm reflected in the microcosm, here turned inward into a living consciousness of the presence of the divine in his human soul. He had many moments of mystical experience, but the strong individualism of his ethics, the persistent activity of genius within him, show that he was not of the type of the passive mystic, content with utter absorption into the infinite, but of that higher type, whether religious or other, who put mystical moments to high creative uses, practical or artistic.

In Wordsworth one finds a closeness to the green earth as real as that of Burns, a poignancy of spiritual experience as actual as that of Blake, with an immediacy of perception of the divine, not, as in Blake, a conception of man, as spirit, prisoned in a world of sense, but a consciousness of the divine coming directly through the senses, as if eye and ear and finger tip were paths through which one drew near to spirit.

In this awareness of organic unity between man and nature, all sense of barrier, of separation between the divine and the earthly vanishes; nature, the world of meadows, streams, and mountains, of animals, of all that with which one comes into contact, is gathered, not only into the the physical and emotional life, as in Burns, but into the world of spirit, mysteriously sharing the processes of the inner life wherein lies reality.

Wordsworth's best work was done in the early period, when he was most keenly aware through sense and through spirit of his organic relationship with nature. The *Lyrical Ballads*, of 1798, Spring shoots of genius bourgeoning and blossoming, and the work of the great period, to 1807 or 1808, presenting, in great simplicity, nature, children, animals, experiencing human souls, are full of perception of his oneness with all life. The divine in nature is to him more than a thought; he found living contact with it. Throughout this period the "light of sense" was quick and keen, the flashes swift and many, and there was hardly a gleam of leaf or blossom, or flash of star, that failed to stir him with a consciousness of "something far more deeply interfused." When he is writing of bird, of flower, of the homely concrete of nature, he is aware all the time of the spirit which "rolls through all things." All these living things, butterfly, daffodil, daisy, linnet, celandine, are concrete manifestations of the "one life within us and abroad," and Wordsworth's reverence in the presence of the humblest things in nature shows his constant sense of indwelling spirit. It is this which gives the strange mystical quality to his nature interpretations; here spirit seems to be taking wing, unfolding into petal, shining in distant star and in the glow-worm at his feet. His treatment of the simplest aspects of nature has deep significance; many have made the mistake of thinking the idea as well as the object simple. The lines:

> A primrose by a river's brim
> A yellow primrose was to him,
> And it was nothing more,

often rouse derision, but might far better give pause for thought. They suggest a profound nature philosophy, a philosophy perhaps most perfectly expressed by another lyric poet of the period, Blake:

> To see a World in a grain of sand,
> And a Heaven in a wild flower,
> Hold Infinity in the palm of your hand,
> And Eternity in an hour.

It is impossible to read Wordsworth's early poetry, recording that significant experience of life in the out-of-door world, without a certain awe, feeling, as did the child Dorothy about the butterfly, fearful of brushing the dust from off its wings. The simplicity, the profundity of his best work at the time give one a sense of drawing near the heart of the mystery of existence and finding the solution of it nearer and simpler than one had supposed. Here is freshness of feeling and of phrase; the language seems new, as if the very words were newly sprung from the bosom of earth to express illumined mood in which every touch of nature reached through sense to spirit.

Truly Wordsworth, in the great moments of his great period, felt living light shining through the clairvoyant senses; it was a long period of perception of that which may come to lesser men in hint or gleam once, perhaps, in a lifetime. The poetry of this period is translucent, like the ferns on the Quantock and the Grasmere hillsides in spring time, with sunlight shining through. In *The White Doe of Rylstone* Wordsworth gives one of the best expressions of his mystical sense of the divine. The recognition of the relationship between living things, of the one life in and through them all, is subtly presented; until, by magic creative touch Wordsworth, in the doe, suggests that inner light, which is the soul of Emily, shining out through the form of the beautiful living creature. This poem, which has a charm, a spiritual suggestiveness that eludes analysis, was written near the end of the period of clearest vision.

II

In Wordsworth, every aspect of interpretation, including the revelation of himself, is given in terms of life; "fair seed time had my soul." Of the slow maturing of his powers to perfectness of insight into a universe

> Which moves with light and life informed,
> Actual, divine, and true,

the poet tells in the *Prelude* in words expressing growth, as of a living thing with roots in the earth, under the influences of sun and wind. That growth is the growth of an individual imagination, penetrating more and more deeply into the divine law of life. He traces his development under the ministry of nature, from babyhood, when the river Derwent attuned his ears to the melody of the universe, through haunting fear, accompanied by

> A dim and undetermined sense
> Of unknown modes of being;

through physical delight, into a "pure, organic pleasure," which was not passive, for his sensibility was "creative," and outer influence found inner, active response:

> An auxiliar light
> Came from my mind.

There is a pulse, a stir of life in his study of himself, as he tells how sensation slips into emotion, and far-reaching and delicate emotions stir the mind, till creative activity wakens within him, and he consecrates himself, aware that he has "the vital soul," in a significant moment of experience, to the service of poetry. The touch of time, of development is upon this story of the creative power of nature at work in the making of a poet finding within himself

> A correspondent breeze, that gently moved
> With quickening virtue;

one is conscious throughout of a becoming, of the promise of the incomplete. And this account of the genesis of poetry, is vital, organic, for the soul of the poet is subtly one with the shaping soul of the universe, and in its turn shapes, expressing that which stirs most deeply within, while nature, through the interpreter senses, plays upon that inner life and activity, deep calling unto deep. So the poet

> In Nature's presence stood, as now I stand,
> A sensitive being, a *creative* soul.

One wonders whether such scrutiny of the inner life, such reverent study of man's consciousness, had been made since the days of Socrates and Plato. Confessions, diaries, autobiographies there had been, but never, before, or since, such a study of the growth of a genius, in singling out that which nourished, fostered the development of his mind and imagination, as he became more and more of an individual. As Pater says of Socrates: "The very thoroughness of that sort of self-knowledge he promoted had in it something sacramental."

The influences touching the soul of the poet were not merely those of the green world about him; observed human experiences, with their subtle intimations of the divine, also waken in him creative activity; and the revelation in the *Prelude* of the poet's development to the point where, through his growing insight, man was admitted to the fellowship of himself and nature, makes one aware of the deepest current of his thought. Not only in connection with nature aspects did Wordsworth know the organic oneness of life; he was aware of the experiences of others, joy, sorrow, endurance, as if they were his own, and he became spokesman. *The Affliction of Margaret*:

> My apprehensions come in crowds;
> I dread the rustling of the grass;

Matthew, in *The Fountain*:

> My eyes are dim with childish tears;

the fragment presenting the aged wanderer who moves so silently that

> The little hedgerow birds,
> That peck along the road regard him not.
> . . . He is insensibly subdued
> To settled quiet: he is one by whom
> All effort seems forgotten; one to whom
> Long patience hath such mild composure given,
> That patience now doth seem a thing of which
> He hath no need,

and many others, are full of direct perception of the deep-rooted relationship of human beings, of belief that one life enfolds all the souls of men. The human nature to which, he tells us, he felt that he belonged, and which he reverenced with love,

> Was not a punctual presence, but a spirit
> Diffused through time and space.

In all this is a new feeling of the deep unity of human lives. It is different from Crabbe's harsh, observant pity, the pity of the helpless observer of human suffering, watching from afar, though that too, in its own way, proved potent in helping waken the conscience of the world. In Wordsworth's recognition of the oneness of all life there was more than mere idea, more than compassionate thought about his fellow men, there was direct consciousness of other human souls, in moments when the physical barrier separating him from his fellows vanished; he was one with them, his spirit with their spirit.

Here too was something of mystical experience. It was not only through the ministry of breeze and grass and flower that Wordsworth felt himself in immediate communication with the divine; more deeply still he felt himself in the presence of the divine in contact with men's souls. There was God, moving in the very instincts, in the deep affections, in the thought that groped toward good; in the will that chose the right. He did not, like the mystic of India, like many a mediaeval mystic, withdraw from human beings to draw near to God, but drawing near his fellow men, he was aware of the presence of the divine through long generations of human story and in the present scene, in the fulfillment of duty, in finding peace in submission to the divine will, in the consciousness of the presence of God in all the concerns of daily life.

For him there was indeed, in those divining moments of insight, a mystical oneness of experience in his contact with others, but that beautiful mystical sympathy involved no thought, for him or for them, of the engulfing of the individual by the infinite. His thought was of the divine spirit manifest in the infinite interplay of individuality, not in blank oneness; there was for him something inextinguishable in personality, in life or in death. Closer contact with his fellows taught him more and more of God; as he found more and more of individuality in their reaction to life, he found more and more of the divine. Their victory, their endurance, were for him revelation.

Wordsworth's theory of poetry and his theory of life are basically one; perhaps this is the reason for his enduring and increasing hold upon the minds and souls of human kind. He interprets art as a life, and life as, potentially, an art, shaped, in such interpretations as we find in *Michael*, *The White Doe of Rylstone*, in the humble lives recorded in *The Excursion*, and in others, in accordance with an underlying idea, with something of the artist's power of selection, rejection, choice. Both arts are based on finding and following divine law, operative throughout the universe.

He was pioneer with Coleridge in a profound conception of the imagination, in the idea of the guiding power in a work of art coming from within, not from outer law, and his thought was ever of the nearness of that power to nature, of influences passing "from earth to man, from man to earth," influences emanating from the "Wisdom and Spirit of the Universe," operative in earth phenomena and in the souls of human beings, the source of the mysterious sympathies between man and nature. Wordsworth's prefaces, especially that of the 1800 edition of *Lyrical Ballads*, wherein he gives reasoned statement of thought and feeling that correspond with subtle flashes of insight recorded in his poems, show that his thought of the poet and of poetry is touched by a mystical idea, reaching far back in race consciousness, of one inner life in all things, and also by fresh organic conceptions that were creeping into men's minds, related to the growing knowledge of oneness of physical structure in the realm of science. A poet, Wordsworth says, "is a man speaking to men," able to be spokesman because he is one of them, bound by fine interrelations that make him one with his fellows; because he "rejoices more than other men in the spirit of life that is in him"; "has a greater knowledge of human nature, and a more comprehensive soul" than are common; finding in his own passions and volitions the key to the interpretation of his fellows, and "delighting to contemplate similar volitions and passions as manifested in the goings-on of the Universe." His thought of the working of the imagination which enables the poet to enter into the personalities of those whom he is interpreting, and even to "confound and identify his own feelings with theirs," is based on a realization of the close interknitting of the souls of men, his heightened consciousness of the life going on in others making him ever more aware of the one life in all.

Poetry, "the image of man and nature," is philosophy also. This "breath and finer spirit of all knowledge," this "impassioned expression which is in the countenance of all Science," involves both feeling and intellect. Springing from passion, it should aim at pleasure in presenting truth, truth that is "an acknowledgment of the beauty of the universe." "The Poet binds together by passion and knowledge the vast empire of human society, as it is spread over the whole earth, and over all time," revealing the one life in humanity. Observation of his fellows, their deep loyalties, affections, convictions, wakened the poet to fuller understanding of the divine working in human life, to further knowledge of the "primary laws of our nature," that make for good throughout the universe. Ever conscious of the one life manifest in the material and in the spiritual world, he affirms that the thoughts, the feelings, the very language of men are purified by nature influences. In the matter of poetic diction, theory doubtless triumphed over observation, a logical mistake, for nature, to him perfect in her working, might be expected to bring forth perfect speech from the lips of those nearest to her. In his own work, he insists, he employs the language really used by men; he chooses incidents and situations from common life. For him minor experiences had value, as part of the one life showing in least things as in great; some of his failures are due to the fact that he could not realize the relative importance of incidents, for all experience had for him eternal meaning. In this thought of poetry, as in his own verse, it is apparent that he strives for the beauty of simplicity, naturalness, truth, for the light of great revealing mood on common things. Humble and rustic life is chosen by him "because, in that condition, the essential passions of the heart find a better soil; . . . because in that condition of life our elementary feelings co-exist in a state of greater simplicity; . . . because the manners of rural life germinate from those elementary feelings; . . . and, lastly, because in that condition the passions of men are incorporated with the beautiful and permanent forms of Nature." Ever grasping more deeply nature as a shaping power in human lives, Wordsworth delights in bringing out the close relationship of man with earth. "What then does the Poet? He considers man and the objects that surround him as acting and re-acting upon each other, so as to produce an infinite complexity of pain and pleasure." All that he says of the nearness of rustic folk to nature, of nature as inspiring and guiding the feelings, shows the organic conception working half consciously, as man is studied in relation to his environment. And, as he writes, his language takes on terms of process and of growth: "passions find a better soil"; "germinate"; "are incorporated with the beautiful and permanent forms of nature." It is noteworthy that his idea of poetry, at this time of the freshest, most vital, most incisive thought about it, is expressed largely in terms of life.

In Wordsworth's study of man and his deep relationship with earth,

> Where deep and low the hamlets lie
> Beneath their little patch of sky,
> And little lot of stars,

the gray stone cottages, the fields, the sheepfolds, the gardens, associated with many years of reverent living, take on something of the sanctities of such life. Because of hereditary faiths and loyalties, fostered by long association, perhaps through generations, with special spots, the very dwelling-places become a part of the lives lived in them. The idea that these tangible things waken consciousness of experience associated with them, of principles there held, might well recall again the Platonic suggestion of entrance into the invisible world being made by touch, impetus from the visible.

All aspects of Wordsworth's thought draw to one; he cannot interpret any phase of human existence except through perception of inner vitality. There is, in his idea of the family, something of the organic conception and its spiritual counterpart, each member performing the part, the function especially belonging to him in the life of the whole, and the same tendency is manifested in his social and political theories. In thinking of nations, of races, the collective idea is emphasized; a people are held together by inner loyalties, not by kings and constitutions. He has a deep sense of the common bond; by espousal of a common cause they become one; each people rebelling against the Napoleonic tyranny is as a single soul, for the souls of nations are as real to him as the "souls of lonely places." Note the sonnet in which he speaks of the winds and waves bringing power to the brave,—the organic suggestion of earth relationship slipping into the spiritual:

> One decree
> Spake laws to *them*, and said that by the soul
> Only, the Nations shall be great and free.

In the long series of *Ecclesiastical Sonnets*, wherein he touches salient points in the history of the Church of England, crucial moments, great personalities, he reveals something of that idea which came into being, at this period, of the organic nature of great human institutions of both church and state, of their development as constituting a collective growth and experience, of the indissoluble relationship between present and past, which Burke held, and of which Coleridge became the most philosophic interpreter in England.

One is grateful for the privilege of reliving, in part, another life, entering into another personality, seeing with eyes more far-seeing than our own, at one of the crucial moments of the world's history. Wordsworth's *Prelude*, the heroic sonnets, *The Excursion*, his interpretation of the experience of himself and others, take us farther into an understanding of the time than we could have gone by ourselves if we had lived then. Living, writing at the heart of this crucial period, Wordsworth has given the deepest, as well as the subtlest, interpretation of much that was best in it, not only in connection with the profounder impulses at work in the French Revolution, but in his often unconscious suggestion of new thought, new intellectual trends and tendencies. He is spokesman for the period, and for something deeper than the period.

Much of that which was to be the distinctive note of the century that was being ushered in, the interpretation of life in terms of life, which was the characteristic method of the nineteenth century, appears in him. Of the organic idea, a sufficient number of expressions have already been given to show that the processes going on in the minds of advanced thinkers, Robinet, Herder, Goethe, and others, were matched by poetic intuition in Wordsworth, that which was creeping into theory of scientist and philosopher finding in him subtle interpretation, in concrete poetic expression. The idea of development which, in both its physical and its spiritual aspect, was to be the basis of the knowledge and the hope of the nineteenth century, the dynamic interpretation of life, appears in his study of his own growth in the *Prelude*; and the thought of the boundless possibilities of existence, which was beginning to dawn on men's minds, could hardly find more significant expression than in Wordsworth's words in the *Prelude*:

> Our destiny, our being's heart and home,
> Is with infinitude, and only there;
> With hope it is, hope that can never die,
> Effort, and expectation, and desire,
> And something evermore about to be.

III

From how many sources came suggestions touching the mind and imagination of Wordsworth in the working out of the nature philosophy which has rightly come to be regarded as distinctively his own, who shall say? The quickening influence of the green earth about him was reinforced by earlier divinations and suggestions; influences there were; to deny all sources would be to deny the idea at the heart of the deeper critical thought of the period, the idea of development. In this world chance miracles do not happen, only the age-long miracle of unfolding. Obviously Wordsworth had inherited much; the eighteenth century nature poets had established a tradition, and from Thomson on, observation of nature, manifestions of love of the world of out of doors had become a habit. To suggest the characteristics of the successive poets of the descriptive school, from Thomson's genial, objective accounts of landscape under sun and shower in the round of the year, of hills, streams, and pasture lands, is not our task. Wordsworth is not primarily a descriptive poet. He admired Thomson, and was aware of the sincerity of his personal reactions, but the urge of his own deeper nature appreciation showed in an endeavor to escape from the tyranny of the eye, "the most despotic of the senses," whose over-use tended

> To lay the inner faculties asleep.

It would be more pertinent to follow those processes of intellectual and spiritual development whereby the "painted scene" of certain eighteenth century descriptive poets, Thomson's successors, became less an object of vision of the outward, and more an object of vision of the "inward eye," coming to be the subtle messenger, interpreter of spirit, as the poetic-philosophic conception of oneness, and of spiritual oneness, came into being. Came, rather, into fuller being. To recognize in Wordsworth the exquisite and individual expression of an idea that reaches far back in the life and thought of the race is no disparagement; realization of the long heritage enhances rather than lessens the significance of this deep and persistently recurring intuition of truth.

How far back does it reach, the idea of oneness, underlying the varied phenomena of life? Long antedating the spiritual is a purely physical conception of oneness in the material universe, for whose dawning one must recall the rise of thought among the Greeks, in the Ionian physicists with their conjectures: was it earth, air, fire, or water, this one element that pervaded all things? recall Heraclitus, whose view "that reality is alive," marked the beginning of evolutionary thought. The idea of a world-soul, denoting at first but physical life, had appeared early, to recur later, at different times, in different countries, one of the basic ideas, gathering, as time went on, depth and significance in a growing inwardness. First named by Plato, and presented by him in the *Timaeus* in a dualistic conception of the creator weaving together mind and matter through the action of this power, the idea took a great step forward in Plotinus, in whose thought the world-soul, wherein all souls are one, emanating from the Deity, touches on the one side pure intellect, on the other, Nature, the two being one in the higher unity of their source, God. Already here was the idea of the tangible, visible, existing only in spirit, its origin and inmost reality, as it is the origin and inmost reality of the soul of man. Plotinus' favorite figure, setting forth his conviction of the inherence of the divine in all that is, was light.

This Neo-Platonic conception, in its drift down the centuries, influenced thinkers of widely different turns of thought, appearing in the idea of the One, whose divine self-expression is the life of the universe, of the mystic, Boehme; in the mathematically reasoned exposition of Spinoza, of the "one infinite substance excludent of all self-determination and negation from itself, the one being in every being,—God"; in others also, whose ideas mark the deepening thought of the race, in the conception of spirit slipping into and transfiguring the idea of matter. Neo-Platonism played an important role in the intellectual life of Renaissance Italy, and in England, after the Cambridge Platonists spoke, became a part of the atmosphere of thoughtful meditation. From the first it lent itself to different phases of development, as its inheritors laid emphasis on the encompassing soul, or on the integrity and vitality of the individual soul.

The world-soul conception may have become pantheism in Bruno, in Spinoza, in Schelling, but in those to whom Plotinus' conception of the individual soul, of all souls as a part of the world-soul, made deep appeal, the trend was away from pantheism, in a direction more truly in line with the thought of Plotinus, of the development of the individual soul through its longing for closer union with the divine, whence its being emanated. For those who cherished this aspect of his thought, the idea of transcendence lingers through all the idea of immanence, however it may fade in the minds of other thinkers. Boehme, Shaftesbury, Wordsworth are among those who need the conception of transcendent deity to complete, explain their apprehension of human individuality, and its relation to the outer universe. Wordsworth achieves "the synthesis of transcendence and immanence" which, as Windelband says, is sought by Plotinus.

Wordsworth, one of the many heirs, whether directly or indirectly of the thought of Plotinus, would seem to have a special affinity with that early idealism, in its idea, noted by Akenside in his *Pleasures of Imagination*, of the twin birth of nature and the human soul, the divine expressing itself alike in the beauty of natural things, and in the instinct in man that apprehends this beauty; hence the hidden correspondence, the inner sympathies, the mystical meanings of natural things. These ideas come to exquisite flower in Wordsworth, who had a living perception of corresponding life in primrose and daffodil, linnet, glow-worm, and overshadowing tree. He wrote joyously:

> To her fair works did Nature link
> The human soul that through me ran;

and he pondered

> How exquisitely the individual Mind,
> (And the progressive powers perhaps no less

Of the whole species) to the external World
Is fitted; — and how exquisitely, too, —
. . . .
The external World is fitted to the Mind.

A blending of ancient thought with fresh intuition of a way of approach to the divine is suggested in Wordsworth's reference to

Those hallowed and pure motions of the sense
Which seem, in their simplicity, to own
An intellectual charm.

He affirms the existence of a

Spirit that knows no insulated spot
No chasm, no solitude; from link to link
It circulates, the Soul of all the worlds,

whose "most apparent home" is the human mind. His expression, "the souls of lonely places" gains new significance as one recalls this early intuition of truth in Neo-Platonism, enriched by the life and faith of many a mystic in the intervening years. Plotinus' idea of the world-soul touching on the one side pure intellect or spirit (*nous*), on the other, nature is recalled by Wordsworth's invocation:

Wisdom and Spirit of the Universe!
Thou Soul that art the eternity of thought
That givest to forms and images a breath
And everlasting motion.

There are passages in Wordsworth that can hardly be understood without some knowledge of this ancient thinker, such as:

Winds blow, and waters roll,
Strength to the brave, and Power, and Deity;
Yet in themselves are nothing! One decree
Spake laws to *them*, and said that by the soul
Only, the Nations shall be great and free.

In Book XIII of the *Prelude* he speaks of Nature as

> a Power
> That is the visible quality and shape
> And image of right reason.

The vision, in the *Prelude*, Book XIV, in its recondite sublimity, becomes clearer to the reader if he recalls Plotinus' conception of all-pervading intellect, emanating from Deity (the One), filled with divine compulsion toward creative activity, and realizes that the passage contains an over-compressed statement of thought which the Neo-Platonic philosopher developed at length. Wordsworth says that the grandeur of the mountain scene

> appeared to me the type
> Of a majestic intellect, its acts
> And its possessions, what it has and craves,
> What in itself it is and would become.
> There I beheld the emblem of a mind
> That feeds upon infinity, that broods
> Over the dark abyss, intent to hear
> Its voices issuing forth to silent light
> In one continuous stream; a mind sustained
> By recognitions of transcendent power,
> In sense conducting to ideal form,
> In soul of more than mortal privilege.

Wordsworth, inheriting, it would seem, the deepest divination of Plotinus, in the thought of the indwelling eternal, a power beyond a power, transcending nature's working, goes beyond him. His life-long attitude is that recorded of an early moment of revelation, enhancing all his powers:

> Gently did my soul
> Put off her veil, and, self-transmuted, stood
> Naked, as in the presence of her God.

The trail back to the source of the refreshing springs of Wordsworth's nature interpretation is long but full of beauty. How much the influence of Plato and of Neo-Platonism may have counted, how much the influence of Christianity, in the working out through the ages from the purely physical conceptions of the earliest thinkers the finely spiritual conception that we have in Wordsworth, of spirit immanent and transcendent throughout the universe, no one could determine. Man can no more define or limit the influence of Platonic idealism or of Christianity than he can define or limit the all-permeating ether.

In the thought of the ancient Hebrew, God had infinite power, was a person, fashioning from afar earth, star, and man, — a conception magnificent, poetic, external, lending itself to drama. The flowering of all conceptions of personality came in Christianity; it is noteworthy that the race which had the strongest conception of personality in regard to the Deity is the one which has most deeply influenced the inner life of humanity. Through natural philosopher and poet, in this period of the birth of our modern world, in the blending of the best of the Greek, the idea of power within, oneness, and the best of the Hebrew, personality, came a new and profound conception of God working within all phenomena. If the world of science, in its interpretation of cosmic law, has since rejected this hypothesis, so swift now, in the interpretation of the universe, is the growth in the spiritualizing of matter that to-morrow it may come back.

The idea of the unity and the perfect working of nature slowly and happily permeated much of eighteenth century poetry, but it by no means approximated the thought of Wordsworth as expressed in *Tintern*. The Deists did not reach the organic conception; to them the universe was indeed one, but mechanically rather than vitally one. It was a beautiful product, cunningly fashioned by the Deity for man, who was interested observer, and, at his best, grateful recipient of benefits to use and enjoy; at his worst, an enigma, showing tendencies toward evil nowhere else apparent in an otherwise perfect universe. In Shaftesbury's followers, the Deist poets, Brooke, Pope, and others, the universe was one, except for God and man, two marked exceptions; God, outside, created; man walked about on the face of that which was beautifully and harmoniously wrought, and reaped the benefits. It was left to Wordsworth to make good the lack in the Deist doctrine of the full revelation of God in the physical universe. Those earlier poets had no glimpse of the need of revelation not only in planet and in insect but in the human soul, though Shaftesbury had a glimmering of the idea, and urged man to try to fit his own nature into the encompassing harmony. In the Wordsworthian conception the universe is one, and inly alive. The great law of good works at its heart, acting in and through all living creatures. His "rolls through all things," "and in the mind of man," far transcend all that had been thought and said by the Deists; perhaps the reason for the restfulness, the peace that Wordsworth brings is that he lets man into the Perfect Whole of which those early eighteenth century thinkers wrote without realizing its incompleteness. It was by slow stages of gradually deepening life that the idea of oneness came to include the inner life of man, of one's self, one's fellow men, the perception creeping in of unity as existent in all the variety and individuality of human nature, bringing with it an awakening perception of kinship. The thought of that excluding evil of action, which made man, as Brooke affirms, the "only blot" in an otherwise perfect universe, gives place to the idea that man, by voluntary choice, may become a part of the divine and perfect order, indeed, in his own small way, creator.

Among more immediate possible influences on Wordsworth's thought may have been, as is often suggested, Spinoza's idea of the one substance which constitutes the whole of reality, but it would seem that earlier, simpler declarations of philosophic faith would appeal to him more deeply than the reasoned steps by which formal philosophers reached their conclusions. He explicitly tells us in the *Prelude* that his great assurance was not a matter of logical analysis, but of deepening experience, a synthesis, wherein growing imaginative insight and feeling played their larger part. The pervasive quality of Spinoza's thought in the eighteenth century is well known, and with some of its aspects Wordsworth was familiar, but his intensity of realization of individuality marked the extent and the limitation of Spinoza's influence upon him, if it existed, for that idea of oneness which meant the submergence of individuality could have no finality for him.

Undoubtedly, in English thought, the idea of nature as a perfect whole, of a central good at the heart of the universe, of harmony throughout, owes much to Shaftesbury of the *Moralists*; Wordsworth's

> Dust as we are, the immortal spirit grows
> Like harmony in music,

recalls, while it transcends, Shaftesbury's thought and expression; and the closing lines of the seventh book of the *Prelude*, speaking of Wordsworth's London experience, repeat words on which Shaftesbury delighted to linger, Nature, Beauty, Harmony:

> The Spirit of Nature was upon me there;
> The soul of Beauty and enduring Life
> Vouchsafed her inspiration, and diffused,
> Through meager lines and colours, and the press
> Of self-destroying, transitory things,
> Composure, and ennobling Harmony.

The question as to whether Wordsworth, in Germany, during the winter of 1799 came into contact with the newly wakened intellect in its interpretation of all life in terms of organic development is one that cannot be fully answered. Herder, in his *Philosophy of History*, grappling with problems of the physical universe, and of the entire life of man, strongly affirming a unity in all the boundless diversity, had helped shape the interpretation of the whole toward spiritual ends. With great persuasiveness he had set forth his idea of the unfolding of the divine life in all nature, according to the eternal purpose of One, both immanent and transcendent, and he was, with power and with originality, applying the central idea of organic development to language, literature, history. It is inconceivable that Wordsworth could have spent a winter in Germany, which was seething with Herder's ideas, full of Herder's followers, without coming into contact with those ideas. He was with an intelligent, thinking, talking race, given, at that time at least, to contagious intellectual enthusiasms.

If one speaks, with Herder, of the organic conception, one speaks, with Wordsworth, of organic perception. The spring lyrics of *Lyrical Ballads*, with their poetic suggestion of the senses as avenues through which one may reach reality, *Tintern*, with its affirmation of spirit working in and through all things, are quick with intuitive certainty of truth which needed no confirmation from words of man. Both were written before he went to Germany.

But it is significant that the *Preface* to the 1800 edition of the *Lyrical Ballads*, with its ideas of the dignity of the common man, and of the expressiveness of the speech of the common man, written soon after his return from Germany, suggests the burden of much of Herder's impassioned thought, from his *Fragmente* (1766–7), and his *Von deutscher Art und Kunst* (1773), that poetry is a common instinct among all peoples; that truest poetry springs from primitive folk-feeling, flowering into folk song, with its beauty of simple, musical speech. It would not be surprising if his stay in Germany roused in Wordsworth, as it has roused in many another, an impulse to theorize in regard to that which had been a matter of instinct. Does he owe something to

Herder's thought of the influence upon man of the spot of earth whereon he grows, his constitution, his temperament determined by local forces, his imagination "organic" and "climatic?"

Furthermore, Wordsworth's conception of the poet, as stated in the *Preface*, shows the impress of the wakening thought of his time, in the reflection of an idea that had been ardently expressed in Germany, by Hamann, by Herder, and later by Goethe, springing in part from a new interest in primitive literature and the consciousness of its genesis, in part from the reaction against mere reason, of the entirety of the individual, the need of man's use of all his powers, of the employment of all his faculties of mind and body. "All good poetry is the spontaneous overflow of powerful feelings" . . . to be produced only "by a man, who, being possessed of more than usual organic sensibility, had also thought long and deeply."

This is the ground idea of the *Prelude*, which tells the story of Wordsworth's discovery of the need of all his powers, feeling, imagination, will, as well as mind, for one who would really live, or would be interpreter of the lives of others. Its enduring fascination comes in part from its being quick with the vibration of an individual life, recovering lost powers; in this, and in the more far-reaching insight thus gained, this record of personal experience might well stand for the inner history also of man's deepening thought in a significant period.

One must not, however, in the absence of undeniable evidence, attempt to prove the direct influence of Herder or of other German thinkers upon Wordsworth, however probable this may be, but rather to suggest that mysterious sharing of waves of great influence, in man's intellectual growth, more intercommunicable than spoken or written word, vibrations, perhaps, in the ether, seen in the permeating force of great ideas, whose universal sweep or appeal is in itself proof of the oneness of all life. Quite as significant to the thinker, if not to the thesis writer, is this intercommunication in great periods, through means that often elude detection, as incontestable as the influence that can be proved by parallel passages.

The deepest and most penetrating of the influences that turned the young poet who bade fair only to carry on the tradition of the eighteenth century descriptive poetry into a seer was that of Coleridge. It is worthy of note that, in the *Prelude*, written for Coleridge, the first tribute paid to his friend was to him as a diviner of the unity of all things, no mere maker of distinctions, given over to analysis:

> To thee, unblinded by these formal arts,
> The unity of all hath been revealed.

It will be recalled that Coleridge, in the *Eolian Harp* (1795), written before he met Wordsworth, expressing the perfectness of a happy moment, the fulness of sense impression, the fragrance of jasmine, the murmur of the sea, the beauty of the cloud rich with light, cries:

> O! the one life within us and abroad,—
> Which meets all motion and becomes its soul,
> A light in sound, a sound-like power in light,
> Rhythm in all thought, and joyance everywhere —
> Methinks it should have been impossible
> Not to love all things in a world so filled.
> . . . .
> And what if all of animated nature
> Be but organic harps diversely framed,
> That tremble into thought, as o'er them sweeps,
> Plastic and vast, one intellectual breeze,
> At once the Soul of each, and God of all?

These lines contain the seeds of Wordsworth's nature philosophy, — the one life within and abroad, a power both within and above all, working through sense upon feeling and mind. The figure of the lyre certainly anticipates that idea of the clairvoyant senses that makes so distinctive a part of Wordsworth's nature interpretation. As the passage was written shortly before the meeting of the two young poets, it is hardly to be doubted that the full power of its thought and feeling should have been brought to bear upon Wordsworth. Written the same year in which Wordsworth published his somewhat disintegrated poem, *An Evening Walk*, it shows a depth and a centeredness of thought of which Wordsworth had shown no signs.

The world has delighted to linger over the magic spring of unmatchable experience of Wordsworth, Coleridge, and Dorothy, Coleridge still with "hope like a fiery column before him," doubtless still unfolding in his "deep and sweet intonations the mysteries of Jamblicus or Plotinus," still expounding his

> Subtle speculations, toils abstruse
> Among the schoolmen, and Platonic forms
> Of wild ideal pageantry;
> . . . .
> And unrelentingly possessed by thirst
> Of greatness, love, and beauty.

Coleridge's mind was, at this period, as he tells us in *Biographia Literaria*, full of Plato, Plotinus, Bruno, of Boehme the mystic, and we may add, on other authority, Spinoza, their theories blending in his new conversion to idealism. As the friends together sought "the indwelling and living ground of all things," every growing thing that Dorothy pointed out seemed to them alive with the "universal mind," for Coleridge's dynamic intellect, as he fused his manifold ideas into one — the conception of the central divine life in all things, which in his thought as in the ancient thought of Plotinus, makes the reality of beauty both in nature and in the human soul, — brought its full potency to bear upon the slower, more tenacious mind of Wordsworth, who grasped the idea, and never after let it go.

But of the give and take of poetic minds the processes are more subtle than critics think, and the printed word could hardly give fulness of truth, but we know that

> O the one life within us and abroad!

is one of the best expressions of that deep experience of contact with the soul of nature which bound Coleridge and Wordsworth so closely together. To its deepening contributed in the minds of both the sense of oneness in their friendship on the Quantock Hills, the sea in the distance, and over it all the veiled loveliness of atmosphere which so often in England "draws all things to one"; the friendship itself, the deep feeling of personality in the friend lending something to the apprehension of personality in the "one life within us and abroad," in the "spirit that rolls through all things."

> But who shall parcel out
> His intellect by geometric rules,
> Split like a province into round and square?
> Who knows the individual hour in which
> His habits were first sown, even as a seed?
> Who that shall point as with a wand and say
> "This portion of the river of my mind
> Came from yon fountain?"

It is delightful to make conjectures about sources and influences; it is often presumptuous to reach too dogmatic a conclusion. They who venture too near an exhaustive explanation of the exact working of the mind of genius, and of all that nourished it to the fulness of its strength, show that they have little appreciation of what genius is, — that living, central, creative power that makes all things new.

Influences may have come to Wordsworth from many sources, but, in the last analysis, his insight is his own. Whatever earlier intimations there had been, his is the most profound poetic rendering of the organic conception, in his interpretation of nature and of the individual, in the spiritual conception of the one life throughout the whole. Man has not made, nor can man ever make a more perfect expression of the idea than Wordsworth has given us in *Tintern*, and it has rightly come to be known as his, for the fulness and beauty of the treatment, and his abiding sense of the presence of the one life, not only in the vast sweep of the universe, in the starry skies, but in the least and humblest things in nature, as in the mind of man. That exquisite rendering in the early poetry of the touch of the one life, "a motion and a spirit," upon the individual human soul, through all the concrete of nature life, bird, flower, touch of wind, gleam of star or of glow-worm; his thought about poetry as revealing the common experience of mankind; his story in the *Prelude* of the making of a poet; his thought of the working of the imagination, shaping from within, of the working of the will, are "the very breath and fragrancy" of the organic idea. We should be thankful that we have so beautiful a rendering, in creative form, of a significant phase of human thought.

In Wordsworth the sense of oneness was so acute that he felt the forces which quickened in him the will toward the right operating throughout the universe, guiding the heavenly bodies. For him this was more than idea; it was experience, organic experience, for the deeper wisdom of Wordsworth seems not to have come from thought only, and from following an idea by the mind alone to its logical conclusion, but to have come from experience, in which, thought, feeling, imaginative insight were quickened into oneness, sense becoming translucent, transmitting to mind, through feeling, light from the central source of light.

V

WORDSWORTH: "THE IMAGINATIVE WILL"

THE phrase is Wordsworth's. More fortunate than many of the expressions whereby man attempts to convey through the inadequate medium of language the processes of the inner life, it contains, in its significant compression, his solution of the problem of existence, his conception of the power whereby the soul of man touches reality.

Wordsworth gained his insight in a deep crisis of experience, in which both personal factors and crucial questions in regard to the fate of nations were involved. It was a time when, in natural protest against manifold tyrannies and abuses of power, the world was full of political doctrines, placing the weight of men's destiny upon outer conditions, political wrong and right. Among the many voices raised in denunciation, the most authoritative was that of William Godwin, in *Political Justice* (1793), protesting against the existence of kings and governments, against all institutions of church and state, and proclaiming that all would be well with man when such outer restraints were removed. Let him, by revolution, turn evil circumstances into good, and his troubles would be a thing of the past. The youthful Wordsworth, fresh from intense experience in France, at the storm-center of the Revolution, full of sympathy with the generous impulses that wrought there for the betterment of the human race, and sharing Godwin's faith in revolution, was captivated by his doctrine of Necessity, an abstract determinism, declaring that "the nexus of cause and effect governs the moral world like the physical." Godwin, radical, freethinker, had been trained in early life in Calvinistic theology, from which he had revolted; but he was still a Calvinist at heart, keeping in method of thought much of that baseless dogmatism, his doctrine of Necessity winning only this over the theology he had discarded, that it does not affirm as the source of its predestination the capricious will of a Creator. Wordsworth's ardent mind was, for a time, while the French Revolution went on its tragic way, given over, like that of his master, to analysis, syllogism, proof, the troubled heart of youth, then, as now, searching for the single intellectual formula that would solve the complex problem of existence, until despairing of the hope of finding ultimate proof of anything, experiencing a

> treacherous desertion felt
> In that last place of refuge, my own soul,

he was reduced by this dogmatic fatalism to depression that was well-nigh despair.

The crisis of that strong disease, the soul's last and lowest ebb, he says, was a questioning as to the reality of the existence of the human will, of the power of choice, and of the adequacy of the reason to give grounds for choice. Reason proved of least use when wanted most; it could give no test of good and evil, nor grounds for the enforcement of right choice.

The story of Wordsworth's recovery, as recorded in the *Prelude*, is one of the great chapters in human biography. In reaction from temporary submission to this doctrine which interpreted man as the driven victim of external forces, and in response to his own need for help, the young poet discarded all theory of either compulsion or salvation as coming from outer circumstances, and came to his own rescue, newly conscious, in moments of fortunate experience, of creative power within. The poetic work of his great period, 1797–1808, is vitalized by the impulse of reaction from a shallow philosophy that ignored the fundamental realities of man's nature, and his discovery that a man could draw himself together, find and employ hidden sources of strength in his own nature, shape and create his life as a poet shapes and creates his poem, with the same process of selection, choice, direction through inner energy, was one of the deep springs of that pure joy in life which gives to the poetry of this period its distinctive character. His faith in "the imaginative will," as a creative power, capable of vivifying the human soul at the pure sources of being, he ever after expressed in his poetry and followed in his life:

> Here must thou be, O Man!
> Power to thyself; no Helper hast thou here,
> Here keepest thou in singleness thy state;
> No other can divide with thee this work:
> No secondary hand can intervene
> To fashion this ability; 'tis thine,
> The prime and vital principle is thine
> In the recesses of thy nature, far
> From any reach of outward fellowship,
> Else is not thine at all.

"The imaginative will." What did Wordsworth mean by it? Insight, and the power to live and act in the light of that insight:

> Access for you
> Is yet preserved to principles of truth
> Which the imaginative Will upholds
> In seats of wisdom, not to be approached
> By the inferior Faculty that moulds
> With her minute and speculative pains
> Opinion, ever changing.

Wordsworth's reaction from Godwinism has a two-fold aspect. Over against the arid rationalism that reduced man to an abstraction, and truth to the meager littleness of formal logic, he affirmed a belief in individual insight, imaginative power, a power not evading, but transcending thought,

> which, in truth,
> Is but another name for absolute power
> And clearest insight, amplitude of mind,
> And Reason in her most exalted mood.

"Amplitude of mind." Wordsworth's rebirth came through the discovery that he was the inheritor of a larger life than that of thought alone, and that mere thought was impotent to solve the deep problems of existence without the concurrence of all the powers of the human soul. Largeness of life came to him through the inflowing life of nature, and the passage in which he tells of his recovery has the freshness of the moment when the ebbing tide turns to the incoming tide, or when sap begins to run in springtime to the outermost twigs of tree and shrub; it is full of stir, and life, and motion. Elsewhere he says:

> Nature's self
> By all varieties of human love
> Assisted, led me back through opening day
> To those sweet counsels between head and heart
> Whence grew that genuine knowledge, fraught with peace,
> Which, through the later sinkings of this cause
> Hath still upheld me.

The deep experience of the time gave Wordsworth his greatest wisdom, and was with him through the years. The vital record of this is given in the *Prelude*; later, in his more reflective period, when the *Excursion* was written, he set forth more fully in philosophic phrase the meaning of the power he had discovered within himself. In both the record of experience and in the theory we find Wordsworth's "superb vindication of the emotions in the attainment of highest truth." He rightly affirmed that "to abstract the hopes of man out of his feelings" was not only a contradiction in terms, but a contradiction of man's nature. In the finding of truth no part of man's powers can be spared. He discovered that the mind, that late comer in the house of life, cannot, unaided, solve all the problems of the longer and deeper experience of mankind. Through the vital union of thought and feeling is born insight, that swifter logic, a power not evading but transcending thought, by means of which man gains wholeness of individual perception, passing beyond mere analysis, argument, proof, and pierces to the truth at the inmost heart of the universe. It is

> he whose soul has risen
> Up to the height of feeling intellect,

who sees into the truth of things.

This clear vision of essential meanings comes through Nature, which quickens the entire human being into action,

> A power
> That is the visible quality and shape
> And image of right reason.

Through this came to Wordsworth a sense of the potential greatness of man's life, in the employment of all his faculties, and the wakening to the full use of the powers within him must have been like the recovery of full physical strength by one partially paralyzed.

In this conception of imaginative insight as an active faculty, quickened by the inflowing life of nature, the organic idea is subtly present. Man, like nature herself, is one and alive, and responds by inner energy to all stimulus from outside. The soul is no blank, at the mercy of external controlling forces, but has power of wakening to independent action. As Kant in the realm of philosophy had passed beyond Hume, with this theory of the self as "a complex of numerous swiftly succeeding ideas," into the certainty that, without the central activity of the mind there can be no understanding, so Wordsworth, through experience and through poetic intuition, discovered that life and thought are synthesis.

Man, possessor of complex powers, is an individual; his insight is individual insight that can not be possessed by another. The discovery that man is not a generalization but a person brought abounding joy to the young Wordsworth, and started him on his quest of study and interpretation of human souls, the unique response of each to the challenge of circumstances. For no two human souls are alike, as no two crystals, no two snowflakes, no two twigs or stems are alike; Nature's ultimate hoarded secret is individuality. Each man has power to create life in the light of his peculiar insight; his insight and his act of choice can be duplicated in no other lives.

For, quite as significant is the briefer word in Wordsworth's chosen phrase, Will, representing his reaction from Godwin's doctrine of Necessity. In the many and increasing interpretations of the poet far greater emphasis has been placed on his interpretation of the imagination than on his interpretation of the will, his faith in the power of man to shape and create his destiny. Justice has been done to his insight, but hardly to his strength.

Matthew Arnold's charming tribute to Wordsworth:

> And Wordsworth! Ah, pale ghosts, rejoice!
> For never has such soothing voice
> Been to your shadowy world convey'd
> Since erst, at morn, some wandering shade
> Heard the clear song of Orpheus come
> Through Hades, and the mournful gloom.
>
> He too upon a wintry clime
> Had fallen, on this iron time
> Of doubts, disputes, distractions, fears.
> He found us when the age had bound
> Our souls in its benumbing round;
> He spoke, and loosed our hearts in tears.
> He laid us, as we lay at birth
> On the cool, flowery lap of earth.
> Smiles broke from us, and we had ease,

misses wholly one of the greatest qualities in Wordsworth, the heroic.

Doubtless many readers would agree with Arnold that the poet's secret lies in bringing rest, making one passive, receptive, but Arnold fails to grasp the steady, central energy of the Wordsworthian quiet. Ease was hardly the aim of the author of the *Ode to Duty*, and of the heroic sonnets, or of him who set forth the strenuous resignation to the divine purpose in *The White Doe of Rylstone*. At times, apparently passive, merely receptive, he wrote:

> The eye — it cannot choose but see;
> We cannot bid the ear be still;
> Our bodies feel, wher'er they be,
> Against or with our will.
>
> Nor less I deem that there are Powers
> Which of themselves our minds impress;
> That we can feed this mind of ours
> In a wise passiveness,

but to Wordsworth, as to Blake, the universe was alive and quick with spirit. In these passive moments he waited only the message inciting to the seer's ardent contemplation, or to divine endeavor. The stanzas suggest his faith in the quickening power of Nature, forever carrying on in man the process of creation, as if the divine energy within were still shaping him, awakening him to deeper reality of life. Even the impulse from the vernal wood teaches man of moral evil and of good, which is a matter of striving and of choice.

In more reflective mood the poet explained his idea of Nature's ministry:

> Hence Genius, born to thrive by interchange
> Of peace and excitation, finds in her
> His best and purest friend; from her receives
> That energy by which he seeks the truth,
> From her that happy stillness of the mind
> Which fits him to receive it when unsought.

Rest in Wordsworth means reviving the soul at the sources of being, becoming one with the whole, not for mystical annihilation, loss of identity, but for greater life, Nature, in that profound union, summoning him to deeper individuality.

Man is more deeply a part of nature than the world had suspected; the word is hardly used in the sense in which the landscape poets had portrayed it. For him who

> Felt the sentiment of Being spread
> O'er all that moves and all that seemeth still,

the term implied not merely the ministry of leaf and breeze, running brook, but something both within and beyond the green earth and the encompassing sky, the inmost essence of things, — very Being, reality, this visible, tangible world acting as intermediary. "One impulse from a vernal wood" represents not the simple didacticism with which it has often been credited, but Being speaking to being.

Nature, in whose keeping lie all human powers, can, it would seem, act upon that complex creature, man, in such fashion as to waken all of his powers into unity and concert of action, discover within him a deeper self. To Wordsworth, the very heart and inmost core of individuality is the will; it is the binding, fusing power, the creative force that welds the varied powers into one; the very center and secret of individuality; in its exercise is the act of creation whereby man creates himself an individual. In his interpretation of human experience, in the work that records his close and patient study of human life in himself and others, is manifest his faith in a power of shaping existence to fine ends, a creative power, in exercising which man becomes most like God. His unconquerable belief in this inner vitality he expressed both in his life and in his thought, bringing his own experience to bear upon his interpretations of his fellow-men.

His discovery of this inner law of freedom came from his own need. Turbulent, wayward by nature, born to live deeply, he found strenuous effort necessary to achieve self-control, to bring his nature into accord with the central good; hence the naked, terrible strength of him, the sincerity, as vital truth was found through vital experience. Perhaps no one less wilful by nature could have found — of course through long self-discipline — such ardent faith in the power of the will. No mere good man, or passively good man, but transgressor, he won his own forgiveness slowly, and found his liberty in self-conquest. Passivity has been too much emphasized in interpreting Wordsworth's experience. The influence of Dorothy, the influence of Coleridge are so constantly stressed that the reader might, at times, almost forget that there was a Wordsworth there to be influenced, but Wordsworth did his own living; his energy of inner struggle has hardly found an interpreter.

Imaginative will shows also in the shaping of his life as poet, his choice of poetry as vocation. He dedicated himself to it, in solemn and irrevocable dedication, "else greatly sinning," and throughout his life, even the great lyric period, the period of delight in largeness of life shared with all living things, bird, flower, glow-worm, fellow human being, echoed his resolution, "to brace myself to some determined aim." He believed himself to have found the inner law of his individual life, whereby he could go on in conformity with the divine, creating in harmony with the creative power forever at work at the heart of things.

Wordsworth's belief in the will implies faith in a law of good at the heart of the universe, and in the power of the individual to find it out and direct his life in harmony with it:

> So build we up the Being that we are;
> Thus deeply drinking in the soul of things
> We shall be wise perforce; and, while inspired
> By choice, and conscious that the Will is free,
> Shall move unswerving, even as if impelled
> By strict necessity, along the path
> Of order and of good.

This is from a passage written early, perhaps as early as 1795, significant as showing the poet in the act of coming to life, and to a realization of the power within him, after the deadening and disintegration of his faculties under the influence of Godwin. Here is expressed the organic idea in an intellectual application, the one life, quickening the individual to energy of choice. Perhaps the word necessity suggests a lingering of the Godwinian vocabulary, but the word here has a different import, for it implies an inner compulsion to follow the highest, an inner need to choose the right, the spiritual counterpart of that idea of an inner urge toward perfection of type that was creeping into the tentative evolutionary thought of the day. Godwin's necessity was a power outside of individuality, this, a power within, the very core and heart of individuality, the power of the will, the inner law of man's own being.

The *Ode to Duty* is Wordsworth's most explicit statement of belief in a universal law of good, and of the power of man to find and follow that law; it represents, not, as has been suggested, a change of view, but an expression in words of the faith in which he had been living. It is a deeply personal utterance. As clearly as in the *Prelude* is given the story of the wakening of the imaginative will in connection with creative art, is here presented the creative power of the individual in the moral life; the power to choose, to bring the will into conformity with the divine will, manifest in the stars in their courses, and in the human soul:

> Stern Lawgiver! yet thou dost wear
> The Godhead's most benignant grace;
> Nor know we anything so fair
> As is the smile upon thy face:
> Flowers laugh before thee on their beds
> And fragrance in thy footing treads;
> Thou dost preserve the stars from wrong;
> And the most ancient heavens, through
> Thee, are fresh and strong.

Something of the drift of thought, from Shaftesbury's time, of inner beauty and harmony throughout the universe is apparent here, vitalized and energized by the stubborn strength of Wordsworth's nature. Life gives opportunity upon which man must seize, bending his will to the great will whose infinite purpose is manifest throughout the universe. His inner necessity to follow the path of order and of good comes from his kinship with the divine. In all the turmoil of perplexing circumstances, with apparently no outer guide, man may fulfil his high destiny and effect his own deliverance, by calling upon the powers within him, not facing, in Stoic negation, life with mere endurance, standing in opposition to all that is, but working in harmony with "great allies." The winds, the sky, the face of the green earth afford encouraging sympathies, are ministers of the good at the heart of things; as is man also, when rightly observed, deeply observed, in his affections, his faiths, his loyalties.

This voluntary obedience to inner law is achieved by man through the imaginative will; insight into truth, and power to act in the light of that insight, to choose. Here are two affirmations: that man by listening to the voice deepest in his own soul is finding and following the great law of the universe; that man has the power to choose the right.

Wordsworth's was an individualistic doctrine, and individualism was the note of the period, but it is wholly different from the chaotic individualism that many at the time of the German Romantic movement professed, the "geniuses" who were a law unto themselves, who, in thought and action alike, were tangential, erratic, irresponsible. To Wordsworth, the interpreter, it was given to find the innermost spiritual meaning and right interpretation of individualism, in the voluntary following of a great inner law, drawing man nearer and nearer the central good.

To the shaping of his idea of the good went much of his contemplation of lives lived in the light of great faiths; the faith and the practice of his ancestors, of those about him, loyal to belief in the spiritual nature and the eternity of man's life, in the need of kindliness, integrity, self-control, worked upon the mind of genius, wakening it to deeper insight. Keeping as much of his spiritual heritage as he could make a vital part of himself, profoundly thinking, and pondering the thought of philosopher and poet, he found, as man must find, that truth came to him from complex sources, but his deepest awareness was always of such truth as has been lived; and thought and feeling were shaped into concreteness by his consciousness of man's need in this human predicament, of the necessity of wakening active power within in answer to that need.

The imaginative will is for him a power shaping not only life, but thought: the will to act; the will to believe. Mere knowledge can go but a little way, sense and intellect being so limited; much in the conduct of life must be left to man's larger powers:

> We live by Admiration, Hope, and Love.
>
> . . . .
>
> Through love, through hope, and faith's transcendent dower,
> We feel that we are greater than we know.

There are varying hypotheses as to what we may believe; Wordsworth's rebuke was stern to those who hold the lesser faith. Man has had glimpses of high hopes; he is renegade if he lets them go. Of the Solitary he writes:

> But he broke faith with those that he had laid
> In the dark earth,

as if faith in enduring life were indeed a factor in its continuance. Here, in the thought of immortality, as in his thought of God, he holds the higher faith by act of will.

And, whether a Presence, touching a mind quick with instinctive certainties, as in

> A motion and a spirit, that impels
> All thinking things, all objects of all thought,
> And rolls through all things, —

or, as belief in the existence of

> a Being
> Of infinite benevolence and power;
> Whose everlasting purposes embrace
> All accidents, converting them to good,

he was very sure of God. "Soul of our souls," he writes a few lines later, exhorting to "Faith absolute in God."

There is no such gap as is often claimed between Wordsworth's earlier and later faith, that which, through tradition and teaching, he had learned of the divine, blending with his own fresh experience of the world of sense and the world of spirit. After his period of negation and denial following his return from France, in the spiritual struggle wherein he discovered that to man belongs the dignity of the will to act, the will to believe, he regained faith in God, not alien to the faith he had been taught, but deeper, in that it was no mere acceptance of dogma, but living, through his own concurrence.

Wordsworth's discovery of this power in man, the imaginative will, not only marked a crisis in his life, a passage in himself from mental sickness to health, but it became the key to his interpretation of his fellow-men, and he worked out a social philosophy, the antithesis of Godwin's, based on a belief in the creative soul, the power of the soul to choose, to act in the light of that choice. He made a close and patient study of human life, not only in himself, but in others:

> The lonely roads
> Were open schools in which I daily read
> With most delight, the passions of mankind, . . .
>
> There saw into the depth of human souls,
> Souls that appear to have no depth at all
> To careless eyes,

and both experience and observation confirmed his faith in the existence of a power in man's soul, capable of shaping existence to fine ends.

One may be pardoned for coming back, as we all come back, to these interpretations, hardly knowing what it is that calls us, touched to new vitality by this contact with living experience.

There is Michael, *integer vitæ*, in spite of the assaults of circumstance. The years fall upon Michael as the snows and rains fall upon the hills among which he lived; they strip him of his joy, of his comfort, of his hope in his son, of whom he thought, not so much as a support in his declining years, as of an heir to carry on the faiths, the sanctities of life associated with this hereditary spot of earth. In spite of the chaos wrought by events, Wordsworth makes you feel the outer forces fading into insignificance before the inner, the "unconquerable" soul. Michael is a creator, his steadfast character built, thought by thought and act by act, through energy of will, brought into harmonious submission to the great will. His life, like the winds, makes a "sub (or supra)-terranean music," in harmony with the universe.

For the old Leech Gatherer life is stripped of all that the world of time has to offer, bare of comfort, of human companionship, of mere sustenance, yet his soul still has a dignity, a power to withstand. Not for him is the cool, flowery lap of earth, but the stark, naked strength of the very boulders that form his background.

Wordsworth's growth of insight into the power of the will is seen by comparing two lives, that of Margaret, embodied in the first book of the *Excursion*, where it hardly accords with his later and firmer philosophy, and that of Emily, in *The White Doe of Rylstone*. Margaret, of whom he wrote early, when he was still somewhat under Godwinian influence, is conceived as victim, crushed by the shock of circumstance. Here, with deepest sympathy, he sees far into the anguish of human experience, but in the *White Doe* he sees through it, and in Emily's heroic acceptance of griefs almost unparalleled is seen that active co-operation with the will of

God, wherein, Dante says, lies peace. There is pathos, beauty, in Margaret, but there is a higher note in the *White Doe*, as in the heroic sonnets, *The Happy Warrior*, the *Ode to Duty*, — faith in the power of the human soul to rise and conquer, or to face, struggling, that defeat which is victory.

This deepening insight, this vision of "The light that never was on sea or land," came to Wordsworth in part through his grief at the death of his loved brother John. It was given to him to find that sorrow, rightly taken, is insight, so, all suffering, all loss, the impact of all that life can bring to bear; man's creative will is the answer to the assaults of circumstance. He has given us, drawn both from his own observation and his experience, an interpretation of life that still thrills us, for it is life caught in the very act of being life. In the *Excursion* he speaks of a child holding a shell to his ear, and listening intensely with his very soul to the music:

> Even such a shell the universe itself
> Is to the ear of Faith; and there are times,
> I doubt not, when to you it doth impart
> Authentic tidings of invisible things.

Wordsworth also listened intensely, with his soul, his ear to human life, and found there what his finer instinct sought, power, even though girt round with weakness, to hold fast to the higher loyalties, to the best that men had hoped or lived. Something of scientific method went into his study of his fellow-men. He crept close to the heart of human life, watched, observed, listened. To him the facts of the inner life were as truly fact as the facts of the outer life, and, like the scientist, he sought and found his hypothesis to explain, include, existing facts. So he gained his knowledge of the "primary laws" of man's nature; significant, to him, in all this observed experience, was the power of holding fast to the human affections, the sanctities of home, the responsibilities involved in human relationships, the inherited belief in man's spiritual nature and destiny. In all this he discerned, whether working consciously or unconsciously, the imaginative will at work, man creating his faiths as well as showing creative power in acts. Man is sentient, alive, choosing; the dignity of the creator rests upon his shoulders.

As in Wordsworth's interpretation of nature there is something active, individual, creative, so in his interpretation of human nature. A passage incorporated in the *Excursion*, but written early, in the crucial period of his career, shows the imaginative will at work in interpreting his fellow-men:

> For the Man
> Who, in this spirit, communes with the Forms
> Of Nature, who with understanding heart
> Both knows and loves such objects as excite
> No morbid passions, no disquietude,
> No vengeance, and no hatred, needs must feel
> The joys of that pure principle of love
> So deeply, that, unsatisfied with aught
> Less pure and exquisite, he cannot choose
> But seek for objects of a kindred love
> In fellow-natures and a kindred joy.
> Accordingly he by degrees perceives
> His feelings of aversion softened down;
> A holy tenderness pervade his frame.
> His sanity of reason not impaired,
> Say rather, all his thoughts now flowing clear
> From a clear fountain flowing, he looks round
> And seeks for good; and finds the good he seeks:
> Until abhorrence and contempt are things
> He only knows by name; and, if he hear,
> From other mouths, the language which they speak,
> He is compassionate; and has no thought,
> No feeling, which can overcome his love.

The power to think nobly of the human soul, after observing and studying it in action, and so to increase the sum of good, is here finely manifest. The will to believe in your fellow-man is one with your will to believe in God, in the Good; the thought of one's neighbour, like the thought of the possibilities of one's own soul, is an act of faith. Sympathy is a necessary part of this insight that penetrates below the surface into the inmost reality of personality, the sympathy that is born of understanding. So, subtly, for the poet was no mere observer of mankind, the struggle of his fellow-man becomes his struggle, through

> Those mysteries of being which have made
> And shall continue evermore to make
> Of the whole human race one brotherhood.

From humble following of duty by lowliest men, shouldering their responsibilities, through the whole scale of his observation, to the heroic, exemplified in Milton, in Toussaint L'Ouverture, in the heroes who fought, in Switzerland, in the Tyrol, in Spain, against Napoleonic aggression, in the whole series of heroic sonnets we have ringing testimony to Wordsworth's belief in man's power to choose the high road and and the hard.

Not only individuals but nations are able thus to choose and to act, and the theme of his heroic sonnets is, the power of the soul of a nation to discern the right, to act in the light of that insight. In that period of special emphasis on the potency of government, of legislation to secure human good, at the cost of revolution, if necessary, his was the voice that proclaimed that

> by the soul
> Only, the Nations shall be great and free.

To develop this soul, to help quicken the imaginative will of his England, to aid her in finding and following the deeper law of her being, he recalls, often in glorious verse, past glorious phases of her history:

> We must be free or die, who speak the tongue
> That Shakspeare spake, the faith and morals hold
> Which Milton held,

calling upon his fellow-countrymen to cherish old standards, earlier insights, where these make for good, reminding them:

> But who would force the Soul, tilts with a straw
> Against a Champion cased in adamant.

In this, as in the conduct of his own life, and his interpretation of other lives, there is a certain spiritual thrift, for he was a son of the north country, a hoarding of moments of special insight, special resolution, keeping all the "gleams" for future guidance and for help in further choice. The "soul-animating strains" which he sang to hearten the wayfarer, be he nation or individual, along the chosen path

> Summoned up the honorable deeds
> Of ancient Story, thought of each bright spot
> That would be found in all recorded time,
> Of truth preserved and error passed away;
> Of single spirits that catch the flame from Heaven.

But his pleas for the wakening to deeper life of both England and France are companioned by rebukes, wherein he speaks as to a person. France has forgotten the greatness of her struggle for freedom, and now, slavish at the feet of Napoleon, is impatient to put out the only light of liberty that yet remains on earth; England stagnates, given over to worship of wealth, to outside show, to selfishness:

> Plain living and high thinking are no more:
> The homely beauty of the good old cause
> Is gone; our peace, our fearful innocence,
> And pure religion breathing household laws.

England

> is a fen
> Of stagnant waters; altar, sword, and pen,
> Fireside, the heroic wealth of hall and bower,
> Have forfeited their ancient English dower
> Of inward happiness.

England is threatened by danger from within as well as from without. The power to meet that danger is an inner power. His England must be pure of heart, and simple, fine in aim to conquer. Stern in his chiding, heroic in his clear call to action, he rebukes, he challenges the best in the soul of the nation.

In his call to the present, in the name of the past, giving reasons why Englishmen should still continue to make themselves free, as in the *Ecclesiastical Sonnets*, where, to quicken spiritual life, he recalls great moments of the past, he reveals something of that idea, which came into being in this period, of the organic nature of great human institutions of both church and state, of development through active choice, the indissoluble relationship between present and past, which Burke held, and of which Coleridge became the most philosophic interpreter in England.

In a time of protest and of plea in regard to the rights of the individual, of a new sense of the worth and the dignity of man apart from all consideration of wealth and titles, his voice was the surest and the deepest in regard to the nature of that dignity. He feels, and makes his reader feel, a reverence for the human soul, a reverence for the living such as that which is usually felt only in the presence of the dead. This reverence is most deeply based on man's power of keeping faith with the higher hopes, the deeper intuitions, the loftier aspirations of mankind; in the power of the human being, by choice, to bring his will into conformity with the divine will, so that this breathing creature, creature of a day, by voluntary act may express the eternal.

Wordsworth's was the most potent message in that period so full of wakening life in all departments of human thought and activity. His was a living creed, wrought out from observation and from experience; his articles of faith were human souls in action; these were present proofs and prophecy of the immanence of the divine in human life. He asked no further proof in dovetailing Old Testament prophecy and New Testament fulfilment, nor was his belief founded on dogmatic theological formula; this life is too complex, too subtle, too varied to be interpreted by a single formula; truth is too vital to be apprehended by any other than the entire living, groping human being. In the world of spirit, man can lay hold on life only by living.

In this philosophy of life, as nature touches the poet's soul, awakening it to creative powers, so that he interprets nature with significance and beauty not there without him, so life, in Wordsworth's thought, with its sorrows, its difficulties, temptations, wakens within man creative will, and he, if he so choose, may shape life into enduring beauty, not there without him. The dignity of the creator rests upon his shoulders.

In such a theory the organic idea is subtly present. The universe is alive, is one; there is reciprocal action between the mind of man and the outer universe, the shock of circumstance, events in the world of space and time. Though there is much of mystery, there is no despair, because the processes of development constantly going on, in which one plays an active part, irresistibly denote growth, whose end is not yet.

Of the influences, aside from those already suggested, of ancestral character and tradition, that helped to form Wordsworth's philosophic and ethical convictions, it is difficult to speak with certainty. It is hard to believe that he was unaware of the chief principles of the Kantian philosophy, so fully in accord with its major premises are Wordsworth's intuitive insights and the conclusions drawn from experience: the limitation of knowledge, the law of duty, the direct contact with reality through conscience. How much he had read of Kant we do not know; how much he gained from Coleridge we may surmise, for Coleridge made it his special study, and Coleridge was a singularly translucent medium for the expression of great ideas, his own and other men's. Kant's

Categorical Imperative rests upon belief in the creative power of the human soul, in the ability of the individual to make his being, in thought and in act, an integral part of the law of the universe. For both Kant and Wordsworth the answer to the riddle of the Sphinx lies in the will.

Perhaps more and more men will turn to this significant period of human development, when the world of thought took on new vitality in passing from the static conceptions of earlier centuries to the dynamic of the nineteenth; from the conception of a world finished and done to the conception of a world still in the making; from the conception of rigid immutable laws, mechanically active, to the conception of a continuous process of creation. It was indeed a rebirth.

The passing from the static to the dynamic conception found one of its first, as one of its profoundest expressions, in the realm of ethics. Deepest, or most significant of all mainfestations of this new life were the thought of the greatest of modern philosophers, Kant, and the greatest of modern poets, Wordsworth. Philosopher and poet alike turned from finding God in outer fact or in written dogma to find in living human consciousness a witness to the divine, the one giving reasoned theory, built up point by point through strict logic, the other finding truth by swift intuition, trying it out upon the pulses. Kant's Categorical Imperative, Wordsworth's Imaginative Will, are both affirmations of faith in a law of good at the heart of the universe; of faith in the power of man to find and follow that good.

There is indeed refreshment in Wordsworth, but it is a deeper refreshment than Arnold knew, a quickening of spiritual force into new energy. Its secret lies in his discovery in an age of analysis, of disintegration, of pulling apart, after a devastating experience in which the analytical powers had been exalted to sole supremacy, a discovery that the human powers must act in unison, for this hard problem of life to be solved; that man must exercise the fullness of his powers of intellect, feeling, imagination, will, — must "move altogether if he move at all."

We are privileged indeed whenever we are permitted to share the experience of one who has touched living truth. Such contact startles, stimulates, inspires, whether we draw near poet, philosopher, or saint. There are times when, going beyond all that man has established by formal proof in regard to the human soul (how little, after all, in the long ages of his thinking!) we come to rest, in our human bewilderment, upon the insight of the seers, aware that those of greater intellect, greater power of feeling, keener imaginative vision than ourselves may have immediate contact with truth which we do not divine. They touch some live chord within, truth we know at the heart of us; their witness to the presence of the divine in human life is part of our enduring heritage.

We may well trust this seer, who, in his great moments, saw into the very "life of things," and knew that it is given to man, if he will but draw upon all the powers within him, to create the good in which he wishes to believe. That which he utters in regard to man's potential insight and his will is enduring truth drawn from vital experience, and comes to us vibrating with the life of the universe, making one feel as if working with God in the dawn of creation, on the day of the making of man.

VI

KEATS' IMAGINATIVE APPROACH TO MYTH

I

THERE is fascination in going back and trying to follow those groping mental and emotional processes whereby primitive man, attempting to explain aspects of nature phenomena, came to interpret them in terms of his own life. That the Greeks were able to express their thought in regard to the natural wonders of sunrise, the movements of the sea, lightning, wind, the growth of green things on the earth, in color and line, making them manifest as radiant imagined personages, is cause for thankfulness for succeeding generations, not only for the light it throws on primitive thought, but for the heritage of sheer beauty. Horror was there too, and fear, but this people, as they developed, chose rather to dwell on loveliness, the flash of Iris against the dark cloud of mystery, and through all the succeeding centuries something of blitheness has come down to us in their interpretation of the powers that environ existence.

Earth processes, through perception of the life within them, — the life in grass and tree and flower hardly differentiated from the life in man himself, — slowly took on personality. At harvest time, imagination wakened by the sight of the high-piled threshing floor, under the open sky, conceived the figure of a woman, holding out gracious gifts — Demeter, already known through the waving grain of early summer, which became the rustle of her garments. The swift flight of the early beauty of spring, that first freshness of leaf and twig and flower, became her child, the maiden Persephone, carried away by that death which was the scorching heat of summer, to come again in the resurrection of another spring, but sought all the year long by the mourning mother. This legend gathered into itself not only regret for the lost charm of spring that dwellers in the country feel throughout the year, but the sorrow and the hope of those whom grief had stricken, for its later growth, in the mysteries of Eleusis, taught what had been implicit from the first in the apprehension of growth, decay, and growth again, — enduring life. Aurora was born of the surprise of the beauty of dawn, which was even as the effect of a sudden glimpse of the radiant beauty of a girl. And Zeus, who drew his being from sky phenomena, spoke sometimes terrifyingly in lightning that destroyed, sometimes in the thunder which sounds in full sunshine from the clouds that draw so near the habitations of men in the clear blue sky of Greece, in not unfriendly fashion, as of one uttering reminders of a power dwelling behind the mere appearance of things. So myth gathered into itself and held the beauty of earth and sky and primitive thought, as a rainbow holds flitting tints of color, as beech leaves in spring hold the light.

How much of intimacy, of comradeship with nature is here, in long hours, under the open sky, of those who tilled the fields of Greece! Their sense of earth nearness is hardly conceivable by us, but the old myths reveal as much as we can understand of their sense of close relationship with earth and sky and all that happened there: bone of their bone, fibre of their fibre, — they were one with the processes of growth and ripening. It was through observation of the operative powers of nature that man's mind, earth-bound at first, wakened, and out of natural processes, the coming of spring, the passing of summer, was born his thought. These happenings on earth and in the sky, in the sea, and under earth and sea, he explained in the only terms he knew, — himself, finding in them kindred powers, naturally conceived as akin to his own highest powers; his slow-growing consciousness was a part of the processes which he watched, and interpreted as personality. Nature was to these early thinkers wholly animate,— one of those early, instinctive Greek guesses at truth which sometimes prove, as in the case of evolution, to be truth indeed. In the making of myth the insistent sense of personality pressed in upon them from their whole environment with gift of grace or of ill-doing, like unto their own, but greater, and in the later stages of Greek myth, the gods are personages, even as they, but with enhanced human powers. Growth of human personality is mirrored in the growing personality of their gods.

Primitive nature interpretations, as already suggested in the Persephone legend, with its expression of man's longing for immortality, revealed in time some dim reflection of the inner life, as growing thought and insight found utterance in myth. Of all, the story of Prometheus is the most significant. In this is presented the struggle of the human consciousness between the old attitude of submission to authority imposed from without, and obedience to an inner voice, authority from within, bidding Prometheus help mankind. The central tragedy of the ages, of all political and religious martyrdoms is foreshadowed here. So myth changes, seeking higher levels, as groping human thought expresses in this fashion new insights, new aspirations. Thus, in some cases, it becomes prophetic, suggesting in concrete terms spiritual growth and development of the years to come, not perhaps in clearly thought out idea, but foreshadowing deeper thought to be. Thus, prophetically, the Prometheus myth gives in the proposed ending, in which the wounded Centaur Chiron was to take Prometheus' place, the farthest reach of pagan thought toward vicarious sacrifice.

II

The coming of a new era brings always need of fresh forms of expression. In the transition period of the late eighteenth and the early nineteenth century, when the world was undergoing fundamental change, some mode of utterance was necessary for young poets to set forth an apprehension of man, his relationships and his destiny, that did not go with the legalized conceptions of abstract man, with the current coin of eighteenth century thought and diction. Neither the poetic vocabulary nor the habits of mind of the preceding period sufficed to reveal the wakening and enlarging thought of the time, the sense of the greatness of life pressing in upon mankind; Keats and Shelley turned to myth, recapturing imaginative insights of an earlier day, finding a way of expressing thought such as was employed when the world was young. Ardor and fulness of experience, of thought and feeling about experience, a freedom of all the faculties, appear in their works, imperfect as many of them are. Myth helped them reveal a poet's delight in coming to his own again, realizing that one might feel as well as think, imagine as well as reason, aspire, as well as give, or accept, final judgment. A nature myth cannot be stretched too far without parting like a cloud, but the use of myth in early nineteenth century poetry is significant and valuable, a phase of creative activity that we would not willingly forego; it met the need, as a mode of utterance, of these young poets, struggling with the rising tide of life in themselves, and in a new century which was to bring greater life to man. It is small wonder that, in this period of reaction when revolt came against authority imposed from without in regard to both thought and expression myth made so deep an appeal. For swiftly changing, enlarging life, full of new imaginative apprehensions of unbounded possibilities, some medium of expression was necessary that could grow with growing life; that could employ symbol, — that touch of concreteness bringing home to sense invisible reality, — to set forth aspects of thought and feeling too far-reaching for rigid statement. From Keats and Shelley have come aspects of thought troubled with the inner perplexities of a later day, but keeping, through the use of myth as an embodiment of thought, something of the freshness of feeling, the perception of beauty of those who, in the early days of Greece, were slowly waking to thought under the stimulus of the wonder and the beauty of happenings in the world of nature. An important question in regard to these modern poets is: In how far did myth help them to express deep meanings, profound significances, that fuller sense of life that was pouring in upon the world?

For our modern way of interpreting myths as the outcome of the wakening mind and imagination of man playing upon nature phenomena, we owe much to Wordsworth, the first to speak in England of the real significance of myth. In Book III of the *Excursion* (847–887) he described the growth of the Apollo legend in the early days of Greece as springing from imaginative moments in the life of the herdsman stretched out on the grass, hearing from far a sweeter strain of music than he himself could make, and creating, from his dreamy thought and the sunshine, a youth with a golden lute. So the crescent moon, a lovely wanderer, became a goddess, sharing his sport, Diana of the chase. Sunbeams and swift shadows on a distant hill became fleet Oreads; the gracious slaking of his thirst from brook or spring is the kindly act of a Naiad. And grotesque, withered boughs and twigs, with horns of deer or goat showing through, gave his imagination material for the making of Satyrs, the visioning of Pan himself.

When Keats in a letter to Haydon (Jan. 10, 1818) wrote of Wordsworth's *Excursion* as one of "the three things to rejoice at in this Age," one wonders what parts he specially cared for. Prominent, if not foremost among them, must surely have been this myth passage, with its suggestion of the slow coming to the primitive thinker of a sense of personality in nature happenings. With his mind already stored with figures from mythology, from the handbooks, with passages from his loved Elizabethan poets, in whose work the myths of Greece play so large a part, Keats, the nature lover, finds this passage full of suggestive thought, and his young mind and imagination quicken into activity that brings a rich harvest.

The story of the fate of the Greek gods in the days that followed the downfall of Greece is a fascinating story, in so far as it is known. Scattered from Olympus, they become beneficent powers, or demons, as the case might be, in far distant lands. Recalled to life, and to Olympus, by the enthusiasm of Renaissance days, they appeared in literature, sculpture, painting, in masque and pageant, developed personalities, taking on enhanced human form. In much of this humanizing and modernizing of deities there is keen sense of beauty, of vitality, much also of pagan license in depicting the activities of those beyond and above human law. The pseudo-classic period brought vain repetitions of the names of the gods, the tinkle of the accustomed epithet: fair Aurora, chaste Diana, pale Cynthia, blushing Flora; the deities were reduced to a conventional pattern, something in the nature of a decorative border on rationalized verse. As man in the thought of the time became something of a generalized abstraction, each member of the hierarchy became something of an expected quality — strange fate for those vital powers which represented to primitive minds the life in sea and earth and sky to vanish in stereotyped epithet!

It was given to Keats to bring to life again, in a spirit akin to that of their first inception, some of the nature gods of the ancient world; in his work one finds insight into the nature and genesis of myth such as the Renaissance, with its riot of imagined mythical personages, did not have, and myth is put to profounder use than in the Renaissance in bodying forth his distinctive philosophy of life. It became the medium of expression of his deepest apprehension of great significances in human experience. We may ask, but can only partially answer the questions: In how far did Keats interpret primitive Greek myth? In how far did he make myth a form of self-revelation?

III. The Early Poems

In the very early work of Keats, the mind of the young poet moves among swirling sensations, emotions, thoughts, often with an amoeba-like indirectness of purpose. At the mercy of every impression, in his over-sensitive response to the beauty of nature, of poetry, of the friendship of friends and of brothers, stirring responsive affection, he confesses himself at a loss

> Whene'er I venture on the stream of rhyme;
> With shatter'd boat, oar snapt, and canvass rent,
> I slowly sail, scarce knowing my intent.

Tracing the growth of the poet is the great joy of studying Keats. As his nature matures through suffering, and through constant development of his mind, deeper understanding brings more and more the selective power of insight; he learns also, through the influence of plastic art, of Boccaccio, of Shakespeare, of Milton, the supreme secret of the artist, the art of sacrifice, of leaving out. He writes of nature in terms of growth, development, process; one can hardly study him in other fashion than in tracing growth, development, process, making progressive study of his thought and its imaginative expression in their successive stages. His three volumes, the immature poetry of the volume of 1817, together with certain early poems published later; *Endymion*, 1818, and the volume of 1820 bring the material to our hand.

In that early work, with respect to his three chief interests, nature, chivalric story, myth, he shows himself more absorbed in the first two than in myth; there are more allusions to them, and more atmosphere in the treatment. The most distinctive touches are nature touches; there are fine bits of observation here and there, and one finds, in many instances, a vitality, a feeling almost of identity with growing things, of creeping down with the roots into the moist soil, of putting forth branch and blossom, as if he were instinctively aware of the close interknitting of the life of man with the life of earth, of which the natural philosophers had been writing. In the many references to Greek mythology there is little that is noteworthy; he has caught the habit of allusion from the poets whom he loves, and in many cases does not swing free from allusion. The Muses and the Graces, the buds in Flora's diadem, flush'd Aurora in the roseate dawning, chaste Diana in her shady bower, the white Naiad in the rippling stream, the Naiad's pearly hands, and similar expressions bear the stamp of pseudo-classic repetition of mythological names, and are little inwrought with the meaning of the context. Yet from the first he was fascinated by myth, as he was fascinated by every kind of beauty, and in a few cases a freshness of touch appears in a vividness of sense-impression, as in Pan's listening to the lovely sighing of the wind by the reedy stream, young Narcissus in the coolness of the shady spot by the little pool, fauns and dryads "coming with softest rustle through the trees"; and in the fulness of appeal of touch, of sound, of smell in the passage in "I stood tiptoe" where Endymion stands on Latmos' top, and breezes from the valley bring the sound of hymns and the fragrance of incense from Dian's temple below. That unusual power of the maturer Keats of making the remote draw near through sense impression appears here in tentative touches, some fortunate, others crude; and the hint of the homely, the everyday, that often brings a feeling of reality in his work, here, at times, reaches the absurd. After the charm of the lines:

> So felt he, who first told, how Psyche went
> On the smooth wind to realms of wonderment,

he shows us Psyche and Love biting each other:

> What amorous, and fondling nips
> They gave each others' cheeks.

In *Sleep and Poetry*, the young poet expresses a wish to bite the shoulders of the nymphs, — a suggestion, surely, that all his knowledge of love-making at this point in his experience must have come from the household puppy.

Already in the early work is manifest the influence of plastic art, which, in the original, or in pictured reproduction, was to help greatly in Keats' visualizing and recreating mythical personages: some of the art-wonders of Leigh Hunt's studio, recounted in *Sleep and Poetry*; and "the white-handed nymphs in shady places"; in "I stood tiptoe," the "young Apollo on the pedestal," "Venus looking sideways in alarm," Syrinx fleeing Arcadian Pan, surely suggestive of Greek sculpture, show him absorbing in eye and in finger-tip characteristics of an art that was to influence him greatly in his own growth as an artist.

Of deeper insight into myth, and its possibilities as a medium of expression of the inner life of thought and aspiration there are glimmerings in this early volume. In "I stood tiptoe" a conception, profound and individual, but hardly as yet clear to the young poet is struggling through obscure expression. The old myth of the moon goddess and her lover Endymion already symbolizes for him the inspiration of the poet by supreme beauty, inspiration by nature, whose loveliest aspect was to Keats the moon. The moon is praised as the most potent of all nature influences, enhancing all other beauty, closing "lovely eyes to lovely dreams," charming away trouble.

The moon is lover of loneliness and wandering, and inspires the song that comes from the wanderer. Throughout this rambling poem, the mind of the young poet is full of the conception stirred in him by Wordsworth, of the growth of myth from nature happenings, and he is wrestling with his own thought of the way in which myth, in these later days, may be made to set forth exalted ardors and ideas about poetry and about life. This story of the love between a moon goddess and a mortal outshines, for him, all other stories. Was there a poet born, he asks, of this marriage? Yes, from the creative touch of myth and nature, myth itself being born from the creative touch of the human imagination on nature process. It is noteworthy that Keats is already a poet of deep sympathy, from whose mind the thought of human suffering is never long absent, recalling, in the moment of the lover's supreme joy, that the pure breezes stealing through the half-closed lattices were cooling the fevered sleep of the sick and soothing them to slumber.

Something of self-revelation appears in the invocation to Poesy in *Sleep and Poetry*:

> And my young spirit follow
> The morning sun-beams to the great Apollo
> Like a fresh sacrifice.

That groping toward something higher, striving for a closer grasp of the significance of myth in its relation to nature, in "I stood tiptoe," is evident also, in finer expression, and with the personal touch, in his sonnet on the Elgin marbles, which had brought him to a fuller understanding of Greek myth, — of the operative powers of nature embodied in Greek art and Greek myth. He expresses thankfulness that his is not the god's task of keeping the cloudy winds fresh for the opening of the morning's eye. This, with "Such dim-conceived stories of the brain," and the reference to "Huge cloudy symbols of a high romance," in the sonnet "When I have fears," represent the most imaginative suggestions in regard to myth in the early volume; and these passages, with "I stood tiptoe," suggest not only an interest in myth, but an individual attitude in interpreting myth,—show something, even, of myth-making faculty, stirred into action by Wordsworth, by nature itself, and by the Elgin marbles.

In many of the poems of the early volume it is apparent that the young poet is, under the stimulus of the creative urge within him, trying to clarify his thought and feeling by writing, before the thought is quite clear, a natural human, poetic instinct. It is all a tentative expression of wakening and enlarging thought, as of a young bird fluttering, and trying to get the use of its wings. In part of the work he gives you confused aspects of thought and feeling just as they streamed through his mind. What the early work fails to achieve in art, it gains in presenting the very thought-processes of a greatly gifted youth, growing up before your eyes. It is no small boon to be permitted to share the growth of genius.

Of the many aspects of swift growth of the young Keats, — hardly paralleled, whereby from an inchoate swirl of feelings, impressions, ideas, developed the fine singleness of insight and the sureness of touch of the artist in the best work of the 1820 volume, none is more striking than the increasing appreciation of the significances and the potentialities of myth. Brief passages in the volume of 1817, with their tremulous, indeterminate suggestions, had obscurely hinted promise, but nothing in the early rendering of myth had revealed the future interpreter, as the sonnet on Chapman's Homer reveals the future artist. Yet there are shadowy indications in this first volume of his beginning to find in myth a medium of expression necessary for him. He later brought to its interpretation his rich sense experience, his deeply stirred emotion, his deeply groping thought; and myth, with its imaginative suggestiveness, its power of growing and expanding, recording development, became one of his most distinctive ways of embodying the results of experience. The question as to in how far Keats interpreted myth turns into the more interesting question as to in how far myth became the means of revealing his own reactions to life; how far he found it capable of revealing the growing insight, weight of thought, spirituality of the years.

IV. Endymion

Book I

The very beginning of *Endymion* gives proof of great growth of imaginative insight into the significance of myth, and of power to express that insight. Myths are among

> All lovely tales that we have heard or read,

and are classed with "daffodils" and "the green world they live in," with trees and running brooks, as a part of that beauty which is "a joy forever," whose "*loveliness increases*." There is a beautiful and imaginative suggestion of myth as growing out of nature powers, of the nearness of these powers to the thought of man; the truth taught him by Wordsworth had sunk deep. As the music of the name of Endymion goes into his being, *each pleasant scene of the story grows fresh before him as the green of our own valleys*; it buds and bourgeons in him as does the spring in the flushing twigs of old forests, in willow branches. A bit later he says:

> Long ago 'twas told
> By a cavern wind unto a forest old;
> And then the forest told it in a dream
> To a sleeping lake, whose cool and level gleam
> A poet caught as he was journeying
> To Phoebus' shrine; and in it he did fling
> His weary limbs, bathing an hour's space,
> And after, straight in that inspired place,
> He sang the story up into the air,
> Giving it universal freedom.

The opening scene is full of the freshness of a spring morning, and of the young poet's spirit. The life of nature quickens in this myth, which is being re-created, and every sense is called upon to minister to the feeling of reality:

> Rain-scented eglantine
> Gave temperate sweets to that well-wooing sun;
> The lark was lost in him; cold springs had run
> To warm their chilliest bubbles in the grass;
> Man's voice was on the mountains; and the mass
> Of nature's lives and wonders puls'd tenfold
> To feel this sun-rise and its glories old.

Keats was drawn to myth by the simplicity of his relation to nature, as much as by his reading of the Elizabethan poets, or of handbooks of mythology; by his instinctive nearness to nature happenings, his utter content with nature as it is, asking nothing but the touch, sight, sound, fragrance of the moment. He had an apprehension, that was peculiarly his own, of the very life in things, and shared the processes of nature, as if they were within himself, of roots, creeping down into the moist earth; of the growth of flowers; of existence of the sparrow, with which, he said, he pecked about the gravel. He was immediately aware, through all his gifted senses, of the close interknitting of man, body, mind, and soul, with the green world of which he is a part. Reading, when he writes of spring, of autumn, one seems to be, not observing, but experiencing the quickening of spring, the ripening of autumn. That idea of oneness in all life, of organic relationship between all manifestations of life, toward which the natural philosophy of the time was groping, was with Keats, through his very temperament, a sensation, as well as an instinct, an intuition. He was one in whom, by some clairvoyance of the senses, there was immediate consciousness of the "one life within us and abroad," a physical as well as an emotional and spiritual awareness. The influence of his loved *Tintern Abbey* upon him was great, and must have helped him toward a realization of that which was within him and without him, and of the flowing of the one into the other. The spirit that "rolls through all things" brought Keats lingering delight in the loveliness of "things"; in him the "light of sense" does not go out "with a flash that has revealed the invisible world," as in Wordsworth, but lingers, growing "ethereal for pleasure," giving a nearness, a tangibility to the divine. It has been said that Keats was like Shakespeare in the simplicity and the objectivity of his nature interpretations, but he is unlike Shakespeare in this sense of kinship with thrush and sparrow, tree and blossom, this instinctive consciousness of sharing a life that flows throughout the whole. If there is in this sense of organic relationship something that chimes with, illustrates an aspect of the most advanced thought of the time, there is also something akin to the primitive nature sense of the early makers of myths who were hardly able to distinguish the life in themselves from the phenomena of earth and sky. This nature nearness, conscious in Keats, unconscious in primitive minds, gives Keats a peculiar felicity in his interpretation of myths.

Nothing could be more fortunate than the way in which, in *Endymion*, the reader is led into the poet's world of ancient myth, making that difficult transition from the world of fact to the world of the ideal:

> And if from shepherd's keep
> A lamb stray'd far a-down those inmost glens,
> Never again saw he the happy pens
> Whither his brethren, bleating with content,
> Over the hills at every nightfall went.

The lost lamb, straying, passed safely in shepherd's belief, under divine guardianship to

> some unfooted plains
> Where fed the herds of Pan.

The Hymn to Pan is not only a beautiful expression of the growth of myth from perception of nature happenings; it gives unmistakable suggestion also of a great idea toward which the young Keats was groping with all the powers of his mind and body. He has penetrated far into the wakening mind and feeling of primitive people, into incipient religion. Through the sense of awe in shadowed places, under overhanging trees, with their eternal whisperings of birth, life, death, through the feeling that there is more here than meets the senses, the deity is summoned out of mystery. Wholly Greek, a bit of pure nature myth, is the appealing touch of emotion in the melody and motion of the reeds swaying in the wind, conceived as giving Pan his love, Syrinx, and taking her away.

In the self-dedication of the growths of the earth to the deity, strawberries offering their coolness, bees their golden honeycombs, the chuckling linnet its five young unborn, in the sense of the presence of the god in all aspects of life, and in the invocation to him to be near, coming on every wind that nods the mountain pine, to be near and to protect, we follow the growth of nature worship in primitive minds. The deeper service of this deity to man and lambkin, and to those between beast and human, fauns and satyrs, is conjured up out of sights and sounds and nature processes; he who is so near is implored to listen. Exquisitely right is the young poet's interpretation of this growing feeling of a protectingness in nature, protecting and playful, joy-giving. Keats was never nearer the truth in regard to the genesis and the significance of primitive myth than in his interpretation of the local god of Arcadia, who, like other local gods, slowly took on increasing powers in the minds of a people with whose development needs increased, and assumed the many-sided attributes tending toward a conception of an omnipresent deity.

Pan is become the universal protector, and the realization of this stirs the minds of the worshipers to deepest reverence:

> Dread opener of the mysterious doors
> Leading to universal knowledge — see
> Great son of Dryope,
> The many that are come to pay their vows
> With leaves about their brows!

At the end, the deeper mystery of life is suggested; questioning slips into worship, and the worshipers stand, lowly bending, with uplifted hands shading their foreheads, on a mountain top sacred to Pan:

> Be still the unimaginable lodge
> For solitary thinkings; such as dodge
> Conception to the very bourne of heaven.

That suggestion, at the outset, of bird and bee, butterfly, corn, and flower fulfilling their lives through the presence of the god has led on through the account of universal protectingness to a suggestion of human fulfilment beyond the reach of mere thought.

The Hymn to Pan is a penetrating and beautiful interpretation of the pagan sense of one life in which all things have part, well preluding a philosophic poem in the garb of myth, whose import is the quest for oneness in all the powers of man, their fusion through the supreme power, love. It is no accident that the god who stood in ancient thought for the mystery of life in all things should be invoked at the beginning.

Turning from the way in which Keats, in these passages, interprets the genesis and the nature of the Greek myth to the way in which, in the main story, he makes the Endymion myth interpret him, become a means of self-expression, we find ourselves confronted by a harder problem.

The old story of the love of the moon goddess for a mortal, the love of a mortal for the moon goddess, born of the sight of the moon in her rising or her going down seeming to rest for a moment on the top of Mt. Latmos, interpreted exquisitely in ancient faith as her visit to her lover on the mountain top, is reborn in the imagination of a young poet, and is made to carry, with full sense of its appeal as a love story, the deep burden of the struggling thought of youth, just finding life and its meaning, coming to symbolize for him the quest of the soul of the poet for beauty and for truth. Unsure in method, it is sure in purpose. From the outset, when Endymion asks:

> Wherein lies happiness? In that which becks
> Our ready minds to fellowship divine,
> A fellowship with essence;

through all his wanderings he cherishes

> A hope beyond the shadow of a dream;

his solitary thinkings

> dodge
> Conception to the very bourne of heaven.

He affirms:

> I did wed
> Myself to things of light from infancy.

These, and many another saying, are part of the "wild and harmonized tune" which his "spirit struck from all the beautiful" in searching for the supreme Beauty. The quest of the poet for ideal beauty, of the lover for ultimate truth, leads him, — the difficulty symbolized by the wide extent of his wanderings, — through and beyond the world of matter, earth and under the earth, under the sea, and through the air, to the heart of human life, to the discovery that love of the ideal and human love are one. Love, in enlarging conception, is the ground thought of the poem, for love is the power that draws to beauty and to truth.

There can be no question of Keats' purpose in *Endymion*, long ago suggested by Mrs. Owen, followed, with or without acknowledgment, by most intelligent critics of Keats, lately denied by Miss Lowell. How could a poet of such depth and reverence of purpose as is manifest in *Sleep and Poetry*, with such concentrated longing to achieve the greatest, embark, in his second venture, on a mere fantastic meaningless tale,—a child's fairy story? How could a disciple of Spenser tell such a tale of adventure without holding ever before him the inner significance of the adventure? It is easy to see why this bit of myth captured his imagination. Even in the old story, in the nature phenomenon itself, there is something of piquing, of incitement to the quest. The visits of the moon goddess to her lover; the haunting beauty of that crescent tip touching Mt. Latmos, as if coming to rest; her wide path through the heavens, and her changing phases, — truly here, even to the primitive mind was a something provoking pursuit, in the idea of meeting, separation, meeting again; and, to a modern mind, the mind of a disciple of Wordsworth and a lover of the *Intimations*, something that well symbolized

> Those obstinate questionings
> Of sense and outward things,
> Fallings from us, vanishings;
> . . . .
> High instincts before which our mortal Nature
> Did tremble like a guilty thing surprised.

It is apparent that, in the depth of subjective reaction, the old tale, which was growing green in the young poet's mind, takes on ulterior meanings, showing his growth of insight into the potentialities of myth, its possibility of symbolizing the inner life of man. If myth is primarily naïve imaginative interpretation of nature processes, whereby nature powers take on personality and act out a destiny in some way bearing on the life of man; if allegory is the conscious use of the concrete, in story and in presentation of character, to set forth abstract idea, *Endymion* hovers between the two, the myth, as was often the case in the later developments of primitive myth, assuming aspects of allegory. Myth was primarily percept, passing often into concept as thought developed; here, something of concept is present from the first, embodied in myth, which slips at times, especially in Book IV, into rather bald allegory. There is much of symbolism throughout, this becoming a means of expression for thought and feeling too subtle to be expressed in any other way. With invention not always fortunate, Keats employs minor myths, as well as the tale of Endymion, to set forth his meaning, adding one bit of myth to another in attempting to express the underlying idea of the poem, with, at times, a resultant effect of exposition, of forced adjustment, rather than of wholeness of imaginative perception. The many additions which he contrives at times bewilder and confuse. It is so crowded with myths that no critic could comment on all, but some aspects of the major and of the more important minor myths can be discussed; in both are many passages suggesting fresh perception of the significance of primitive myth, and many which finely symbolize the inner experience of the hero.

At the outset, through fortunate concrete touches, Keats induces a sense of reality in this myth world; truly, one may not only see, but hear, touch, catch the fragrance of the moment, in this open space, on the side of wooded Latmos, edged round by dark tree tops, where often

> A little cloud would move across the blue.

The dark forest, imagined, is yet rooted in actuality. The scene of worship, the incense, the ministering priest, the damsels bearing flowers, the sunburnt shepherds, the homely touch of the mothers beckoning their sons to silence, the singing of the hymn to Pan while the flame leaps on the altar are full of that peculiar power of Keats of convincing you through your senses of that which existed only in the imagination. Greek plastic art not only gave him insights, helped him in his apprehension of the nature of Greek gods, but suggested a method of expression which one finds throughout his work; in many a line, sweeping drapery, the dancing feet of nymphs, a noble pose, reveal the influence of sculpture on the poet. The Parthenon reliefs, as has often been suggested, influenced him in creating this scene of worship; the initial description of Endymion, in his fair-wrought car, like a carved figure in some Greek relief, gives a clear picture, with firm, outstanding lines; but, if Greek plastic art gave him the outline, the "lurking trouble in his nether lip" betrays the modern.

The beautiful and haunting scene where Endymion, with the spring morning in his veins, sits with the aged priest among the old shepherds, and all save Endymion tell their dreams of fulfilment, carries further the humanizing of the myth. The old dream of fulfilment beyond earthly life; Endymion, wrapt in youthful wise in the dream of fulfilment in this, self-centered, is cold and dead to their wistful sympathy, nor has he sympathy with them.

Endymion throughout, in spite of the large element of the fantastic in his adventures, is made real by his self-absorption, his freshness of sensation, his young amorousness and crude taste, his swift response to all that he meets, sees, imagines, — in short, his very youth; his sense of the beauty of the outer world, and his intuition of its inner meaning. He has youth's utter longing to find the way. His words, when, later, Peona has won him by her sympathy to tell her of his trouble and his hope, might well stand for the chosen youth of all ages, in all returning springs:

> Yet my higher hope
> Is of too wide, too rainbow-large a scope
> To fret at myriads of earthly wrecks.
> Wherein lies happiness? In that which becks
> Our ready minds to fellowship divine,
> A fellowship with essence.

The note of Keats' period is apparent here in the introspectiveness, the attempt to think out the problem of his individual life and potential growth, and in his awareness that truth must be sought through experience. "Axioms in philosophy are not axioms," he wrote in one of his letters, "until they are proved upon our pulses." "Nothing ever becomes real until it is experienced — even a Proverb is no proverb to you till your Life has illustrated it."

A student of Keats finds always the recurrent idea of development manifest in his thought about himself and about his art. Endymion, like the young Keats in *Sleep and Poetry*, is aware that he must pass through various phases of growth to win the truth. The gradations of experience somewhat obscurely outlined in *Sleep and Poetry* were interpreted by Mr. Bridges as having the import of Wordsworth's steps toward reality, recounted in *Tintern Abbey*. He recalls the famous passage in the *Letters* (May 3d, 1818) in which Keats writes of the stages of the poet's experience: the infant or thoughtless chamber; the chamber of maiden thought where we are intoxicated with the light and atmosphere, but gradually come to a realization of misery and heartbreak, pain, sickness, and oppression, and feel the burden of the mystery.

The second chamber is paralleled in *Sleep and Poetry* by

> First the realm I'll pass
> Of Flora, and old Pan: sleep in the grass,
> Feed upon apples red, and strawberries,
> And choose each pleasure that my fancy sees.

The deeper phase of experience by

> And can I ever bid these joys farewell?
> Yes, I must pass them for a nobler life,
> Where I may find the agonies, the strife
> Of human hearts.

A longer and more searching interpretation of the gradations of experience is given in the speech of Endymion to

Peona in Book I, a significant and puzzling passage of which Keats said: "My having written that argument will perhaps be the greatest service to me of anything I ever did."

Here, as always in his deeper thought, he is busy with the idea of development, and this passage, the most important in Book I, traces again the pattern of his thought of life, as suggested in his early poem, and outlined in his letter. His idea of development as presented in this passage, and as followed in the successive books, has not been sufficiently emphasized, and this neglect has led to a misinterpretation of some of the love passages. Professor de Sélincourt has made illuminating comment upon it, but I think that a further idea is struggling toward expression here, — an idea of all life as fundamentally one. Even early, unthinking phases of sympathy with human story, Endymion says, bring union with one's kind. He speaks of aspects of past experience, of battles long ago:

> Feel we these things? — that moment we have stept
> Into a sort of oneness.

A deeper unity comes from personal experience; love and friendship are "far more self-destroying,"

> leading, by degrees
> To the chief intensity,

which is

> fellowship divine,
> A fellowship with essence.

Of all the powers, the most potent is love, which not only brings the fullest development of the individual, but is a cosmic force, operating through all life, shared not only by all humanity but by all nature, producing "more than our searching witnesseth." It has within it a greater power than that which means delight in itself; it can sting and beckon toward the highest reality, can make mortal being immortal.

And here is suggested a profounder oneness, the ultimate reality, wherein are blended in completeness all the imperfect experiences that have gone before.

The slender thread of the moon myth is too slight to carry the weight of the young poet's groping thought. In his story of Endymion's quest for ultimate reality, his pilgrimage to the world's dusky brink, not only other myths, but incidents akin to those in old romances, and in the *Arabian Nights* are brought in, sometimes in puzzling juxtaposition, but Keats is not the only youthful writer who has sometimes obscured his meaning in trying to make it clear. In one respect the myth is held throughout: it is a tale of love, and Keats' theme throughout is love, for the stages, the gradations of experience have become stages, gradations in apprehension of love, its nature, its mystery, its potentialities: the puzzle of the passion aspects of love; the love that grows out of sympathy; the love in the Platonic sense, that draws toward the Beauty that is Truth, for

> In that which becks
> Our ready minds to fellowship divine,
> A fellowship with essence,

Keats places love as the highest. Love in enlarging conception is the ground thought of the poem, and the phases of growth representing the different aspects of love, are presented in successive steps, corresponding with the different books. After this attempt, in Book I, to think out the matter, in youthful fashion, we have: in Book II, love that is passion, that has in it appetite; this leads to understanding sympathy with similar experience, and enfolds the seed of something higher; in Book III, love that is ideal, the pursuit of Beauty; this leads to a higher type of sympathy, sympathy with suffering; in Book IV, love that weds the spirit of sorrow; the real and the ideal become one in realized entirety of human life.

Book II

The recurrent thought about the stages of experience appearing in *Sleep and Poetry*, in the *Letters*, in Endymion's discourse in Book I has been noted, but no one has, I think, suggested how entirely Endymion's adventures in the second book reflect and interpret more deeply that second stage of experience, represented in *Sleep and Poetry* by

First the realm I'll pass
Of Flora, and old Pan: sleep in the grass, —

in Endymion's discourse, by a delight in old story:

Then old songs waken from enclouded tombs,
Old ditties sigh above their father's grave.

Keats speaks in the *Letters* of this second phase as follows: "We have become intoxicated with the light and the atmosphere; we see nothing but pleasant wonders, and think of delaying there forever in delight." So Book II of *Endymion*, with its marvels and portents, the sparry hollows, marble gallery, diamond balustrade, and chasms; its delight in adventure for its own sake; its revelling in myths, Vertummus, Pomona, Triton, and others is an effort to present in narrative form this phase of experience of uncentered youth, of sheer detached, inexperienced delight in adventure and old story.

Much of Book II brings to the reader a sense of disappointment; this underworld is interpreted with no such joy and understanding as is the world of meadows, trees, and sunrise of Book I, and the underground adventures hardly bear out the beauty of the passage which introduces them:

And like a new-born spirit did he pass
Through the green evening quiet in the sun,
. . . .
and, far away, the blue
Of ocean fades upon him; then, anew,

> He sinks adown a solitary glen
> Where there was never sound of mortal men,
> Saving, perhaps, some snow-light cadences
> Melting to silence, where upon the breeze
> Some holy bark let forth an anthem sweet,
> To cheer itself to Delphi.

It would be difficult to find in poetry passages which bring a greater sense of letting down than the love passage in which Endymion and his mysterious visitant, whom he does not recognize, are united, coming after the high ideality of the finer passages. Nothing of "dim-conceived glories of the brain" appears here, or, for that matter, in the goddess described by her lover in Book I as appearing in his dream with "pearl round ears," "blush-tinted cheeks, half smiles, and faintest sighs." The love scene in Book II seems the very nadir of Endymion, representing the feverish fancy, and unappeased sex-appetite of a boy. "Those lips, O slippery blisses!" might well be accounted the worst of many bad lines in *Endymion*. The experience is given at great length; perhaps it represents, not mawkish delight in voluptuous sensation, as would seem at first glance, but the urgency of the young poet's feeling of the importance of what he is trying to say.

The voice that, at the outset, bids Endymion descend

> Through the hollow,
> The silent mysteries of earth,

is not speaking at random, and has deeper significance than has generally been recognized. Dark and mysterious doors, he says in the *Letters*, open out of this second chamber of experience. In the record that follows of symbolic experiences in the underworld the poet's thought is penetrating more deeply into the problems of life than in that second phase of experience, suggested in *Sleep and Poetry* and in the *Letters*. Surely this passion verging into appetite is intended by Keats to stand for a lower phase of experience to be passed through and outgrown, having in it the seed of something greater, for all his thought of life is of a passage from lower to higher. Undoubtedly he would not mean to suggest full attainment of the ideal at the outset of the quest. The amorous responses to Endymion's utterances, the promise of "an immortality of passion," represent, not so much the goddess visitant as a youthful state of mind. For the moon goddess is not, as is usually suggested, a static, but a dynamic conception, representing successive stages of growth in the young poet's idea of love; the early crude imaginings, dwelling on the external, the physical; the early sensuous experience of passion are outgrown as the hero develops, in his struggle toward the ideal. Lovers and critics of Keats soften with apology their dismay over this passage as betraying the author's undeveloped taste, but a different view of its significance, as not representing full union with the ideal, but an early experience to be gone through in the quest for the ideal, would acquit him of luxuriating in the semi-sensual at crucial moments of *Endymion*, though no one could claim that the expression of the idea is adequate. There is nothing in Greek myth that could help him say what he is trying to say here. Keats wisely wrote: "The imagination of a boy is healthy, and the mature imagination of a man is healthy; but there is a space of life between in which the soul is in a ferment."

In such a ferment is the soul of Endymion in this scene, which represents not attainment, but the blurred experience of youth in all the dualism of nature, on the one side, the dream of the ideal, on the other, chaotic passion. Already in his struggle he has prayed to Diana:

> Deliver me from this rapacious deep!

The "known Unknown" who visits him says, significantly, after an allusion to Venus:

> His soul will scape us.

Yet, after the unfortunate love scene,

> Now I have tasted her sweet soul to the core
> All other depths are shallow,

suggests that already he has achieved "a sort of oneness," that something deeper than the experience has wakened through the experience, that out of passion has come power, insight that leads him on:

> Ye who have yearn'd
> With too much passion, will here stay and pity,
> For the mere sake of truth,

the poet writes, in regard to this passage.

Book II is the book of passion; this is the central theme of the incidents recounted, and the deepest of all the mysteries encountered underground, of which Mother Cybele is the symbol, in that finely descriptive passage which has part in the atmosphere, if not in the narrative. The visit to the hero of the Unknown, the Venus and Adonis myth, and that of Alpheus and Arethusa, represent the working of passion, and over against these, finely contrasted, is the most beautiful of the pictured myths in this book, that of the quivered Dian, seen far off through a long, pillared vista. This is the Diana of the Greeks, known through poetry and through plastic art, quivered, forested, chaste, and free. There is new life in the young poet's interpretation of the old attributes, and Endymion is represented as glowing with a sense of her power to help. All the joy of nature sweeps over him as she comes "on light tip-toe divine" to him, engulfed in experiences that rob him of his nature freedom. He pleads for the feeling of the breeze, for the linnet's song;

> O Haunter chaste
> Of river sides, and woods, and heathy waste
> . . . thou dost taste
> Freedom as none can taste it, nor dost waste
> Thy loveliness in dismal elements.

He gives a distinctive appreciation of this nature goddess, already in his thought a huntress of the souls of men; and his prayer to her: "Deliver me from this rapacious deep," shows that she, not his later visitant, keeps him in mind of the ideal for which he is questing.

Already in Book I has come recognition of love as cosmic power, a force in all life, flowers, river, wood, and vale, and the hearts of human lovers; it is there connected with the higher operations of the soul. Keats, in Book II, uses the Venus and Adonis episode to express his idea of this universal, all-compelling power. Seeming indirect, it is, in its meaning, directly in line with the underlying idea of this book. Shakespeare's *Venus and Adonis* is recalled in the over-elaboration of the presentation of passion; plastic art helps the young poet in the description of Adonis. But the most significant aspect of the treatment is the recognition of the universality of the passion of love; a sense of organic nature process, inherent in the ancient vegetation myth, appears in the rendering of the winter sleep and the spring awakening:

> Safe in the privacy
> Of this still region all his winter-sleep.
> . . . Then there was a hum
> Of sudden voices, echoing, Come! Come!
> Arise! awake! Clear summer has forth walk'd
> Unto the clover-sward, and she has talk'd
> Full soothingly to every nested finch.

In presenting, through the story of these lovers, the life of love in all nature, Keats is struggling with a great idea, not fully clarified, is growing into perception of great truth. He is thinking in myths, whose primitive imaginings help him to express aspects of thought and feeling which he could hardly have expressed in all their vitality and complexity in any other way. If his mind seems overcharged with the beauty of old story, one must recall his need of stating his meaning imaginatively, his statement in the Letters that he "never can feel certain of any truth but from a clear perception of its Beauty."

Curiously interesting, with reference both to Keats' power of appreciating and interpreting primitive myth, and with reference to his way of making myth interpret the inner life of his hero, is the Alpheus and Arethusa story, of the nymph, vowed to Diana, who fled from the love of the river god, and escaped by being changed by the goddess into a fountain. The rush and ripple of the water become the voice of Alpheus in his ardent wooing, and his plea to Arethusa to follow him to his hidden source in Arcadian forests, and where his coolest waters flow through mossy rocks or brim round flowery islands, are fortunate nature-myth imaginings, with a primitive touch. The story of passion and pursuit, misfortune and disappointment, wakening sympathy, has deep significance in Keats' development of his theme. In trying to set forth the all-importance of love, his mind gropes among its actualities and its potentialities, passion, personal joy, and that higher something which beckoned the soul of the young poet from the first. Endymion's self-centeredness is broken by an entering wedge of sympathy; the understanding of passion is as far as his sympathy can go in this early stage of his experience. To add a word to Mrs. Owen, not only the fact of his sympathy, but the progressive nature of the phases of his sympathy are interesting and significant, for in this, as well as in his experience of love, can be traced the measure of his growth. "There was a cooler light," the poet says; "He saw the giant sea above his head," and the reader is aware that Endymion is going on to finer insights, subtler sympathies.

Book III

Perhaps it is in the third book that we first realize how fit to become the symbolic expression of life as a spiritual quest the old myth has proved in the young poet's interpretation of it; "its loveliness increases." We pass on here to higher levels of being, and throughout we feel

> The moving waters at their priestlike task
> Of pure ablution round earth's human shores.

After the execrable opening lines, among the worst in all Keats' early work, he slips into the melody and majesty of

> No, there are throned seats unscalable
> But by a patient wing, a constant spell,
> Or by ethereal things that, unconfin'd,
> Can make a ladder of the eternal wind.

The highest note yet sounded in connection with the moon legend is struck in the opening lines, through 190. In lines 90–102, and 142–190 the poet comes nearer than he does anywhere else to expressing fully what he had groped for in "I stood tip-toe," his thought of the moon as the symbol of the highest beauty which had haunted him, beckoned to him in all aspects of life: in the visible, audible, tangible beauty of earth; in the growth of flowers; in all nature, — river, glen, mountain top; in ardor, aspiration, poetry, wisdom; in friendship; in love:

> O what a wild and harmonized tune
> My spirit struck from all the beautiful!

In the presentation of the visible beauty of the moon, given in many imaginative touches there is an exquisite blending of the primitive myth-maker's perception of nature-phenomena with a young philosopher's thought. His way of making the nature myth play into the spiritual conception, the spiritual conception into the nature myth shows distinct gain in symbolism. In this moon, stealing unobserved into her throne, while Apollo's gold breath is misting in the west, the stars waiting for her "silver-footed messages," is there not, in the suggestion of the moon as symbol, shedding her beauty on all things, her loveliness wan on

Neptune's blue, on sleeping kine, on nested wren, and the boughs of ancient trees, revealing the meaning of the sage's, the poet's message, of friendship and of love, — is there not a dim conception of a power at the heart of all things, a subtle influence, "drawing all things to one"? Love is apostrophized:

> O love! how potent hast thou been to teach
> Strange journeyings! Wherever beauty dwells,
> In gulph or aerie, mountains or deep dells,
> In light, in gloom, in star or blazing sun,
> Thou pointest out the way.

Love is the power that draws to the beautiful, and throughout there is the sting or summons of Love in the search for Beauty. Instinctively a Platonist, instructed by Spenser, by his friends, — or possibly the name Plato connotes less an individual thinker than a finer tendency of human thought,— he has the idea of love as the moving force in the spiritual universe; already in Book II it has been presented as the moving force in the physical world. Beauty at the heart of life and of death is suggested here:

> Thou leddest Orpheus through the gleams of death.

There is perhaps something greater than Platonism in the conception of love as manifest not only in light but in gloom, and in the *gleams* of death; and in the passage in which Endymion, in an ecstasy of idealistic aspiration, sees the path to the Beautiful open before him, but does not recognize it:

> He saw far in the concave green of the sea
> An old man sitting calm and peacefully.
> Upon a weeded rock this old man sat
> And his white hair was awful, and a mat
> Of weeds were cold beneath his cold thin feet.

Endymion's feeling of repulsion when hailed by the aged man in appeal for help,

> By Pan
> I care not for this old mysterious man!

his attempt to repel, by memory of love that was passion and appetite, a wakening love which is sympathy and self-forgetfulness; the dawning realization that he is in the presence of sorrow, and the enlarging of his nature that comes as his heart begins to warm with pity, are finely suggestive. The hero-poet passes into a deeper phase of experience, into a realization of misery and heartbreak and pain; his feet are irrevocably set upon the path that leads to highest beauty; and the old myth, which was a simple tale of love, takes on, in this sympathy with age, with suffering, a conception of love unknown to any ancient myth.

The sea background of Book III is presented with an imaginative interpretation of nature charm that might well challenge comparison with Keats' interpretation of the green world in Book I. "Do you not hear the sea" through all this? Keats' own feeling about the sea is attributed to Glaucus, the delight in its coolness, the longing to be one with its "mighty ebb and flow," and this affords a welcome contrast to the smothering quality of Book II. By projecting something of himself into this minor ancient myth Keats has recreated it, making it very vivid in those passages interpreting the loved element in which its hero moved, his fibres interknit with the swell of the wave. Glaucus, in part through the quoted description of him, which owes much to Keats' appreciation of plastic art; in the idealism of his tragic love experience; in his growing young again as he sees helping youth approach, is made very human, in spite of the fantastic happenings. The bare legend of Glaucus and Scylla, mere circumstance in Ovid, is elaborated, transformed, given an ethical import, so that we might almost feel ourselves being "bullied into a certain Philosophy," as the indignant young poet felt in reading Wordsworth.

Many a reader, many a critic has thought the story of Glaucus irrelevant, but its meaning is deeply a part of the poet's thought, whether or not he has fully objectified it.

This blending of a minor with the major myth, Glaucus and Scylla, with one of the nature-power myths, one of the lesser, more fanciful, with one of the more imaginative, is made, with some wrenching, to serve his deeper purpose. The expanded minor myth in part repeats the main story, with stronger emphasis on certain features, the young poet stumbling among many ways of driving his idea home.

The spirited version of the Circe story is part of his large meaning regarding love which draws to beauty, sin against love to degradation. This is a story of love which has suffered from its own betrayal. In that fine, if overdone, grotesque, rendered with such force of inward meaning, with its presentation of the bestilizing effect of yielding to the evil spell, it is impossible to escape the significance. The young medical student brings knowledge to bear on his imaginative rendering, in showing premature age coming upon the victim of Circe, who says:

> But such a love is mine, that here I chace
> Eternally away from thee all bloom
> Of youth. . . .
> Ere many days be overpast
> Disabled age shall seize thee; and even then
> Thou shalt not go the way of aged men;
> But live and wither, cripple, and still breathe.

Very striking in this recreation of an ancient myth, is the symbolic shipwreck of the lovers, brought about by "hell-born Circe":

> All the billows green
> Toss'd up the silver spume against the clouds.
> The tempest came;

and the release of the bespelled lovers, after the breaking of the wand upon the lyre, not free until they had escaped the spell of Circe, has haunting significance:

> Thus went that beautiful multitude,

as fast as "Swallows obeying the south summer's call," and another multitude came:

> On a wide sand they met,
> And of those numbers every eye was wet;
> For each their old love found.

The charm of Book III is a broken charm; fantastic bits are mingled with passages of genuinely imaginative description and characterization, and of vivid narrative. Deservedly famous is the description of Neptune's Hall:

> And as the blue
> Doth vault the waters, so the waters drew
> Their doming curtains, high, magnificent.
> . . . .
> A light as of four sunsets, blazing forth
> A gold-green zenith 'bove the Sea God's head,

suggestive in its fashioning of a dwelling place in the world of dreams for the sea-god. But the hymn of Neptune brings no such largeness of imaginative interpretation as does the hymn to Pan; of course it is admittedly a less significant myth. This has a pseudo-classic inflation in thought, feeling, cadence. Would that Keats could have given it the music of the sea, as in his earlier lines:

> Old ocean rolls a lengthened wave to the shore,
> Down whose green back the short-liv'd foam, all hoar
> Bursts gradual, with a wayward indolence.

Deeper than the appeal of the objective descriptions is that of the spiritual insights. The spirit of Beauty moves on the waters and under the waters all through Book III, impelling to sympathy, to disinterested action. The key to the meaning, as the way opens before Endymion to greater love for his fellows, is given by Glaucus:

> Aye, hads't thou never lov'd an unknown power,
> I had been grieving at this joyous hour.

The "great enfranchisement" is not only for Glaucus, for the drowned lovers, but for Endymion, the Endymion who, in an earlier phase of his experience, had felt

> How crude and sore
> The journey homeward to habitual self.

Now that he has found through experience the freedom that comes from entering into the lives of others through constantly refining sympathy, a message from Cynthia, — and this is finely imagined, — is written in starlight on the sky above, and Endymion finds rest, in one of those charmed moments which Keats knows so well how to interpret, of utter content in the simplicity of his response to the simple things of nature:

> And forest green,
> Cooler than all the wonders he had seen,
> Lull'd with its simple song his fluttering breast.

Book IV

It would seem that in Book IV, while the thought of the young poet is expressed more explicitly than in other parts of *Endymion*, the rendering of myth is less fortunate than in other sections, notably Book I and Book III. Creative imagination flags; in setting forth the clearly-conceived idea that human love and ideal love are one, the simple ancient myth fails him; he has to invent, and he invents rather bald allegory. Oddly enough, in the incident wherein this idea is expressed, and the dark Indian Maid whom Endymion loves reveals herself as, in reality, the goddess who had inspired his quest, the poet misses a primitive nature-myth suggestion of the dark of the moon in the first and second quarters as symbolizing the Indian Maid, or, if he means this, does not make it clear that he is thinking in terms of nature process. Seldom in this book do we find the fine, primitive apprehension of nature happenings slipping into personality as in Book I.

There is frequent mention of myth, but much of it is fanciful, external, as in Endymion's dream of playing with the attributes of the gods, trying Phoebus' golden bow, bracing Pallas' shield upon his arm, attempting to wield a Jovian thunderbolt, again suggesting that early chamber of experience where one is lingering outside the door of life; and in the scene which shows the gods, inspired by the music of Dian's hymn, feeling a sense of heightened powers; Hesperus snaps his lucid fingers merrily; Castor has tamed the planet Lion; the Bear has mastered Pollux; the Centaur has his arrow ready. Here is none of the high imaginative quality of the hymn to Pan; a later development of myth is suggested, in which nature deities have slipped into human personalities. The finest bit of rendering of this phase of myth comes in the splendid Bacchic procession, which has a wealth of interpretation of heightened feeling. Music, color, line, action make vivid the coming of the god and his followers, in achieved poetic art to which both sculpture and painting contributed, as is shown in Mr. Colvin's *Keats*. The music and tumult representing Earth's uttermost joy are finely contrasted with sorrow; Keats could find among the bright figures of Greek mythology none that could body forth his meaning here; his Indian maid is of his own fashioning. Wisdom outstripping his brief experience is expressed in this passage, upon which Mr. Thorpe has made the most illuminating comment that has yet been made, that the poet cannot come into his full power until he has wed sorrow.

Though the central conception of Book IV is genuinely imaginative, in its insight into the heart of life, much of the treatment is over-allegorical and whimsical. The journey with the Indian Maid on winged steeds to the clouds; Endymion's dream of trying on the powers of the gods; Sleep fantastically journeying to Olympus, and Diana's feast have not the charm at its best of Keats' interpretation of myth, or its use in symbolizing the development of the inner life. Yet one nice touch comes where Endymion and the Indian Maid sleep among the clouds, and the hero-poet is wakened from his dream by Diana, crescented, to higher things. From a dark cloud

> The moon put forth a little diamond peak,
> . . . .
> Bright signal that she only stoop'd to tie
> Her silver sandals.

The beckoning tip of the moon, the call of the ideal, the fading and falling of the earthly love, the dangerous drifting toward the Cave of Quietude ("the centre of indifference," Carlyle would say), a place of spiritual exhaustion, — "There anguish does not sting, nor pleasure pall," "where hopes *infest*"; the clarion call of the music of Dian's feast, and the consequent wakening of the winged steed of the imagination on which he had mounted to the heavens, — surely the thought-import of the allegory is not hard to follow here, as, summoned by sight of the beckoning tip of the moon and by the sound of the trumpet to achieve his utmost, he is borne by the winged steed to the ground, and alights on a misty hill, thus winning one step nearer the reality which he seeks, the oneness of the real and the ideal.

If it is, at times, difficult to tell in *Endymion* where instinctive myth slips into purposeful allegory, one finds no such difficulty in this allegorical bit where, as in *Sleep and Poetry*, and in Wordsworth's *Prologue* to *Peter Bell*, the flight on wings of imagination ends with coming to rest on the earth. To Keats, as to his master, Wordsworth, the imagination must have its foundation in reality. The struggle begun in the clouds is continued on earth. In his feeling after his fall to the ground that the call of the ideal is a sin against human love:

> Oh I have been
> Presumptuous against love;
> . . . . . .

No, never more
Shall airy voices cheat me to the shore
Of tangled wonder, breathless and aghast.
Adieu, my daintiest dream,

as in his feeling, when among the clouds, that love for the Indian Maid was a sin against the ideal, we get the very ferment of the mind of youth — "O state perplexing!"

Keats' thought is of great interest here, in the passage in which Endymion entices the Indian Maid, his earthly love, after he finds her again, to rest content with him in the perfection of sense experience:

See, through the trees, a little river go
All in its mid-day gold and glimmering.
Honey from out the gnarled hive I'll bring
And apples, wan with sweetness, gather thee.
. . . .
Those lips shall be my Delphos . . .
Say, is not bliss within our perfect seisure?
O that I could not doubt!

Her deeply significant answer is:

I may not be thy love: I am forbidden.

Does not her refusal mean that earthly love cannot be perfect without the ideal, as Endymion has found that the ideal cannot be perfect without the real? Is she forbidden by a deep law of life, always urging toward higher development? Each, alone, is inadequate.

There is beauty and significance in the ending, where Endymion, feeling himself about to die, having lost his hold on both the real and the ideal, resting his head upon a grassy hillock, recalls his apparently wasted purpose:

I did wed
Myself to things of light from infancy.

In a moment of sudden revelation, when light reflected from silver flame comes into the Indian Maid's face, he knows, as many a critic has noted, that warm human love and passion for the ideal are fundamentally one, and consecrates his union with the humanized goddess by three kisses, while Peona, as well she might, goes home through the gloomy wood in wonderment. Love has drawn him to completeness of existence in which real and ideal are blended; to fulness of poetic gift which recognizes this fusion; the ending of the poem leaves us deeply conscious of the greatness of the conception of love of this young and inexperienced poet.

No one would claim, the author least of all, the form of *Endymion* as successful. Few poems have worse faults, so far, as one is sometimes tempted to think is the case with nature itself, does the creative impulse outstrip the shaping power, yet few immature poems show more poignant promise of high excellence in the poet. It would be hard to find worse figures, worse diction, worse flaws in taste than may be found in parts of *Endymion*; the many word-experiments are as appalling in some instances as they are fortunate in others. Yet it is throbbing with vitality, physical, intellectual, spiritual; thought and feeling too great for perfect expression surge up in the young poet, crying out for clear utterance which they often fail to gain. There is a largeness about it, a sense of greatness of spirit, searching out the way of beauty in all the tangled mazes of earth. In the treatment of myth we find the allusions more inherent, more a part of the psychology of the moment than is the case in the first volume. If there are, at times, amusing and almost absurd lines, in the attempt to recreate myth imaginatively, as in Hesperus "snapping his lucent fingers merrily," there are also interpretative suggestions of haunting beauty, where a single line may sum up the whole of a bit of ancient myth, as in the often-quoted

> Like old Deucalion mountain'd o'er the flood,
> Or blind Orion hungry for the morn;

or in

> 'Twas a lay
> More subtle-cadenced, more forest-wild
> Than Dryope's lone lulling of her child;
> And nothing since has floated on the air
> So mournful strange.

The grace of motion suggested in the delicate lines of a Greek relief appears in the glimpse of the moon stooping to tie her silver sandals.

Endymion is quivering throughout with a sense of the beauty of these old stories, which Keats brings to life by descriptive touch, or word of sympathetic feeling. The main myth, vitalized by his whole inner life of thought and feeling, breaks under the weight of meaning which he attempts to make it carry, but the import of this poem of spiritual quest is perhaps too great for any one, even a mature poet, to express perfectly. In giving this and the minor myths inner significances, treating them introspectively, as symbolizing the complex experience of aspiring youth, he shows himself determined to make the concrete set forth pure idea. There are broken passages, sheer, sometimes strained allegory, and incidents which seem at first reading irrelevant, but which prove, on close study, to have subjective connection, which the young artist was not able to objectify. But in the labyrinthine poem it is fascinating to search out and find again the thread that one may have lost; hear again the note sounded at the beginning; work on to the unmistakable clarity of the ending. Though the imagination of the poet often fails, falters, is lost, there is great imaginative power in the poem, revealed not only in the insight which pierces far into a great meaning of life, shown in the central theme, but in the shaping power manifest in many a passage, a wide variety: beautiful interpretation of nature and of myth; characterization of mythical personages with new and deeper import; narrative and descriptive bits of haunting charm:

struggle toward great meaning and great expression; unforgettable passages of pure idealistic thought.

So an ancient myth, born of brief recurring moments of nature beauty in the minds of primitive, beauty-loving people, is reborn, and is made to carry the deeper thought of a young poet of a later day, subtle, spiritual, growing wise, keeping, in this later expression, a radiance caught from early imaginings. An old and simple love tale has developed in Keats' mind into a potential symbol of all aspects of love. Love in great philosophic conception is here, and love as known in homely human experience; the call of the ideal; the tug of passion; the mysterious relation of passion to spirit; the self-centeredness of both aspiration and passion, until greater love grows out of early, incomplete experience to include others with self. There is increasing significance in the conduct of Endymion throughout. Love is the first he finds and the last he finds, but in the end it is love transfigured, gathering up into itself all the intellectual and spiritual possibilities of his soul.

At times the thought is imperfectly wrought out, the poet's mind as bewildered as experience itself is in early years, when youth is drawn two ways, many ways, between the claims of the physical, the claims of the spiritual, body and soul not yet wrought out into oneness, not yet fused, as at the end of *Endymion*. Keats, conscious of the significance of this struggle, reveals Endymion, torn between the conflicting influences of Diana, crescented, and the Indian Maid, shows himself troubled about his own identity:

> What is this soul then? Whence
> Came it? It does not seem my own, and I
> Have no self-passion or identity.

The hero-poet in the end, completed, perfected, in a love that combines the real and the ideal, is one with himself, the dual creature drawn to one. In this conviction that a man's nature must grow into unity, as in the conviction expressed throughout the poem that the life of man must be one, in sympathy and understanding, with the life of his fellows, the organic conception of life is present, of the individual as a part of a vast living whole. Individual development cannot be perfected without recognition of all aspects of human nature, or without full recognition of the subtle interrelations that bind man to man. Keats employed a rather cumbersome method of giving his reaction to a new apprehension of life that was creeping into men's thought in this period, but it is unmistakably there, the idea upon which our modern social theories, our ethics, nay, religion also, are based, — of oneness of life in all things.

An inherent part of the organic conception of life was the idea of development; that which lives, grows. Under the influence of a new order of thought, a new way of interpreting life was coming into being, based on what Herder calls "the sacred book of experience"; recognition of the "trial and error method" of facing its problems was creeping in imperceptibly, perhaps fromt he study of development which was beginning to be the method of science. *Endymion* is thrilled through and through with a sense of development and the possibilities of development, of growth, in which the wisdom that comes through experience is a factor, to greatness which could not be fully stated at the outset, or held in a purely intellectual conception:

> Effort, and expectation, and desire,
> And something evermore about to be.

It is interesting to compare *Endymion* with that pale vision of aspiration and thwarted hopes, Shelley's *Alastor*, a much more finished poem, but far less profound in conception. In *Alastor* there is no idea of growth; the difficulties that beset the soul crush instead of inciting to more vital endeavor. Keats held a firm conviction that difficulties "nerve the spirit of a man." In his journal letter to George and Georgiana Keats (beginning February 14, 1819) he says: "Do you not see how necessary a World of Pains and troubles is to school an Intelligence and make it a soul? A Place where the heart must feel and suffer in a thousand diverse ways."

His idea expressed in this remarkable letter, of individual souls as sparks of God's own essence, of the world as "The vale of Soul-making," in which individuality is acquired only through struggle, anticipates the conception of spiritual development which dominated Browning's whole life and work.

Endymion is an embodiment of Keats' thought and of his early experience. If we have not, throughout, clarity, adequacy at all times, of expression, it is much to share, even in an imperfect work of art, the struggling life of a young poet of surpassing imaginative gift and great humanity, who reveals his deep thought and feeling in this tale of Endymion, finding his way through constantly enlarging and refining love to Beauty, to "the very white of truth."

V. The Volume of 1820

In coming to the volume of 1820 one notes, in certain respects, as great a step forward in imaginative insight into the meaning and the possibilities of myth as in coming to *Endymion* from the volume of 1817. It is not, for the most part, in the odes that this evidence of growth appears. Allusions there are; in the *Ode to a Nightingale*: Lethewards, the light-winged Dryad of the trees, Flora and the country green, Bacchus and his pards, and the queen Moon on her throne; and the *Ode on Melancholy* brings saddening suggestions in the ruby grape of Proserpine, the mournful Psyche. It is to be noted that these are not, as is often the case in the volume of 1817, interpolated allusions; they are wholly relevant, one with the mood. The *Ode to Psyche* is the only one based on myth. From early days he had been charmed by the thought of

> How Psyche went
> On the smooth wind to realms of wonderment.

In spite of the wonderful and varied sense appeals in the nature passages, and the magic of descriptive suggestion; in spite of the tremulous emotion with which a phase of ancient worship is rendered, the reader misses something. Inherent in this late-born myth was a spiritual meaning that Keats does not suggest; one would have expected from the poet of *Endymion* a deeper interpretation of Psyche, the soul. It is true that this, like the *Ode to a Nightingale*, gives something of the living presence of flowers, the whispering of the leaves, the incense of worship and of blossom, that sharing of life-processes of nature out of which myth grew, but it belongs distinctly to that early phase of experience, the "realm of Flora, and old Pan," in *Sleep and Poetry*, of unchallenged pleasure in life and story, that second chamber in which "we see nothing but pleasant wonders."

In the *Ode on a Grecian Urn* there is little myth, but there is a master-stroke in the wonder at whose shrine among the gods those believers in the little town had gone to worship. It is one of the unanswered questions roused by the Ode; some god of compelling power, for all were gone.

In *Hyperion* Keats' deepening power in the interpretation of myth is apparent, and the use of myth in expressing his own thought. The unfinished poem is full of the vivifying force of imagination whereby personified nature powers, mythic gods, Titans, and giants of the ancient world are interpreted in terms of their own life, or those activities which the Greek imagination conceived as life. With the exception of the beginning of *Endymion*, and especially the Hymn to Pan, *Hyperion* is much nearer to a primitive sense of things, to the minds and imaginations of early makers of myths than is Keats' earlier work, and at the same time it bears the stamp of mature thought and experience, a riper wisdom than he has before expressed.

From an old and fragmentary story told by Hesiod, representing an earlier phase of legend than the Homeric, and revealing the thought and feeling of primitive people, groping blindly among the mysteries of Earth and Sky, the dispossession of the Titans, of whom the most important are Saturn, supreme ruler of heaven and earth, and Hyperion, god of the sun, by Zeus and Apollo, and the struggle therein involved, Keats has created a poem whose deep appeal comes from the blending of that earliest stirring of man's thought as shown in the nature myths with a very modern philosophy, the inner significance of change and the beauty of change. Whether the import of Keats' unfinished poem is the "evolution of man's mind from trust in brute force and the imperfect knowledge of mere reason to the god-like wisdom of intuitive understanding," as Mr. Thorpe says, or as Margaret Robertson affirms, "intellectual supremacy makes physical force feel its power and yield," we perhaps need not inquire. Suffice it to say that it stands for development, growth; for passing from a lower to a higher order; for belief that necessity for such progressive change is inherent in the order of the universe.

In *Hyperion* the central idea is presented through a process, unfolding in the situation, in the characters, more fused with the material and more clear in import than is the case with *Endymion*, which has more of artificial invention and combining. It is here presented, simply and naturally, in a succession of scenes, more dramatic than epic, dealing rather with the inner life than with the action of the gods, as they undergo profound individual experience, face a great crisis: the fallen Saturn, consoled by Thea; Hyperion, threatened with loss of power; the council of the dispossessed Titans, with the coming of Saturn and Hyperion; the summoning of Apollo to his kingdom. In the delineation of the gods there is much suggestion of that early phase of myth in which nature processes began to take on personality; much too, of the later stage, when, becoming more humanized, they walked earth and sky in the manner of persons. The great charm lies in the lingering of the former in the latter, surprising the reader with the freshness of imaginative perception in the work of a young nineteenth century poet. And the deepest that Keats knew about human nature and its destiny becomes interpretative of these ancient gods.

The fallen Saturn, in the opening scene, is wonderfully rendered, both inwardly and outwardly. The silence of the opening lines gives both look and state of mind; even the description of him, which owes much to plastic art, so much had Keats learned from the Elgin marbles, suggests the inner experience: "quiet as a stone"; here is the stillness of age, the stillness of sculpture:

> His old right hand lay nerveless, listless, dead,
> . . . .
> While his bow'd head seem'd list'ning to the Earth,
> His ancient mother, for some comfort yet.

His suffering is made known to us in the depth of Thea's grieved sympathy, Thea, his sister, goddess of the moon. Great imaginative power and insight into primitive myth are shown in her telling in terms of nature process of the loss of power of this ruler of earth and sky:

> All the air
> Is emptied of thine hoary majesty.
> Thy thunder, conscious of the new command,
> Rumbles reluctant o'er our fallen house;
> And thy sharp lightning, in unpractis'd hands
> Scorches and burns our once serene domain.

When Thea moves, it is as if one of the pediment goddesses of the Elgin marbles had risen and moved; and plastic art shows its influence in

Old Saturn lifted up
His faded eyes and saw his kingdom gone.

But neither plastic art nor appreciation of primitive myth gives Saturn and Thea their greatest reality. If, in this revelation of the gods in terms of nature life, Keats touches the elemental with a wealth of fine shades of perception, akin to the Greek, delicate, subtle, in the inner character interpretation as revealed in action or situation, he transmutes, transfigures. Thea has no thought of her own loss of power, as, her hand in sympathy upon Saturn's bended neck, in loveliness of gesture, she comforts him:

> There was a listening fear in her regard.
> . . . .
> But oh! how unlike marble was that face:
> How beautiful, if sorrow had not made
> Sorrow more beautiful than Beauty's self.

In the interpretation of Saturn, penetration into the mind of age, with its sense of waning power, and the momentary surging back of energy, of creative force, brings the master touch: "Where is another chaos?" Keats' remarkable insight into the human, his deep imaginative sympathy with aspects of sorrow not yet his own, his gift of losing his own identity in that of another, show here, and make real a primitive god in a way in which no primitive nature god had ever before been made real. Saturn, in all the pathos of his age, his failing power, — the poet's grief is even as Thea's in seeing him overthrown. Keats was full of sympathy with humanity on its weary way; those aged faces that stand out from the fresh, leafy beauty of his work, — the Bedesman, Angela, Glaucus, suggest that he was aware, through all his youthful limbs, of the ache of old age, the pain of the falling away of life. It is strange that he, whose sense of the welling up of life was so full, should have had so keen an understanding of its waning, the rarest of all sympathies, that with faltering age. As he writes this poem, presenting

> Many a fallen old Divinity
> Wandering in vain about bewildered shores,

a greatness clings to it, something universal, for he interprets not only the dispossessed gods, but aging humanity, the lot to be borne by all.

Less near the poet's penetration to the heart of life is Hyperion, the sun god, active rebel against the fate which is overtaking him; no remembered aged, life-and-death-stricken faces in hospital beds came to the poet's mind to help in this great imagining! But the elemental touches, that primitive sense of the powers of nature verging into personality is remarkably keen. Hyperion is represented in struggle wherein one may feel the fiery energy of the sun; the sunset glow of his wrath, the miasma night-chill of his misgivings, the sunrise glow of his hope, seen in reflection upon mountain summits and in the faces of his fellow Titans, are finely described, and are very near the primitive. In the struggle, the inward agony, the resolution to conquer and reinstate Saturn, Keats shows the potential dramatic power within him, as he does in the Council of the Titans in Book II. Hyperion, though imaginatively rendered in many ways, is not so wholly Keats' own as are Saturn and Thea, Oceanus and Enceladus, inasmuch, as has often been noted, he owes much here to Milton.

There are not wanting minor touches whereby, in Keats, as in Homer, the Gods of Greece become more credible by taking on minor aspects of human feeling and human failing:

> Blazing Hyperion on his orbed fire
> Still sat, still snuff'd the incense, teeming up
> From man to the sun's god, yet insecure.

Wrath and vanity are convincing, but Keats slips into the over-homely when he makes Hyperion stamp his foot and so jar the whole golden region. Now and then we find that over-elaboration of detail which dispels the reality of the suggested unreal. In Book II, Ops, the mother of the gods, described with black folded veil, pale cheeks, forehead wan, and eye-brows thin and jet, is overhumanized into nothingness, a great falling off from the presentation of the same goddess under another name, Cybele, in Book II of *Endymion*.

Book II, with its Council of the Gods, imperfect as it is, affords a wealth of material in regard to Keats' insight into primitive myth, and his use of myth in setting forth his own deeper thought. There are many fine elemental touches whereby the gods are interpreted in terms of nature process and earth structure, as in the early stage of myth. Typhon and Porphyrion, fire-breathing monsters, with many more, are presented:

> All their limbs
> Lock'd up like veins of metal, crampt and screw'd;

the "sanguine feverous boiling gurge of pulse" suggests a point where the mind of the medical student meets primitive imagination. Enceladus, god of wrath and of volcano, meditates, plots,

> And even now
> Was hurling mountains in that second war.

There were no such imaginative geologic suggestions in *Endymion*, Book II, underground. Genuinely imaginative is the way in which the nature gods are represented as being scarcely distinguishable from their background, the over-shadowing crags seeming to have monstrous horns; the slaty ridge, "stubborn'd with iron" on which they sat, was as part of themselves:

> Scarce images of life, one here, one there
> Lay vast and edgeways; like a dismal cirque
> Of Druid stones, upon a forlorn moor.

Among the grouped many,

> No shape distinguishable, more than when
> Thick night confounds the pine-tops with the clouds.

No touch of the elemental is more fortunate than that in which sunrise in the mountains represents the coming of Hyperion to the council of dismayed and bewildered gods, bringing to each face a gleam of light, "but splendider in Saturn's":

> And every gulf, and every chasm old,
> And every height, and every sullen depth,
> Voiceless, or hoarse with loud tormented streams:
> And all the everlasting cataracts,
> And all the headlong torrents far and near,
> Mantled before in darkness and huge shade,
> Now saw the light and made it terrible.

Then the sight of the face of the dejected king of day brings to them all deeper despondence.

One interesting aspect of this creation of nature powers in terms of their own life, seen in Saturn, Thea, Hyperion, Coelus, Oceanus, Enceladus and others is that much is given in nature sounds, coming as voices of unseen beings. Sound and silence play a larger part in this than in any other poem of Keats, and bring poignantly home to us this moment of experience of the early gods; earth deities speak in the music of earth. There is great beauty in many of these passages. Thea's words of sympathy and grief are likened to the sound on a summer night, when

> Tall oaks, branch-charmed by the earnest stars,
> Dream, and so dream all night without a stir,
> Save from one gradual, solitary gust
> Which comes upon the silence, and dies off,
> As if the ebbing air had but one wave.

The murmuring of the many gods, preluding Saturn's voice at the council of the Titans, is like "a roaring in the bleak-grown pines"; the voice of Oceanus, the sea-god, began to sound

> In murmurs, which his first-endeavouring tongue
> Caught, infant-like, from the far-foamed sands;

and of his sea-daughter, Clymene, it is said:

> So far her voice flow'd on, like timorous brook
> That, lingering along a pebbled coast,
> Doth fear to meet the sea.

The overwhelming voice of Enceladus rises:

> The ponderous syllables, like sullen waves
> In the half-glutted hollows of reef-rocks,
> Came booming thus.

Hyperion's roar is "as if of earthly fire."

Book II gives not only the elemental, but much of the later stage of Greek myth, of developed individuals, and with this something of dramatic interplay of personalities, of the unfolding of character into action. The best instance of this is in the effect of wrathful Enceladus upon Saturn,

> The supreme god
> At war with all the frailty of grief,

who would have sunk to despair with the rest but that the awe in Enceladus' eye came like an inspiration; Saturn feels ready for action, but the only creative power left him is that of anger: he knows not what to do. Not primitive, but modern, yet finely imagined and harmonious is his attempt to unriddle the mystery of the universe:

> Not in my own sad breast,
> Which is its own great judge and searcher out,
> Can I find reason why ye should be thus:
> Not in the legends of the first of days,
> Studied from that old spirit-leaved book
> Which starry Uranus, with finger bright
> Sav'd from the shores of darkness,

is there cause for the doom which has befallen them.

Coelus (Uranus) in Book I, expressing grief for fallen Saturn, pity for threatened Hyperion, his sons, says:

> I saw him fall,
> I saw my first-born tumbled from his throne!
> . . . .
> Yet do thou strive; as thou art capable;
> . . . .
> I am but a voice;
> My life is but a life of winds and tides,
> No more than winds and tides can I avail: —
> But thou canst.

This father, Uranus, in Hesiod, vows vengeance on these Titan children who had supplanted him; the words which Keats makes him utter suggest the growth of man's spirit in the long centuries between. Pity, sympathy, vicarious suffering are inwrought throughout the poem; even the individualizing touches suggesting sculpture are full of feeling, imaginative renderings of inner experience alien to Greek plastic art. The pity of Thea for Saturn; of Coelus for his sons, pitying Hyperion while the stars pity him; Hyperion's chivalric impulse to reinstate Saturn add a divinity to these imagined personages beyond the reach of those who first imagined them. Brief, fragmentary as Keats' work is, he added to Greek mythology an element which appears only in the Prometheus legend; this disinterestedness, this love sprung of pity, adds a beauty of spirit that Greek myth, with all its loveliness of color and line, did not know. Help is given by the gods for other reasons than personal preference or mere caprice. So he interprets the gods subtly in terms of the inner life, and his insight here is a measure of his growth from the days of romantic wonder

> How Psyche went
> On the smooth wind to realms of wonderment, —

through the subjective interpretation of the moon-goddess in Endymion, his Cynthia representing his own idealistic state of mind, to his conception of the gods in *Hyperion*, losing none of their ancient majesty as interpreted by poet or sculptor, but humanized, warm with the affections of the Keats family, loyal with the loyalties of his group of friends, and some of them, endowed with spiritual insights. They are more than men, being gods, and more than gods, being men, with human hearts of sympathy.

The characterization suggests one reason for Keats' inability to go on with *Hyperion*. The idea of dispossession by supreme beauty is the dominant idea. But what greater beauty is there, one is inclined to ask? He had made some of his falling rulers so beautiful within that one wonders what could surpass them; there was no room for fighting in a world thrilled through with disinterested sympathy and pity. Reading Saturn's account of his rule, it is hard to conceive what rule could be greater:

> I am smother'd up
> And buried from all godlike exercise
> Of influence benign on planets pale,
> Of admonitions to the winds and seas,
> Of peaceful sway above man's harvesting,
> And all those acts which Deity supreme
> Doth ease its heart of love in.

It remains for Oceanus to tell us the frailty whereby Saturn failed, of personal demand:

> But for this reason, that thou art the King,
> And only blind from sheer supremacy,
> One avenue was shaded from thine eyes,
> Through which I wandered to eternal truth.

Among the dejected gods the dispossessed are not the most discouraged; Apollo, who is coming into his reign, betrays a keener anguish. The fragment of Book III has a different tone from the other books; its relation to the underlying idea of *Hyperion* is not wholly clear. Though the music of the sea is aptly suggested as ushering in a higher reign in which there was to be a kind of music throughout, a Platonic harmony, —

> Throughout all the isle
> There was no covert, no retired cave
> Unhaunted by the murmurous noise of waves,

Apollo, the sun god, poet, musician, about to fulfil his high destiny, is stricken with utter grief. One might have expected joy and triumph; the tears of Apollo at this moment have remained an enduring puzzle to students of Keats, but the jibes that have come from some critics are unwarranted. This passage may not be good art, but it is most suggestive in regard to the thought of Keats.

Is not the secret of Apollo's sorrow the very secret of Keats' own heart, as suggested in various passages in his poems and his letters, as touchingly revealed in the *Fall of Hyperion* (pathetically less in poetic value than *Hyperion*, but indispensable to our knowledge of Keats, the man), the inability to reconcile the poet-singer career, with the first and greatest of all aims, to relieve suffering? It was a dilemma worthy of the tears of a god.

Truly, Keats, like other makers of myths, had to find the key to his interpretation of the god in terms of his own experience, his own insight, his own personality. The central trouble at the heart of Keats, from the early days when he longed to

> Find the agonies, the strife
> Of human hearts;

longed to reconcile the calling of the poet with that of the healer, had been intensified by the days when he walked the hospitals, by the hours of suffering and grief when he watched by the side of his brother Tom's sickbed, hours in which he worked on *Hyperion*. The woes of human kind pressed in upon him; his mind in his earliest endeavors to be a poet is on the languid sick in their fever's sleep; and in *Hyperion* he reveals his knowledge that

> The laden heart
> Is persecuted more, and fever'd more
> When it is nighing to the mournful house
> Where other hearts are sick of the same bruise.

In his letters he says: "Were it my choice, I would reject a Petrarchal coronation — on account of my dying day, and because women have cancers." Elsewhere he speaks of his hope of dying for a great cause. He was always in doubt about the justification of his being a poet; inheritor of all beauty, of all suffering, his problem was acute. Even so Apollo, who says:

> O why should I
> Feel curs'd and thwarted?

This is not the triumphant

> God of the golden bow,
> And of the golden lyre,
> And of the golden hair,
> And of the golden fire,

who had haunted Keats from early days, but an Apollo overcome by grief, by doubt, by misgiving. We see a god recoiling before a task too great: the weight of the world's sorrow; the gift of song. He had been watching the suffering of the dispossessed; he suffers; only he who has suffered can attain supreme insight. Was not this suffering intended to be the necessary preparation for the god to become such a poet that his singing would be justified because of its healing and consoling power?

Nothing is more significant in this unfinished fragment of Book III than the fact that Mnemosyne, the goddess of Memory, is to be the muse-inspiration of the ruler of the new era. Perhaps the idea was inherited. In the *Prometheus Bound* of Aeschylus it is said that Prometheus gave men

Memory, "that sweet muse mother," but undoubtedly Keats had a meaning of his own. Apollo says:

> I can read
> A wondrous lesson in thy silent face.

The life that is past so presses in upon Apollo that he feels as if he were becoming immortal through an elixir:

> Knowledge enormous makes a God of me.
> Names, deeds, gray legends, dire events, rebellions,
> Majesties, sovran voices, agonies,
> Creations and destroyings, all at once
> Pour into the wide hollows of my brain,
> And deify me, as if some blithe wine
> Or bright elixir peerless I had drunk,
> And so become immortal.

In the fact that Apollo is nourished on memory is suggested an idea, working at the heart of the period in which Keats lived, and destined to triumph over revolutionary doctrines, of indissoluble connection between the past, the present, and the future. In his attitude Keats presents an entire contrast to Shelley, Godwin's pupil, to whom the past was one long blunder, verging into crime, from which nothing could be learned save abhorrence.

It was more than Miltonic diction, Miltonic inversions, which Keats felt hampered him in carrying on *Hyperion*, which made him give it up. He was thinker, philosopher, poet, but never an epic poet; incidentally, he never claimed that he was writing an epic poem in *Hyperion*! It was not the events but the potential significance of the events that drew him to the old story of the passing of great things and the coming of greater. Homer, — if there was a Homer, — would have flinched from trying to think out the meaning of the story he had to tell; he wisely confined himself to the action. Perhaps *Hyperion* is more impressive in its fragmentary state than it would have been if completed.

Apollo, bowing under the experience of the past in facing

the future, undergoes a struggle like that at the gate of death, or liker still to one who should take leave of death and die into life. The poem breaks off when its hero is on the eve of great knowledge, and remains a fragment, profoundly interpretative of the great transition epoch of the late eighteenth and early nineteenth centuries.

The deepest interpretation of the meaning of *Hyperion* comes from Oceanus; few passages in the poetry of this period are more significant than his speech in Book II. With a voice like that of the waves on far-foaming sands he addresses the rebel gods, angry Enceladus and the others, and bewildered Saturn, who has in vain searched his own sad heart and all the universe for a reason for this threatening doom. Oceanus reproves them because they have not yet found the law of development; Saturn, blind from individual demand, has missed the path through which he, Oceanus, has wandered to eternal truth. In his words we are aware of a conception of constant change, inherent in the order of the universe, of change as law working out great destiny.

How much Keats knew of the trend of recent scientific thought in Germany and France toward evolution we do not know. His group of London friends represented a wide range of intellectual interests; records of the conversations of the young are not kept, and lives and letters contain only a tithe of that which we should need to know for full understanding. From the study of science he must have been aware of the organic nature of all life, of the fine interknitting of the whole fabric of existence. Above all, his study would have made him conscious of constant process in all things, growth, decay, and growth again, and the instinct of youth would find it hard to conceive of growth, change as leading to the lesser, for its whole apprehension of life is of going on to greater things.

It was a great moment in the history of thought; the idea of evolution, long whispered from the days of Greece, newly discovered, was taking a fresh hold upon men's minds, and taking on a beauty and a significance never before known. No record of Keats' reading shows direct contact with these ideas, but there is, in any great period, subtle intercommunication of thought for which speech or written word can not wholly account, and assimilation of the deep meaning of ideas that began to permeate the thought of his time is unmistakable in his work. Keats, in *Hyperion*, not only presents in the form of myth the idea of progressive change, but passes from an outer to an inner interpretation, gives it spiritual significance, as Herder had done in his *Philosophy of the History of Man*, an interpretation which nineteenth century science was pleased to forget, though nineteenth century poetry remembered; and twentieth century science seems about to recall it.

With no effect of incongruity this ancient nature deity is made to voice the very heart of modern thought in his utterance: "We fall by course of Nature's law"; and beauty drawn from the thought of Greece mingles with the modern:

> So on our heels a fresh perfection treads,
> A power more strong in beauty, born of us
> And fated to excel us . . .
> . . . for, 'tis the eternal law
> That first in beauty should be first in might.

The imaginative insight that makes the god of the sea spokesman for the beauty of ceaseless change that means law needs no comment. So Oceanus expresses man's immemorial longing to find a meaning in the happenings of life, the constant change and process, becomes interpreter of the deepest intellectual conception that was being worked out in the age in which Keats lived, and gives it an inner meaning which neither scientist nor philosopher in England had given it. What wonder that the poet stopped, the vastness of the conception leaving him

> Silent upon a peak in Darien.

An ancient, rough-hewn myth, of war and fighting and change of tyrannies, became the medium of expression of the deepest thought of the age that was being ushered in. To take primitive imaginings, growing out of nature perception; to keep the nature nearness, and to make the early myth expressive of a late, and profound phase of human wisdom, was great achievement. Here is suggested the most fertile idea of modern thought, of all life as unceasing development, with deep vibration of hope in regard to destiny whose greatness is not yet known.

That the idea of passing from a lesser to a greater order, following an inner, not an outer compulsion, should have been embodied by Keats in myth is significant; probably he could not have expressed himself so fully in any other form. The old wonder of the critic that myth could have been at this late date revived is lessened when we recall the importunity of new life both of thought and feeling pressing in upon his generation, and the fitness of myth, with its flexibility, its power of suggestion, to set forth a conviction of promise in the future that went beyond reasoned proof. He was in those early years when one is living thought, trying it out, to use his own phrase, upon the pulses, not affirming and reaffirming abstract dogma; one traces his growth through the growing spirituality of his interpretation of myth, as shown in the three successive volumes. From early allusion, the mouthing of golden names, the tremulous, vague apprehension of beauty in the volume of 1817, it has come to be the expression of his own deepest thought and experience, as well as of the profoundest divination of truth of the age in which he lived.

So *Hyperion* reveals not only a great advance of insight into the meaning of primitive myth, but also the growth of the poet's soul. He shows in this poem, much of which was written by his brother Tom's deathbed, that, if he has entered that chamber of experience, where "Misery, Heart-break, pain, sickness, and apprehension dwell," he has found a door opening into freedom. "Sorrow is wisdom," Keats wrote in one of his letters. The deep appeal of *Hyperion* lies in the meeting here of youth's fresh sense of opening life and promise, with the reverent acquiescence of age. Wisdom one would think beyond the power of his years is in this great submission to the great laws of life. Instead of dimming the brightness of ancient myths, he has taken old earth stories, with their cosmic import, the rendering of physical phenomena, and has made the life of the spirit shine through them.

Especially in the difference between the interpretation of the two major myths can we measure the inner growth of Keats. In *Endymion* we have the experience of the individual, the one; in *Hyperion*, the universal, the race experience, and the adjustment of the individual to the whole order of being. Endymion is a youth who feels all beauty coming within his eager grasp, — beauty of nature, of human life, of spirit; he can win them all. In *Hyperion*, the youthful poet, through swiftness and intensity of experience, and the great gift of penetrative imagination, is aware of what age is fortunate to have found, that the supreme beauty comes from willingness to let go. *Hyperion* is not much later in time, but is vastly later in depth of experience. Here is the central peace of surrender, differing from Keats' youthful ambition and longing to achieve, from the restless search of his hero Endymion. Reading the two poems, we have read the sonnet through, from

> When I have fears that I may cease to be
> Before my pen has glean'd my teeming brain,

to

> then on the shore
> Of the wide world I stand alone, and think
> Till love and fame to nothingless do sink.

In another sonnet he gives the profound significance of *Hyperion*, the briefest and most poetic expression of that which proved to be the deepest faith of the nineteenth century:

> There is a budding morrow in midnight.

Keats' last great poem, the *Ode to Autumn*, though not ostensibly based on Greek myth, is very near the heart of it, a perfect expression of the phase of primitive feeling and dim thought in regard to earth processes when these are passing into a thought of personality. The moment brings a sense of fulfilment, and Autumn becomes a gracious woman, born of the bounty of the fields; even so, in the minds of early Greeks, Demeter was born. Recalling primitive myth-makers who could hardly tell the life in their environment from the life in themselves, it is the very self of Greek myth coming to be, representing an earlier phase of it than any other so far found in Keats except the Hymn to Pan, and there is a difference; that is an appreciation; this, an experience.

It is the culmination in the work of Keats of all that quiet and entire delight in Nature as she simply is, — the sharing of the creeping down of roots; the pleasure, which he said was his greatest, in watching the growth of flowers; the mingling of his being in the fragrant dusk in the *Nightingale* with the being of flowers; and we are again conscious of that enhanced perception that seems to come in Keats from the perfect harmony of all the senses, as if a new mode of perception had been acquired through their deep accord.

Always the tendency of Keats' poetic life was toward the rendering of perfect moments of experience; this lingering over moments of delight sometimes delays the narratives; it gives to the odes their fulness of appeal. More than mere thought, more than mere feeling is involved, a wholeness of experience wherein the poet reaches out to completeness of existence. In the *Ode to Autumn* his deep, organic nature sense of being one with all that blossoms and ripens under the sun makes him aware of a deep law of life; a harmony at the heart of things, apparent at no other moment of the year, is revealed. Mystics who aver that the secret of existence is written on the face of things if we could but see might find here one who had read and understood. Primitive perception of nature life and process and his matured and chastened thought blend in perfectness of experience; with the gifts of autumn the gifts of his young spirit are garnered up as in an offering. In this sense of Being fulfilled, there is perfect acquiescence in the great laws of life and perfect insight, sense and spirit in fine accord. If *Endymion* means the eager quest for Beauty, and *Hyperion* the assurance that Beauty is on the way, the *Ode to Autumn* means that Beauty is here.

VII

THE YOUNG BROWNING

I

TO BE born at a time when the intellectual and spiritual forces of a new era are sufficiently astir to make themselves felt in many tentative ways, and to be born with genius able to assimilate the best of new thought wakening in the minds of men, is perhaps as great a gift as the gods can bestow. In this, as in most ways, Robert Browning was fortunate. His youth was passed in a period, suffering, it is true, from the failure of hopes roused by the French Revolution, but beginning to be stirred by fresh thought in a profounder realm than that of the political world, concerned with ideas more far-reaching than those regarding the fall of kings and the rise of republics, thought still in its tentative stages, of a growth, evolution, in all forms of life upon the earth. It was a period of the re-birth of science under the stimulus of a new idea, tentatively suggested by both natural philosopher and scientist. Robinet's *De la Nature* appeared in 1761–8; Erasmus Darwin's *Zoönomia* in 1794; Lamarck's *Recherches sur l'Organization des Corps Vivans* in 1802; Sir Charles Lyell's *Principles of Geology* in the early thirties of the nineteenth century, the years in which Browning was doing his first work; in 1807 Hegel had published his *Phaenomenology of the Spirit*, for the thought of ceaseless development was beginning to embrace the whole life of man, not the body only, and its environment, but the mystery of the inner life. In 1800 had been printed in England an excellent translation of the *Philosophy of the History of Man* by the natural philosopher, Johann Gottlieb Herder, setting forth in impassioned phrase the deep-lying principle of inner growth throughout the universe, culminating in the development of man's soul. It was a world alert with the wakening consciousness of a new era, entering upon a way of thinking that, throughout the century, was to give impetus and sweep to the interpretations of man's life, those influences already operative which were to bring to the Victorian Age its peculiar sense of progress, of life shaping toward great ends. Browning, child of his age, and contributor through penetrating imaginative power and keenness of vision to its deeper thought, found a new and original way of expressing the profoundest intuition of a great period.

II. Pauline (1833)

In reading Browning's first poem, *Pauline*, one is aware of a vast energy of life, undirected, trying to find its way. It is full of physical, intellectual, spiritual vitality, which lends vividness, poignancy, to the inner struggle that is here depicted; its burden is the anguish of non-fulfilment of the supreme ideals of thought and faith and conduct which the speaker had set before himself. It is unique among the first poems of young poets in its unawareness of aught save the great things in life; there is in it a largeness, a sensitiveness to great issues, an ignoring of all petty aims; the soul, the soul's destiny is the one concern. Browning strikes here the high note that was to be his through great length of life. The hero, conscious of the greatness of the forces that have nourished and impelled his spirit, — nature, myth, art, literature, Plato, and Shelley, who were to him literature and something more, suffers remorse for having failed that which they had given him; for having betrayed his own powers; for having failed Pauline.

As he thinks of the past, he becomes aware of a lesser self within him, which had hampered the greater self, a cynical, questioning spirit, which had mocked his faith in the further reach of his spirit, had betrayed him into using less than his full powers. Thus, will has failed him; feeling is no longer a stimulus; that which had been his great gift, imaginative insight, is paralyzed; his sin is in part the sin of passivity. Born into life to act, to create, baffled by the apparently mistaken direction of his efforts, he has fallen into a kind of floating inaction; he is bewildered by his own letting go. The heart and climax of his failure is that he can love nothing; love, which had blended love of a woman with love of art and love of humanity, has gone.

It is a poem of ego-centeredness. Inflowing influences have but intensified the life of the ego; the hero of *Pauline* had not found the right outflowing. His energy had surged toward this and that outcome, in the world of thought, the world of art, the world of beneficent deed in behalf of his fellow men, any one of which activities would have meant escape, but had fallen back on self, discouraged. There is a lack of awareness of anybody else in the world except Pauline, and she is but a projection of himself; the fellow men he had tried to help are in his mind but shadows of shadows. He is functioning alone in the universe, isolated, dislocated, and he suffers the pain of being cut off from living contact with his kind.

Pauline reveals the very mind and soul of the young Browning. The rapid streams of thought and feeling are revealed just as they rushed through his mind; the reader shares his naked inner consciousness, the throes of his struggle. It is a very ferment center of young thought and feeling, for genius is at work, revealing its dim desires, its inability to clarify itself, its groping, through all mists, toward the highest. In the swift rush of the phrases it is hard, at times, to understand, but there is an immediacy of shared experience, so that you see the growth of a young mind, as certain skilfully taken motion pictures have enabled us to see the very growth of flowers, the groping down of the roots, the growth upward of the stem. The same is true in regard to the early poems of young Keats, but Browning is less passive, less at the mercy of sensation, more intellectual than young Keats. Here is vast energy of thought, hardly as yet knowing its direction, but clarifying itself with utterance, so that at the end you are aware that growth has been going on throughout.

From the first, Browning shows daring originality, strikes at the outset the note of his own individuality. None of his youthful contemporary poets, so far as we know, thought his thoughts. Early influences fostered the development of his peculiar genius. We get the impression that the boy Browning, though surrounded by affectionate home life, was, in his comparative freedom from school restrictions, much alone, yet was incapable of being alone in a world filled with individualities, not only people, but bird, beast, insect, all living things in hedgerow, meadow, and hillside. Camberwell, at the time of Browning's birth, was a suburban village, green with its many trees, grass plots, and gardens, an old church at the foot of the hill. Of the world of his fellowmen he was thoughtfully aware from early days. Mr. Sharp records that, on holiday afternoons, he would lie under the elm trees upon the hillside, gazing at distant London across the river: "Something of that mighty complex life, so confusedly petty to the narrow vision, so grandiose and even majestic to the larger ken, had blent with his being from the first."

The hero of *Pauline* draws from Browning's inmost personality, reflects the early experience of the youth whose mind, body, soul were tingling with vitality. Here is passion to know all, experience all, take on the whole and make it part of himself; longing to live in the fulness of his powers. It is a mood of youth, the mood which the Faust legend has gathered into itself, as known in succeeding centuries. It is more than mood; mind vibrates as well as desire in this hunger for more than the human being can compass, both of emotional and intellectual experience:

> My selfishness is satiated not,
> It wears me like a flame; my hunger for
> All pleasure, howsoe'er minute, grows pain;
> . . . .
> This restlessness of passion meets in me
> A craving after knowledge:
> . . . .
> I am made up of an intensest life,
> Of a most clear idea of consciousness
> Of self, distinct from all its qualities,
> From all affections, passions, feelings, powers;
> And thus far it exists, if tracked, in all:
> But linked, in me, to self supremacy,
> Existing as a centre to all things,
> Most potent to create and rule and call
> Upon all things to minister to it;
> And to a principle of restlessness
> Which would be all, have, see, know, taste, feel, all —
> This is myself; and I should thus have been
> Though gifted lower than the meanest soul.

Surely this introspective desire to know all, possess all, is not unrelated, by way of inheritance and descent, to the state of mind that had greeted the vastness of the universe opened out through seventeenth century science, through Spinoza's vision of the infinite, that had led the Deists into their attempt to explain the whole. The explained still proving inexplicable, thought, deepening, led to a desire to know the whole more inly, more profoundly, to penetrate the world of the inner life, in its relation to the outer all.

One power he has which has saved him in all the chaos of unfulfilled desire and aspiration, his imagination, and this bit of self-analysis gives truth. It is an imagination penetrating at this point and that; wandering about, full of a sense of freedom; receptive, but not yet skilled in shaping power to definite ends. There is an interesting revelation in the suggestion of an imaginative attempt to realize himself in other lives:

> I have made life my own.
> I would not be content with all the change
> One frame should feel, but I have gone in thought
> Through all conjecture, I have lived all life
> When it is most alive, where strangest fate
> New-shapes it past surmise.

Puzzled by the mystery of existence, to whose interpretation he has no key, feeling mankind in the hands of fate which may mean doom, or may mean right fulfilment, he finds himself paralyzed by the sympathy which comes from imaginative insight into the "throes of men":

> Why else have I sought refuge in myself,
> But from the woes I saw and could not stay?

In the world of nature, too, imagination enables him to enter into more life than his own, bringing him a happy sense of sharing, untroubled by the puzzle that besets his thought of human life:

> I can live all the life of plants, and gaze
> Drowsily on the bees that flit and play,
> Or bare my breast for sunbeams which will kill.
> . . . .
> I can mount with the bird
> Leaping airily his pyramid of leaves,
> And twisted boughs of some tall mountain tree.

Nature brings him an inner realization of grasping the whole which he does not get in connection with human life, though that is what he longs to enter into and understand. Into the world of bee, of plant, of mountain tree he can escape, can know himself a part of it, baffled as yet in entering into the vast and varied world of human consciousness, human experience, human individuality, which demands a deeper divination. He has an intense consciousness of self, but is not assured that his conjecture touches reality in that imaginative approach to other selves, despite his longing to penetrate the infinite variety of life, to be all, see, know, taste, feel all, fathom, in short, all experience. Pauline had inspired him to a task beyond his power:

> And then thou saids't a perfect bard was one
> Who chronicled the stages of all life.

Here are the birth throes of a dramatic poet, a poet who is to be interpreter of human individuality in its life processes, becoming more and more individual; of Browning, whose early, intense sense of his own consciousness in *Pauline*, whose eagerness to enter into the consciousness of others, developed into the power to do so, to "live all life when it is most alive."

Nature nearness is more apparent in *Pauline* than in any poem which Browning afterward wrote, and his reaction to nature has marked originality. The world outside is not there to be described; it is not mere background; it is actively a part of human consciousness, for there is an imaginative sharing of process in nature that has the distinctive note of a new period, the human reaction making those who watch and feel partakers of that life. In the passage beginning

> No, we will pass to morning —
> Morning, the rocks and valleys and old woods,

there is a sense of life shared with the wind in the tree tops, the birds living on high boughs, the spray from the waterfall, the wild hawks, and all that goes on in bank and stream

> Where the pale-throated snake reclines his head,
> And old gray stones lie making eddies there,
> The wild mice cross them dry shod.

In Browning's mature poetry the spirit of a new life flows, as clear and exhilarating as that of a mountain stream, a spirit that asks no questions, knows no fear, but lives, and is conscious of growth. In *Pauline* he has not reached this instinctive assurance, but he is on the way. The spirit of all earth's springtimes, revealed in some of his early nature passages, is later to permeate his grave studies of human life:

> And spring's first breath
> Blew soft from the moist hills;

and in *Paracelsus*:

> Earth is a wintry clod:
> But spring-wind, like a dancing psaltress, passes
> Over its breast to waken it, rare verdure
> Buds tenderly upon rough banks, between
> The withered tree-roots and the cracks of frost;
> . . . .
> savage creatures seek
> Their loves in wood and plain — and God renews
> His ancient rapture.

That feeling of being in the process of nature life, of bird, beast, growing things is apparent throughout *Pauline* in the mind and spirit of the young hero of *Pauline*; it is in the early years of *Paracelsus*; in the lyrics of *Pippa Passes*; and in the all too few later nature lyrics, as "O to be in England, now that April's there!"; *Meeting at Night*; *Parting at Morning*; *Home-Thoughts, from the Sea*; in some of the later lyrics:

> Such a starved bank of moss
> Till, that May-morn,
> Blue ran the flash across:
> Violets were born!

Here the thrill of life in the universe is felt in the lyric rendering of human mood in terms of nature. It is cause for regret that, in his later years, Browning became so wholly absorbed in interpreting the inner life of man that he presented far less often than in his early work the life of the green world vibrating with the life of humanity.

The influence of Shelley is apparent in the nature passages of *Pauline*, as in the contrast of shining light against the dark in the spring passage:

> The black-thorn boughs,
> So dark in the bare wood, when glistening
> In the sunshine were white with coming buds.

Browning's attitude toward the "Sun-treader" is that of a worshiper, ready, like Keats, to let his

> Young spirit follow
> The morning sun-beams to the great Apollo
> Like a fresh sacrifice.

There is haunting beauty in his tribute to Shelley, expressed in nature terms:

> But thou art still for me who have adored
> Though single, panting but to hear thy name
> Which I believed a spell to me alone,
> Scarce deeming thou wast as a star to men!
> As one should worship long a sacred spring,
> Scarce worth a moth's flitting, which long grasses cross,
> And one small tree embowers droopingly —
> Joying to see some wandering insect won
> To live in its few rushes, or some locust
> To pasture on its boughs, or some wild bird
> Stoop for its freshness from the trackless air:
> And then should find it but the fountain-head,
> Long lost, of some great river washing towns
> And towers
> . . . .
> Then girt with rocks which seek to turn or stay
> Its course in vain, for it does ever spread
> Like a sea's arm as it goes rolling on,
> Being the pulse of some great country — so
> Wast thou to me, and art thou to the world!

Feeling akin to Shelley's vivid sense of nature process is in the nature passages in *Pauline*, as in Browning's other early work, the ceaseless action going on in earth and sky phenomena, and in the movement of the waters, but in Browning is something very different from Shelley's impalpable, impersonal nature renderings, that abstract presentation of constant movement seen in *The Cloud*, in the sunrise in Act II of *Prometheus Unbound*, and in Act IV. Browning had from the first a strong sense of personality in all living creatures; Shelley never had a strong feeling of personality in regard to man or God. Nature was alive to Shelley with cosmic force, "the one spirit's plastic stress," and Browning, influenced by Shelley, kept throughout his many years a vivid consciousness of the one force sweeping through all life. But to Browning, who apparently never shared Shelley's keen interest in the inorganic world, shown in the boy-chemist's experiments, nature was individually alive. Here, as in his interpretation of human beings, was an intense feeling of individuality, even in creatures not human. "The morning swallows with their songs like words" strikes a note that reappears in Browning's later representations of bird and beast, and in his attitude in youth toward his many pets: mice, snakes, monkeys, hedgehogs, eagle, toad. The same attitude is recorded in connection with those back-yard members of his family in his later days in London: the owl that was the "light of the household," and the two geese named after the Quarterlies. Perhaps his early, as well as his later love of all the minor folk of hedgerow and meadow reveals his instinctive awareness of the one life shared by all living things. Something of cosmic sense shows in the interchange of sympathies with the least and humblest of creatures, that sense of relationship with all that lives.

The urge of Shelley's eager, impetuous intellectual life stimulated and somewhat intoxicated him, and its influence shows in many ways: in the tributes to him, in the social sense, the hope of serving mankind, in the conviction of the all-importance of love in life, in the Platonic idealism, as well as in the perception of nature action. Passages of *Epipsy-*

chidion echo in the appeals to Pauline to share the promise of new life in an ideal spot. *Alastor* is the only other early poem which can be compared with this in the fulness of revelation of the author's individuality at the outset of his work, but this suggests deeper meanings than *Alastor*, though its execution is far less perfect. *Pauline* is more intimately a part of inner consciousness than is Shelley's poem; it is full of complex and warring currents, more human in its bewildered intensity, its hero searching within, and not over the face of the earth, for the answer to the riddle of life.

The profounder note in the young Browning's work is apparent in *Pauline* in the speaker's feeling of individual responsibility, that consciousness which is the starting point of character, of individuality. The hero of *Pauline* takes it for granted that his failure is failure of the inner self; he ascribes this failure to no external cause. Shelley had, at least throughout the greater part of his life, found evil in the world an external thing. From the first Browning departs from his poetic master in this, and the deepest gap between the two lies in Browning's early knowledge of life as spiritual struggle, versus Shelley's idea of life as struggle against outer force. The saving grace in this youthful ego-centeredness is the recognition of the profound truth that the secret of his destiny lies folded up within himself.

Full realization on the part of the hero of *Pauline* of his failure proves a turning point. The beginning of recovery comes in his discovery that he is isolated, can love nothing; recognition that his greatest failure is that he can love nothing is the deepest intuition of the young Browning as reflected in his hero. It is not only that love for Pauline has waned; with this has gone the creative impulse of which that love was a part, the desire to achieve in art, to benefit humanity, even to enter into the creative achievements of others. Here, where he depicts love of a woman as subtly inwrought with love of beauty in nature and in art, with human aspiration, with love of humanity, Browning, already in this immature work, reveals his belief that love is the central force, the creative power in all life.

Love had been stressed by the Deist nature poets Brooke, Thomson, and others, as an attribute of God, in passages wherein they were attempting to interpret the nature of God as manifested in the making of the universe. In Browning's *Pauline* we have the birth-throes of a great idea; man, conceived by Deist and theologian alike as the passive recipient of God's love, must be able to love, to feel within himself the creative power of loving, or he perishes.

Characteristically for Browning, the moment of apparent defeat turns into a moment of victory: "I can love nothing" changes at the end into

> I the hopeless, I the loveless, hope and love.

The creative wakens again within him under the sting of this realization, and, as the power to love quickens within him, a re-awakening of his life-forces begins to stir through his sense of failure; the fulness and ardency of young life, reviving, striving again toward the greatest, gathers all the resources of mind, emotion, imagination, and dismay yields to triumph as he finds that he has been living in less than the fulness of his powers. The divided self is fused in the returning power to love.

Already Browning is focusing in moments. The idea through which release comes to the speaker flashes upon him at the end, in one of those moments of revelation which Browning delights to suggest as coming at the end of life, throwing light along the backward way. In this groping, through manifold desires and impulses, through aspiration and dereliction on the part of this youth whom only the deepest questioning can interest, only the infinite can satisfy, there had been, after all, an inner directing energy that was God:

> O God, where do they tend — these struggling aims?

he asks, and answers:

> And what is that I hunger for but God?

The cynical spirit within him had mocked his faith:

> Why have I girt myself with this hell dress?
> Why have I labored to put out my life?
> . . . .
> And e'en for all my reason do I not
> Feel him and thank him and pray to him — now?

The import of the passage is that the soul, struggling toward complete fulfillment of itself, of all its desires, impulses, aims, is, whether it knows it or not, struggling through the power of the divine within, toward a transcendent something greater than itself, God. Out of a world filled with self he has found his way to perception of something greater than self of which he is a part. The infinite opens out.

Pauline is vague, uncertain in its art, but not in its meaning, which the young author could not fully objectify. "Good draughtsmanship and right handling," he said in later life, "were far beyond the artist at that time." If, in the swift rush of the phrases, it is hard at times to follow, at the end the reader is aware of a kind of submerged coherence. Through all this swirling of idea and emotion there has been growth, though the hero has not been aware of its direction, and the realization of it comes upon him at the end as a surprise. It is evident that, in the discovery of the truth, the inner reality of life, every faculty is living, dynamic, mind, emotion, imaginative intuition. In this recapturing of lost powers, the discovery of a greater self, is an experience akin to that of Wordsworth recorded in the *Prelude*, as life passed for him from analysis to synthesis, — there far more clearly and impressively presented. Browning here, in the person of his hero, discovers himself, enters upon the heritage of his full gifts and powers, finding that all the faculties, mind, emotion, intuition, enter into the solution of the problem of life.

Though, in *Pauline*, is a seething turmoil of thought, hardly as yet knowing its import, yet certain ideas emerge. Already the organic nature of life is apparent to the young poet; the hero of *Pauline* has failed himself and his fellow men; he has not fulfilled his individual being; he has not succeeded in playing his part in the larger organism made up of the world of his fellow men. In presenting that swirl of undirected intellectual and emotional activity, Browning's mind is groping toward the discovery of that which was to be to him the key to life, the master idea of his poetic work, but he does not reach it. His hero moves through an energy of inner life that is chaos very near to a perception of that energy which is law, a law of spiritual development. He escapes from the tangle into a conviction of the existence of God, of immortality, the swiftness of the revelation coming as a surprise after the indirection of the poem. In the intellectual and ethical questioning, as in the nature interpretation, all is dynamic, nothing static; and the frustrated life of the speaker brings to the reader the need, on the part of both the young author and his hero, in this story of spiritual struggle, of the idea of a continuity of inner experience involving a law of progress, God within.

There is beauty in the promise of the ending, as the poet's spokesman passes

> To where I clearlier see and better love.
> . . . .
> For this song shall remain to tell forever
> That when I lost all hope of such a change
> Suddenly beauty rose on me again.

The poem is full of the promise of one, who, when both science and philosophy were beginning to emphasize continuity, to interpret life as constant movement toward higher phases of being, was, in his youth, reading Plato, with his idea of the growth of man's spirit toward the perfect.

III. Paracelsus (1835)

There are moments in the lives of poets over which the imagination delights to linger, in the hope that some vitalizing touch of larger life may come. Few are more appealing than that which brings us a glimpse of the youthful Robert Browning, treading the streets of Camberwell, climbing Herne Hill, with *Paracelsus* growing in his mind. The inflow of Renaissance ideas, the inflow of ideas from his own period, meet and blend; here is youth raised to the *n*th power. With vast energy of intellect, emotion, imagination, genius begins to find its way, in the clarifying of thought, the clarifying of form.

The wakening intellectual ardor of the Renaissance, as studied in the life of one man, opening new vistas, with unbounded opportunity for knowledge and experience, is reinforced by the wakening intellectual and spiritual ardor of the early nineteenth century, with its tentative conception of a central life in the universe, of a law of unceasing development, the evolutionary idea, about to gather up into itself all that men had thought and dreamed of evolution since the days of Greece, and to carry it further, into reasoned proof. Browning's young mind, already vivified and sensitized by the poetry of Keats and of Shelley, is full of the early stages of thought of two great periods; two splendors meet and fuse: the imagined Renaissance, and the early nineteenth century, with all that is stirring within it, its profoundest apprehension, perhaps, embodied in the idea of the philosopher Hegel, of endless spiritual development.

The elder Browning's fortunate interest in old books and odd characters brought his son the influence that he needed, giving focus and direction to his thought, through the discovery of the significance of an outstanding character in a great period; *Paracelsus*, in three volumes, with engraved portrait, stood upon the home bookshelves. In the seething intellectuality of *Pauline* there was lack of the shaping power of imagination, a predominance of the intellectual and the emotional over the image-making faculty; the poet did not succeed in fully objectifying his thought. In its swift rush, nor time, nor place, nor background is indicated; there is no center , no action, no continuity of development. Meditating on the character and the achievements of Paracelsus against his background of the Renaissance was a liberal education to the young poet. Here, probably, he was first made aware of the influence of currents of thought in a period, of environment, on character. Swirling ideas and feelings emerged, took shape, blended; in following his study of the development of his hero we watch the development of the artist coming to be, escaping from the purely subjective. Something solid, tangible emerges, a great historical figure against a great historical background, his experience a part of the growth of the race in a crucial moment of its development. Studying an individual of conspicuous personality and achievement, drew his mind from the ego-centeredness of *Pauline*; through inquiry as to how this man came to be he began to understand the relation of the individual to the larger body of which he is a part, of inner realities to outer realities. Thinking of that character, the forces operating in the age of the Renaissance began to flow into his imagined face: the wakening to the study of fact; the vast hunger for knowledge; the abjuring of magic; the intense sense of individuality; the power of a single man to achieve. His personal relationships enter in; after the sheer subjectivity of *Pauline* the youth is learning something of the adjustment of character to character, the effect of other personalities on his hero, of his hero on others. Time, place, circumstance, action emerge; character expresses itself in event. Here the art of Browning begins to come into being, in the inflow and outflow of forces, center ing in successive situations, each the outcome of the interaction of character and circumstance which makes the dramatic complexity, and irony of life. If he does not present fully the historical Paracelsus he grows swiftly toward his own peculiar form of art in trying to do so, in search for the hidden springs of life within him, and in the presentation of his growth, wherein are blended that which he received from without, that which he contributed from within.

In this spiritual epic the study of Paracelsus is given wholly in terms of development, into which enter environment, influence of friends, opportunity of the moment, inner energy, impulse, — identified by the hero as God within. He is as vivid against his background as a Renaissance portrait but the comparison is misleading; here, all is mobile, nothing stationary, fixed, — his personality is in process of coming to be, the urge within impelling constant change; the touch upon him of friend or foe, the new experience in strange lands among strangers, the challenge of opportunity, each instant bringing growth. The flowing nature of the time world is apparent in this developing personality.

This experience is presented at five successive moments, in five scenes definitely fixed in time and place, of which I, III, and V stand out as most distinctive. Each scene is a crucial one, and its ending marks a step onward in his progress. If *Pauline* was an eddy in a circle, this is a stream finding its way.

At the outset Paracelsus voices his aspiration to compass the whole,

> To comprehend the works of God
> And God himself, and all God's intercourse
> With the human mind,

in a finely imagined scene in a Würzburg garden, where, in the fragrance of ripening grapes, and the after-bloom of the apple tree, with the stir of life all about him,

> Gray crickets and shy lizards and quick spiders,

tenants of the enclosing old populous green wall, he takes leave of his friends. Their doubts and hesitations become part of his growth in confirming him in his inspired obstinacy in regard to his God-given mission; still more does their conversion at the end of the scene to belief in his venture become an integral part of the strengthening soul within him. Festus is throughout a potent factor in the development of Paracelsus; Michal, who is to influence him still more inly, is exquisitely suggested in the whole, now by a concrete touch, her smile here in the old garden, now by a swift flash of her inmost self upon the soul of Paracelsus, a spiritual contact of human beings as finely suggestive as that in *Pippa Passes*.

The young poet knows the hidden springs of life within the character he is presenting, for they are in himself also, and the scene is full of the vibrancy of youth, wholly alive in mind, soul, body, the wakening intellectual power of a boy in a period of swift intellectual advance stimulating his imaginative insight into the wakening forces of another great era, and into the heart of a lad whose years were even fewer than his own.

The vibration of a moment of intellectual change and awakening appears in Paracelsus' determination, significant of growth both in the hero and in his period, to cast off the old, abjure magic and black arts, and mediaeval ways of thinking:

> 'Tis time
> New hopes should animate the world, new light
> Should dawn from new revealings to a race
> Weighed down so long.

Here is the irresistible impulse of genius, tearing through the fabric of settled beliefs and convictions, perhaps not unmindful of the rents made, but with need to obey the strong inner compulsion. Here is the splendor of the Renaissance passion for knowledge, with the wakening conviction that it is not all to be found in books:

> I go to gather this
> The sacred knowledge, here and there dispersed
> About the world,

well interpreted by this London youth in the early thirties of the nineteenth century, standing on the threshold of an era actuated and inspired by a passion for truth lurking in observable facts, waiting for an interpreter.

One can see how, to the searching mind of Browning, the wandering life of Paracelsus, always in intellectual quest, "through Germany, Italy, France, the Netherlands, Denmark, Sweden, Russia, and probably some parts of Asia," feeling his way along the study of fact, would appeal as an objectification of the intellectual hunger that the young poet knew so well. Paracelsus, it is written, sought information from all and sundry, — from "physicians, surgeons, and alchemists, . . . executioners, barbers, shepherds, Jews, gypsies, . . . fortune tellers," from teamsters and vagabonds on highways and at inns. To the youth with the budding interest in every type of humanity, longing to live "all life when it is most alive," the study of the life of Paracelsus must have meant a great widening of his own human interest, reinforcing that instinct fostered by gazing at London from under the elm trees of Camberwell Hill, — the thought of that adventuring, the pleasant detail of vagabonding bringing to his confused impression of the complex life of humanity something of the defining concrete, as he relived the life of the wayfarer, to whom expression, gesture, clothing of those whom he met must perforce reveal much of their way of life. So did Paracelsus minister to the lad's passion for wider knowledge, experience, and to the young artist's need of the tangible expression of individuality.

Renaissance individualism, as well as the timeless assurance of gifted youth in any period shows, in the attitude of Paracelsus toward the great work he intends to achieve:

> I, singled out for this, the One!

He is interpreted as one of the great men of his time, standing alone, doing great deeds alone, as they stand out in the pages of history, in Renaissance portraits. The taint of passion for power mingles with his passion for knowledge; the dislocation of pride is expressed in the words put into the mouth of this self-chosen leader:

> I never will be served by those I serve.

Longing

> At once to trample on yet save mankind,

he is wisely interpreted by the precocious youth as both in the wrong and in the right, in other words, a human being. In Paracelsus' aloofness from the human race is the eternal tragedy of genius, loneliness. He does not and he can not keep pace with his fellows, for they are incapable of his stride. This isolation differs from the unmotivated loneliness of the hero of *Pauline*; loneliness there came from having let go. In Paracelsus, — and there is tragedy and irony in the thought, — it comes largely from that greater gift that lifted him out of the companionship of his fellows into the solitude of genius.

Festus distrusts not only the purpose of Paracelsus, but his method. Two great aspects of the Renaissance appear in these two men; well set off against Paracelsus' scorn for that which men have attained is Festus' reverence for the written word:

> Call this, truth —
> Why not pursue it in a fast retreat,
> Some one of Learning's many palaces,
> After approved example? — seeking there
> Calm converse with the great dead, soul to soul,
> Who laid up treasure with the like intent.
> . . . .
> But you have coupled with your enterprise
> An arbitrary self-repugnant scheme;
> Of seeking it in strange and untried paths.

What books are in the desert? Writes the sea
The secret of her yearning in vast caves
Where yours will fall the first of human feet?
Has wisdom sat there and recorded aught
You press to read?

Lyell was even then, as the young poet wrote, in the early thirties of the nineteenth century, answering this question in the affirmative.

Paracelsus is bewildered that this leader who had first roused his mind could not understand it in action:

I was not born
Informed and fearless from the first
. . . .
But you first guided me through doubt and fear.

Festus is fearful of his friend's aim, as coveting more than mortal may expect. He differs from Paracelsus about God, — and in this debate lies the intellectual center of the poem, — not understanding his conviction that God is working in his inner longing, impulse, vision; is afraid of his scorn of the gathered wisdom of the ages, and finds the seed of failure in Paracelsus' attempt to drag the infinite into the finite, puzzled by the working of the mind of genius, that further aim, that look:

As if where'er you gazed, there stood a star.

To Paracelsus it seems that Festus, the man of God, is urging him to live as if God did not exist, that is, to ignore the inner impulse prompting him, that through which he is surest of God. God is found in vision, in vast longing for knowledge:

I profess no other share
In the selection of my lot, than this
My ready answer to the will of God
Who summons me to be his organ . . .
. . . .

What fairer seal
Shall I require to my authentic mission
Than this fierce energy? — This instinct striving
Because its nature is to strive?
. . . .
How know I else such glorious fate my own
But in the restless irresistible force
That works within me? Is it for human will
To institute such impulses? — still less
To disregard their promptings?

The mark of a new order of thought is apparent in this Renaissance hero, as interpreted by the young poet of the early nineteenth century, or of thought that seems new with each fresh reappearance. That assurance which has so pervaded our deeper poetry, especially nature poetry, of human consciousness as directly aware of the divine doubtless owes much to Neo-Platonism. Paracelsus was a student of Neo-Platonism, and some of his sayings reveal the hold of that conception, which, when a man has once grasped it, he is not likely to forget, of nature and the soul of man alike as emanations of very deity. Study of Paracelsus was probably one of the sources of that life-long assurance of Browning that human nature is rooted in the divine. It is to be noted that Browning's Paracelsus uses the favorite figure of Plotinus of the divine as light. In Plotinus, the "imprisoned splendor" flows out from the divine intelligence, and becomes that world-soul of which all souls are part. "The external man is not the real man but the real man is the soul in connection with the Divine Spirit,"[10] said Paracelsus.

So study of Paracelsus not only trained the young poet in art, by giving him something tangible to work upon, but influenced his thought, both in regard to thirst for knowledge, omnivorousness for experience, — for he too would see all, know all; and in a tendency toward mysticism. With the desire to search the uttermost parts of the earth is combined in Paracelsus a desire to search the inmost recesses of his own mind and soul, finding there the surest guide to truth:

> But friends,
> Truth is within ourselves; it takes no rise
> From outward things, whate'er you may believe.
> There is an inmost centre in us all
> Where truth abides in fulness
> . . . .
> and to *know*
> Rather consists in opening out a way
> Whence the imprisoned splendor may escape,
> Than in effecting entry for a light
> Supposed to be without. Watch narrowly
> The demonstration of a truth, its birth,
> And you trace back the effluence to its spring
> And source within us; where broods radiance vast,
> To be elicited ray by ray, as chance
> Shall favor
> . . . .
> Hence, may not truth be lodged alike in all,
> The lowest as the highest?
> . . . .
> Therefore, set free the soul alike in all,
> Discovering the true laws by which the flesh
> Accloys the spirit!

His friends, puzzled alike by Paracelsus the scientist and Paracelsus the mystic, bid him God speed, won to faith in the man if not to comprehension of his idea, holding him in a deeper bond than that of mere understanding:

> I go to prove my soul!
> I see my way as birds their trackless way.
> I shall arrive. What time, what circuit first
> I ask not:
> . . . .
> In some time, his good time, I shall arrive:
> He guides me and the bird. In his good time!

Michal. Vex him no further, Festus; it is so!

The Paracelsus of Scene III, at Basel, fourteen years later, is a man developing through what seems to him defeat, growing, partly through self scorn. The scene is finely and definitely imagined, and the emergence of form from nebula, as apparent in *Pauline*, is best studied here, in a situation similar to that, a moment of review of the past and a confession of failure to find the ultimate truth and to benefit humanity. He sits in the evening with Festus by an open fire, in Basel, where his fame is great:

> Heap logs and let the blaze laugh out!

Past, present, and future, the years behind and the years ahead are gathered into this moment, which brings the turning point in Paracelsus' life and thought, as the friends talk until the gray dawn, with

> the melancholy mind astir
> Within the trees
> . . . .
> The heavy darkness seems
> Diluted, gray and clear without the stars.
> . . . .
> Day, like a mighty river flowing in;
> But clouded, wintry, desolate, and cold.

Here is self-reproach, similar to that in *Pauline*, but here it is motivated, objectified; definite characters emerge, definite action, definite background of a great period. The poet takes you to the heart of the university life of the time; you are made to feel the vibrating intellectual curiosity, manifest in the spectacle of youth crowding about a lecturer, with eagerness to know, rather than with eagerness for a degree. The historical imagination, through which Browning was to reveal many individual lives in many periods, is here wakening in this study of his hero against a Renaissance background. There is fine dramatic irony throughout this scene in which Paracelsus, at the height of his worldly success, confesses his own knowledge of his inner failure to Festus, the loyal friend, whose simple pride in the other's great achievement slowly changes to recognition of the fact that a dark road still lies ahead for him to travel with his friend.

Paracelsus reveals his self-contempt for failing in his great purpose; for his remembered willingness to betray his intellectual insight by resorting to the mediaeval methods he had abjured; the exceeding bitterness of winning the applause of men for that lesser success to which he had not aspired has eaten into his soul. Gaining unbounded power over man, he has lost his hold on God. At the outset he had been sure of God within, in his instinct, his impulse; now he has lost that assurance of vital contact with the divine, and his thought of God has changed from that of a voice speaking within to the traditional conception of a harsh master wielding power from without:

> I know as much of any will of God
> As knows some dumb and tortured brute what Man,
> His stern lord, wills from the perplexing blows
> That plague him every way.

Of that remembered inner assurance he has only an ironic sense:

> God's intimations rather fail
> In clearness than in energy.

God had been, he had believed, in his inner energy, his striving will, his power to achieve; now, his will weakening, he is for the time being a determinist, feeling that he has no part to play in his own destiny:

> I simply know
> I am no master here, but trained and beaten
> Into the path I tread.

He conceives himself as victim:

> You are to understand that we who make
> Sport for the gods are hunted to the end.

Though he has lost his assurance of impulse from God guiding him from within he is dimly aware of forces at work in human life which he cannot understand, for which he can find only a cosmic comparison, his predicament leading to thoughts about himself and about world-progress greater than he can explain. The figure suggests that Browning is putting his hero, like himself, on the track of the law of development in the universe, and the geology of the thirties slips into the mouth of the spokesman of the Renaissance; here, as in other places, the distinctive knowledge of the young poet's period, and that other which he is interpreting, both clash and blend:

> I precede my age:
> . . . .
> Come, I will show you where my merit lies.
> 'Tis in the advance of individual minds
> That the slow crowd should ground their expectation
> Eventually to follow; as the sea
> Waits ages in its bed, till some one wave
> Out of the multitudinous mass, extends
> The empire of the whole, some feet perhaps
> Over the strip of sand which could confine
> Its fellows so long time.

His sense of apartness from human kind has not here the arrogance that it has in Scene I. Growth is apparent in his dawning recognition of the selfishness of his intellectual quest:

> I must know!
> Would God translate me to his throne, believe
> That I would only listen to his word
> To further my own aim!

His passionate self-centeredness has isolated him; his loneliness is three fold; he has lost the feeling of vital contact between God and himself; he stands apart from man; and, an added isolation, the magic circle is broken. He had been one with nature, recognizing the instinct that had led him into his quest as shared by other living creatures: "He guides me and the bird":

> And now the forest-creatures fly from me,
> The grass-banks cool, the sunbeams warm no more.

His scorn of humankind marks the depth of his degradation; he has unmeasured contempt for his predecessors, whose books he has burned, seeing no connection between them and himself, and for those gathered about him. This comes in part from thinking of man as stationary, fixed in his present littleness. A tidal wave of intellect like his own could bring them some little gain, but he has no inkling of a power of development as latent in them. He has lost in himself all feeling of growth, and conceives of those about him as at a standstill in their folly and degradation. For himself he sees no way out; he scoffs at Festus' conviction that there is another world to mend the mischance of this.

But the young poet is wiser than his hero; through all this consciousness of utter loss and failure there is growth in Paracelsus, never a second's pause; Browning is as relentless as nature herself in driving man on. Even the downward path through blunder, mistake, sin, leads eventually upward, and Paracelsus, even in the grosser transgression of the following scene, finds no possibility of escaping ultimately the bonds that bind him in profound oneness to man and to God.

At the end of Scene III one may note a mark of gain in seeming loss, a dawning peception of some wholeness of life and power of which Paracelsus had not been aware. There is a reversal of his degraded thought about humanity in his discovery of factors in human experience which make development possible:

> Love, hope, fear, faith — these make humanity;
>
> . . . .
>
> And these I have lost!

His new insight has other sources, besides his knowledge of his own failure. Throughout the scene he has been dimly aware of what Aprile had told him long ago of his lack of power to love, wisdom imparted to him earlier still and with more dramatic fitness by Festus of his danger of becoming a mortal not knowing what love is, Festus, interpreter both in word and in deed of the deeper sources of love. And the scene is full of Michal, more potent than if she had been with them before that fire, her face still wearing

> that quiet and peculiar light,
> Like the dim circlet floating round a pearl;

Michal, whose carols used to drop

> In flakes through that old leafy bower built under
> The sunny wall of Würzburg;

Michal, who had told him that he would succeed and yet be wretched, discerning an aim beyond his aim.

Though at this crucial point in his mid-career Paracelsus has lost his conviction of the immanence of God; though God is to him, as in Scene II, still only mind, and his self-scorn great that he has not fathomed the mind of God, he is on his way to a deeper idea of God, in part through apprehension of that which is greatest in humanity.

In Scene V the stream that has passed through turbulent rapids finds the sea. It is twenty-nine years since he first started out that the furthest point of Paracelsus' development as recorded by Browning comes, and it comes as he lies on his deathbed, in a hospital cell at Salzburg, with Festus at his side. The scene is clearly defined:

> The lamp burns low, and through the casement bars
> Gray morning glimmers feebly.

Paracelsus is still learning, still developing upon his death bed; even death is, in Browning's thought, no rest, but a strenuous thing, and his hero is full of a sense of fresh adventure:

I am dying, Festus.

. . . .

New being waits me; new perceptions must
Be born in me before I plunge therein;
Which last is Death's affair; and while I speak,
Minute by minute he is filling me
With power; and while my foot is on the threshold
Of boundless life — the doors unopened yet

. . . .

I turn new knowledge upon old events.

Assurance that God is and has been within him is strong again at the end of life, though this assurance is purged of all self-conceit. He knows now, in a rush of certainty,

What whispered in the evening, and spoke out
At midnight;

and, for the sacredness of that voice,

I bid these walls
Be consecrate, this wretched cell become
A shrine, for here God speaks to men through me.

For the conception of the great law of being for which he had been groping all his life comes upon him at the end; he had felt this at moments before he could think it; now he knows in thought that which had been implicit in feeling, and can formulate it, this idea of sharing the life of God in development that is endless. The climax of interest in *Paracelsus* comes in this dying speech of the hero, wherein is revealed the truth that his struggling life-experience had brought him, which fuses all that for which Paracelsus the scientist had searched in his wandering throughout the earth, all that for which Paracelsus the mystic had groped in his own soul, that "inmost centre," "where truth abides in fulness."

Standing, in his scarlet gown lined with fur, his signet ring upon his hand, "last, my good sword," he sets forth in impetuous poetic speech the idea of the unity of all life; of continuity, progression through lower forms up through more and more complex forms of organic life to man; of endless growth and development. "Matter is the visible body of the invisible God,"[11] the historic Paracelsus had said. Here is a vivid sense of God as life, as law throughout the universe, manifest in all physical change, in all spiritual and intellectual change, an idea not unrelated to the seventeenth and eighteenth century conception of the oneness of the universe, of Deity in the whole, but the thought of mechanism has changed to a thought of developing life, and here is the individuality of personal reaction to the conception, life touching life:

> I knew, I felt (perception unexpressed,
> Uncomprehended by our narrow thought,
> But somehow felt and known in every shift
> And change in the spirit — nay, in every pore
> Of the body, even,) — what God is, what we are,
> What life is — how God tastes an infinite joy
> In infinite ways — one everlasting bliss,
> From whom all being emanates, all power
> Proceeds; in whom is life forevermore,
> Yet whom existence in its lowest form
> Includes
> . . . Thus he dwells in all
> From life's minute beginnings, up at last
> To man — the consummation of this scheme
> Of being, the completion of this sphere
> Of life: whose attributes had here and there
> Been scattered o'er the visible world before,
> Asking to be combined, dim fragments meant
> To be united in some wondrous whole,
> Imperfect qualities throughout creation,
> Suggesting some one creature yet to make,
> Some point where all those scattered rays should meet
> Convergent in the faculties of man.

The passage is deeply interpretative of the young Browning, and of the profounder thought of the age in which he lived, an age in which the evolutionary idea, beginning to animate philosophy and science, was about to come into its own. Browning, wakened by it, gave, with insight marvelous in a youth of his years, a personal reaction. The dynamic interpretation of the universe is to Browning more than an intellectual conception; the feeling, full of imaginative perception, which he attributes to Paracelsus, is his own, a feeling of being in the life-process, of sharing the age-long growth. Before the intellectual conception dawned on him, he had known, had felt, in spirit and in body,

What God is, what we are,
What life is — how God tastes an infinite joy
In infinite ways,

this God "from whom all being emanates."

Apprehension comes through his whole being; he is wise enough to suggest that it is the touch of nature life, reaching him through the lyric verse spoken by Festus, that quickens in the dying man the thought of sharing, of being part of all living, and brings the instant's flash of insight into the significance of it all, — life, in the music of the stream through weeds and waving grasses, the quick life all about

Where the shrew-mouse with pale throat
Burrows, and the speckled stoat
Where the quick sandpipers flit
In and out the marl and grit.

Par. My heart! they loose my heart, those simple words;
Its darkness passes, which naught else could touch.

Intuition, emotion, imagination are at work in the young poet as he gathers up the groping thought of his own period and vitalizes it by living experience, giving it such interpretation as none other had given it. The sting and thrill of youth is in his presentation of the organization of all life and its development from lower to higher, presented with an ardor that makes the reader feel the life energy throbbing throughout the universe, and leading to the interpretation of the force therein as spiritual, which is the center and heart of Browning's philosophy, theology, ethics. Nowhere in his work is the peculiar vibrancy, the leap of life into the written line, more apparent than here.

The question as to the source of Browning's philosophy of growth cannot be fully answered. He may have got something of the idea from Paracelsus himself, who held that the world is a unit, vivified (*beseelt*) by an active power, an organization, full of vitality, all its parts related, which, in its life-processes, runs through all stages of existence which we find in the individual.[12]

Finding here the kernel of his idea, and recalling Bruno's conception of the world-soul: "Everywhere is one soul, one spirit of the world, wholly in the whole and in every part of it," and of perpetual change throughout the universe, we cannot accuse Browning of anachronism in putting into the mouth of his Renaissance hero an idea that was tentatively finding its way, as fresh discovery, into the thought of his own time.

"In reality, all that seems *proved* in Darwin's scheme was a conception familiar to me from the beginning: see in *Paracelsus* the progressive development from senseless matter to organized, until man's appearance (Part V). . . . How can one look at Nature as a whole and doubt that, whenever there is a gap, 'a link' must be 'missing' — through the limited power and opportunity of the looker? But go back and back, . . . you find creative intelligence, acting as matter but not resulting from it," said Browning in a letter in later years.[13]

Tentative expression of the theory in the later eighteenth century may have helped him discover the law at work

'Mid this dance
Of plastic circumstance.

The idea of growth through inorganic to organic, of continuity of development, through increasing complexity, of a trend toward perfection in all nature processes, of her tentative efforts all pointing toward the production of man, was presented by J. B. René Robinet, in works published in the sixties of the eighteenth century: "Robinet thus laid the foundation of that view of the world as wholly vital, and as a progressive unfolding of a spiritual formative principle," writes Peter Chalmers Mitchell, in the *Encyclopaedia Britannica.*

A possible, rather, a probable source might be suggested in Herder's *Philosophy of History*, admirably translated into English by T. Churchill in 1800. Browning's part-German ancestry may account for his affinity with aspects of German idealistic thought, notably that of Hegel. The likeness of parts of Paracelsus' last speech to passages in Herder, the conception of the singleness of the one life, unfolding itself in all the "inconceivable variety" of nature, and in the moral and mental development of man, as well as Browning's lifelong affirmation of certain ethical and spiritual ideas found in Herder, may well make one believe, even if one cannot prove, that the young poet derived much from the *Philosophy of the History of Man.* This, from beginning to end, expounds the working of "organically operating omnipotence," whose "indwelling powers" are revealed alike "in the lowest order of creatures" and in the whole development of man. The exultation with which Herder sets forth the urge of the one life through all the progressive complexity of being, in its ascending series through the inorganic into the organic world, plant, animal, "till finally, to crown the organization of our Earth, man, the *microcosm* arose," finds its counterpart in Browning. "He, the son of all the elements and beings, their choicest summary and the flower of the creation" is more briefly expressed in Browning's

> Up at last
> To man — the consummation of this scheme
> Of being.

Herder's "We are . . . a summary of almost every species of organization on the earth"; his discussion of the ways in which man partakes of the nature of plant, of animal: "There exists no virtue, no propensity in the human heart which has not somewhere in the animal world its similitude," seems to find an echo in Browning's

> Whose attributes had here and there
> Been scattered o'er the visible world before,
> Asking to be combined, dim fragments meant
> To be united in some wondrous whole,

and in

> Hints and previsions of which faculties,
> Are strewn confusedly everywhere about
> The inferior natures, and all lead up higher.

Many and various are the suggestions in Herder summed up in Browning's "All tended to mankind."

"All the changes we observe in the inferior regions of nature are tendencies to perfection;" to Herder, as to Browning, the law holds good in the higher realms of experience:

"Now if we look back, and observe how everything behind us seems to travel onward to the human form; and again, that we find in man only the first bud and sketch of what he should be, and to which he is evidently framed, either man must proceed forwards in whatever way or manner it may be, or all connexion and design in nature is but a dream."

In Herder's philosophy, within each order of being lies the seed of its own fulfilment, spiritual as well as physical in the case of man, and "*Man is formed for the Hope of Immortal-*

ity." "No power can perish. . . . We have no instance of it in nature. . . . It is a contradiction . . . that a living, acting somewhat, in which the creator himself is present, in which, by energies divine he manifests his residence should be converted into nothing. . . . What the all-vivifying calls into life, lives; whatever acts, acts eternally in his eternal whole."

Of man he says: "Thus much is certain, that there dwells an infinity in each of his powers which cannot be developed here," for the conviction of the logic of the law of continuity manifest in earthly life necessitating belief in immortal life rules Herder's mind, as from first to last, it did Browning's in his interpretation of the experience of man,

> The heir of hopes too fair to turn out false.

Faith in the trial and error method is Herder's also; it was always a part of Browning's philosophy of life:

"He [man] is taught to go only by means of falls, and frequently attains truth only through the help of errour." He believes that evil is not enduring; man has power to retrieve his mistakes, and may learn good from evil: "Thus, conformably to an unalterable law of nature, the evil itself produced some good." "God himself could not divest man of the capability of errour; but he implanted this in the nature of human mistakes, that soon or late they should show themselves to be such, and become evident to the calculating creature."

"All the errours of man are mists of truth," said Herder; Browning held a similar belief.

The final speech of Paracelsus shows Browning coming into his own intellectually; here and henceforth his whole interpretation of life centered in the idea of growth, progressive change, the dynamic operation of inner law. It is significant that Paracelsus acknowledges as one of his chief shortcomings that he had seen in the past only failure, a long record of disgrace, instead of discovering the divine continuity of life. He had failed to grasp the secret of the incomplete in man, and the promise of growth that lies therein. Here Browning purged himself of that aspect of Shelley's thought which had been inspired by William Godwin, and shows himself growing wiser than his master, passing with his age from belief in revolution to an understanding of the slow process of evolution:

> I saw no use in the past: only a scene
> Of degradation, ugliness and tears,
> The record of disgraces best forgotten,
> A sullen page in human chronicles
> Fit to erase. I saw no cause why man
> Should not stand all-sufficient even now.
> . . . .
> I would have had one day, one moment's space
> Change man's condition, push each slumbering claim
> Of mastery o'er the elemental world
> At once to full maturity, then roll
> Oblivion o'er the work, and hide from man
> What night had ushered morn. Not so, dear child
> Of after-days, wilt thou reject the past
> Big with deep warnings of the proper tenure
> By which thou hast the earth: for thee the present
> Shall have distinct and trembling beauty, seen
> Beside the past's own shade when, in relief,
> Its brightness shall stand out.

In a way, Paracelsus' whole experience is a learning of evolution. As he starts on his career he prays for sudden change for all, the democratic impulse of the revolutionary period intruding through the youthful poet's mind into his impetuous speech:

> Make no more giants, God,
> But elevate the race at once! We ask
> To put forth just our strength, our human strength,
> All starting fairly, all equipped alike,
> Gifted alike,

an odd sentiment to put into the mouth of a personage of

the Renaissance, with its individualism, its egoism, its faith in supermen. Paracelsus had burned the books of his predecessors as worthless; now he begins to understand that only an apprehension of the close linking of past and present holds hope for the future.

Shelley, for all the changeful iridescence of *Prometheus*, and that suggestion of ceaseless atomic activity that is present in many of his nature passages, does not grasp the deep secret at the heart of change, law. His thought of change is comprised in the cycle, the year cycle, as in the *Ode to the West Wind*; the cycle of racial life, accomplishment, as in *Hellas*; he moves in a circle, his forward-looking thought of the future curving back to the dream of the long-past Golden Age. Browning, sharing the growth of a new period, finds the spiral.

That impatience for immediate perfection, characteristic of Shelley, Browning is outgrowing, as he makes his hero, Paracelsus, waken out of past mistakes to new wisdom, in a realization of the slowness of human growth:

> I saw no cause why man
> Should not stand all-sufficient even now.
> . . . .
> Nor yet on thee
> Shall burst the future, as successive zones
> Of several wonder open on some spirit
> Flying secure and glad from heaven to heaven:
> But thou shalt painfully attain to joy,
> While hope and fear and love shall keep thee man!
> All this was hid from me.

Browning's ethical convictions, the outcome of his evolutionary philosophy, of his idea of the life of the soul as spiritual development, mark a parting of the ways between him and Shelley, though some aspects of that influence lingered on to later years. Already in *Pauline*, more clearly in *Paracelsus* he presents life as inner struggle, his interpretation based upon a conviction of personal responsibility. From the first, evil is not to him merely an outward thing, embodied in institutions, but it exists within, to be overcome by the individual, for Browning, like Wordsworth, takes his stand upon the individual soul, and, like him, has faith in the divine which is inherent therein. From *Pauline* to *Asolando* Browning presents life as spiritual struggle, and in all this interpretation, evil is conceived as, ultimately, a means of good. As in Herder's *Philosophy*: "Thus, conformably to an unalterable law of nature, the evil itself produced some good," there is a final good in all evil.

An important difference is apparent between Browning's optimism and that of the Spinoza-inspired eighteenth century Deists, Shaftesbury and his followers, Pope, Henry Brooke, John Gilbert Cooper, Mark Akenside, and others, who affirmed the existence of beauty and harmony throughout the universe, which was of such vastness that evil was so trifling as to be negligible. Between their day and Browning's had come a tentative conception of evolution, revealing difficulty as a means of growth; Browning believes not that everything now is in a static condition of well-arranged perfectness, but that man has a fighting chance of perfectness, for of struggle, of possibilities of development there is no end. Shaftesbury, indeed, though affirming the static perfection of the outer universe, was aware of the need of growth and the possibilities of growth of the soul of man, and surely an echo of the faith which he defended with such courageous urbanity sounds in Browning's

> They grow too great
> For narrow creeds of right and wrong, which fade
> Before the unmeasured thirst for good.

The end of *Alastor*, as compared with the end of *Pauline*, shows another significant difference between the youthful Browning and the poet whom he delighted to honor. The hero in *Alastor* goes out utterly: "Now thou art not"; the hero of *Pauline* moves on "To where I clearlier see and better love." Insistence on immortality is still stronger in *Paracelsus* than in *Pauline*; the logic of the idea of continuity leads Paracelsus-Browning, as it had led Herder and, after him, Goethe, to belief in the continuance of life after death:

> If this be all — . . .
> And other life await us not — for one,
> I say, 'tis a poor cheat, a stupid bungle,
> A wretched failure.

Man,

> The heir of hopes too fair to turn out false,

("there dwells an infinity in each of his powers which cannot be developed here," Herder had said) must await that continuing of existence to which its beginning entitles him. The hope inherent in the unfinished is everywhere in the physical world; all evolution implies it; Browning finds it in the spiritual. Paracelsus affirms:

> If I stoop
> Into a dark tremendous sea of cloud,
> It is but for a time; I press God's lamp
> Close to my breast; its splendor, soon or late,
> Will pierce the gloom.

To Paracelsus, who, in Scene III, had scoffed at the idea of immortality, had come, at the moment of his deepest degradation in the following scene, with the knowledge of Michal's death, through the thrust of experience into mere opinion, belief in the continuing life of the soul:

> Know, then, you did not ill to trust your love
> To the cold earth: I have thought much of it:
> For I believe we do not wholly die.

Far more deep as is the belief of Browning that life is spiritual struggle, that evil may come within to be fought and overcome, than is Shelley's, one aspect of his ethical theory owes much to Shelley, the social aspect: man's life is that of his fellows:

> Progress is
> The law of life, man is not man as yet.
> Nor shall I deem his object served, his end
> Attained, his genuine strength put fairly forth,
> While only here and there a star dispels
> The darkness, here and there a towering mind
> O'erlooks its prostrate fellows:
> . . . .
> When all mankind alike is perfected,
> Equal in full-blown powers — then, not till then,
> I say, begins man's general infancy.

Here, surely, is suggested something of the unity of all life, a perception of oneness in the affairs of men: Browning was heir to the gathering feeling of responsibility of man for man, shown in the Shaftesburian idea of virtue as social, in the philanthropies of the eighteenth century, and flowering in utmost beauty in the mind of Shelley. Yet the whole basis of Browning's faith was different from that of Shelley, to whom "progress" was not "the law of life." The significance, in a poem whose deeper import is spiritual evolution, of a need of faith in the power of humanity to develop, needs no comment.

The idea of the organic nature of all life is not presented as mere theory, but is worked out in experience; it took Paracelsus all his life to learn it, and he learned it by means of his own failure. Browning's idea, never lost throughout his lifetime, of attainment through failure, is here more boldly and firmly presented than in *Pauline*: "I am glad, most glad that thus I fail!" Paracelsus, who had failed in part through pride, through lack of recognition of the bond between himself and his fellows, willing to help them but unwilling to be one of them, finds saving humility at the end:

I give the fight up: let there be an end,
A privacy, an obscure nook for me.
I want to be forgotten even by God.
But if that cannot be, dear Festus, lay me,
When I shall die, within some narrow grave,
Not by itself — for that would be too proud —
But where such graves are thickest; let it look
Nowise distinguished from the hillocks round,
So that the peasant at his brother's bed
May tread upon my own and know it not.

The loneliness, the isolation of genius, the fierce individualism of his youth is well set off against the feeling of oneness to which he wins at the end, when he casts in his lot with man and with God. Pride at the outset has given way to humility that reflects a new consciousness of sharing; out of the scorn of human kind, marking the depth of his degradation, has grown knowledge that life unshared is not life. Paracelsus realizes that, fundamentally, his failure had been failure to love humanity:

In my own heart love had not been made wise
To trace love's faint beginnings in mankind,
To know even hate is but a mask of love's
To see a good in evil, and a hope
In ill-success.

There is deep significance in the fact that the burden of failure in *Pauline*, and, to a large extent, in *Paracelsus*, is inability to love. There it is the pained outcry: "And I can love nothing"; here it represents the profoundest phase of that experience wherein, through failure, he finds at last the way:

Love's undoing
Taught me the worth of love in man's estate,
And what proportion love should hold with power.

He has come to recognize love as humanity's best, God's best. In following the development of Paracelsus one follows the development of his thought of God, known at first only in his own intellectual cravings, conceived as mind alone:

> God! Thou art mind! Unto the master-mind
> Mind should be precious. Spare my mind alone!

he had cried, when he feared his own downfall. Many and complex elements enter into his new-found faith; his own failure, the consciousness of his own lack, his awareness of what was the motive power in the highest types of humanity he knew have brought him a greater thought of God. It was through the mystical tendency, keeping him alert to watch the forces working in the human soul, that he has learned to trace love's faint beginnings even in the lesser men whom he had once despised, to recognize God in the deep love and loyalty of his friends. The wisdom of their words, but more than their thoughts and their words their love for him had taught him: Festus, drawing near to Paracelsus in his degradation, loyal to the end, growing greater to the last under the glory and the shame of Paracelsus; Michal, whose love had been penetrating enough to see that what he had at first sought was to be to his deeper self failure. His feeling for Festus, his remembered feeling for Michal, and theirs for him, are part of the insight which he attains at the end.

The last words of Paracelsus, the climax of his message, bring an expression of his belief that the force at the heart of all the process and change throughout the universe is fundamentally love:

> Love still too straitened in his present means,
> And earnest for new power to set love free.

That power whose working he had followed in scientific quest throughout the earth is revealed to him more deeply through the promise that he finds in human life, the "tendency to God," and through his inner consciousness of the stirring of divine possibilities in himself. Clearer insight, won from experience, confirms his early belief that the instinct, the impulses striving within, were from God; an immediate consciousness of the divine supplements and completes knowledge gained from the quest; "truth is within ourselves" as well as without.

Thus early is announced a confession of faith, which, through study of the work of Browning's many years, we know he made his own. Evidently, during the period of his work on *Paracelsus*, he reached a great intellectual and spiritual conception, in the light of which he afterward interpreted many lives of human beings. He believed that the power through which growth comes is love, the supreme dynamic force in a universe which is all action, life moving toward great ends; a new statement in a new age, of "God is love"; a reaffirmation of Dante's "Love which moves the sun and other stars." Paracelsus the scientist and Paracelsus the mystic are both present in the poet's lifelong aim to bear witness that love and power are one. Rabbi Ben Ezra speaks for him midway down the years:

> I who saw Power now see Love perfect too.

In his last utterance of opinion, in *Reverie*, published just before his death, we find:

> From the first, Power was — I knew.
> Life has made clear to me
> That, strive but for closer view,
> Love were as plain to see.

After his own long years of experience, and his long years of study of human life, this is his conclusion: Creative love at the heart of the individual is the supreme power in human life; creative love at the heart of God is the supreme secret of the universe.

IV. Pippa Passes (1841)

After the suffering and pain of *Pauline* and *Paracelsus*, the knowledge that has come out of self-study and study of the experience of another, Browning can afford to play happily with the idea of the oneness of all life, and its irresistible development as it "verges to some goal" in all the variety of human experience. He plays happily indeed with the idea, but not superficially; there is profundity here, for all the lightness of touch.

Never, perhaps, did philosophic idea find more appealing form than in *Pippa Passes*, arresting in its concreteness of presentation, true poetic creativeness showing here in definiteness of characterization and of action. The young poet has learned the lesson of the artist; limiting his subject, after the vast scope of *Paracelsus*, he can shape more completely. Nothing that he ever did in his long life of creative activity is more distinct in line, more fully created than parts of *Pippa*.

The idea of the whole, made clear dramatically, not in abstract statement, of the interrelatedness of all lives, the unconscious influence of life on life, flashed upon Browning, as he tells us, as he walked in Dulwich wood, which stretched over the level ground beyond Denmark Hill, at whose foot Camberwell stood. Through the slight thread of Pippa's song, four different groups of people, wholly unconnected in any space and time relationship, are woven into the one spiritual fabric, life; and in each case, quite unknown to the singer, a decisive change of eternal significance is wrought by the unseen contact. Each scene is the climax scene of a possible tragedy, the turning point of the action: "I have lived all life when it is most alive," said Browning in his youth. The words of the song in each case inspire a decisive choice on which hangs the future destiny of the personages involved.

The difference of the four scenes is as marked as their apparent unrelatedness. The few years that have passed since the writing of *Paracelsus* have brought the poet, through thought and through observation, knowledge of the variety of human experience; the many shades and grades of depth; the incalculable diversity of ways in which human growth is carried on. Here is not only the idea of the organic unity of all lives; here too is the idea of spiritual development, set forth in unique fashion.

In the first scene, wherein dramatic power akin to that of Webster, is oddly linked with a modern type of idealistic thought, is presented passion and its possibilities. Out of seeming evil, a sensual and debasing love, Ottima wakens to creative love which transfigures and redeems.

In the second, the coldly intellectual and artistic Jules, barred from human sympathy and relationship by static canons of supposedly definitive taste, is brought into close contact with human kind and into greater potentiality as an artist, by the wakening in him of love which is pure creative power.

In the third, the young hero, through love of country, mistaking the right way to serve her, sins, but in so doing follows a higher impulse than the selfishness that might have restrained him.

In the fourth and last is the wakening, through temptation, of the pure love of God in an ecclesiastic who had overmuch loved his tradition of family and of Church.

Browning's ethic is presented here through suggestion rather than through affirmation; nowhere else in his work does the conviction of the evanescence of evil, of evil as a means of good, find more convincing expression than in the first scene and the last. It is most apparent in the Sebald and Ottima scene, but it is in every one of the episodes; it is the means by which the soul, tempted, achieves something of the good. From the vague self-centered sense of frustration in *Pauline* the young poet has escaped into a conviction of a divine law operative throughout the whole, a conviction of living truth, and he is beginning to trace its working in manifold aspects of human experience.

Something significant in his thought is shown in the rapidity with which, in each case, deeper life comes. In the swift intensity of experience there is development, yet, so quick it is, the starting point seems goal. Here is no need of insisting, as in *Pauline* and *Paracelsus*, on the unsatisfactoriness of this life, the need of continuation in immortality; here, happily, the instant's flash of experience brings the values of eternity into an instant of time, lifts it out of the time world into a world of eternal values. The poet's mind, groping more deeply, is finding something that is ever after present in his work, an idea inherent in Platonism, of eternity not as an extension of time, but an ever-present value, an intensity.

The lyric in the first scene of *Pippa*, justly famous, reflects the flash of happiness that came with each recurrence of the idea found, after long struggling and suffering, by Paracelsus, who felt joy in dying in the moment of grasping great truth:

> God's in his heaven —
> All's right with the world!

This flake of song expresses that which Deist optimism had attempted to affirm in regard to a perfect God, revealed through perfect nature, and expresses far more, for the Deist world was a world of mechanism, and this is a world of life. Browning's God-ordered universe is alive with God.

There is a haunting charm in *Pippa Passes*; it touches, with its poetic concreteness, minds not philosophic with philosophic ideas, which are not, perhaps, recognized as such. Its happy picturesqueness of expression caught and held popular attention. The great ideas, foreshadowed in *Pauline*, fully stated in *Paracelsus*, of the organic nature of all life, of a law of spiritual development, of the evanescent nature of evil, of the movement onward of all life toward good, are flashed out from a different angle in *Pippa*; that which is expressed in the thought of Paracelsus is here lyrically and dramatically made manifest in actual experience. Not again after *Paracelsus* does Browning explicitly state all his articles of faith, though he comes near it in *Saul*, *Rabbi Ben Ezra*, and *Reverie*, but throughout his work, in lyric, monologue, or formal drama, the meanings flashed out from this or that aspect of experience are related to this central core of young conviction that never grew old. Browning's articles of faith are closely knit into one living body of belief; he has a swift, winged way of mentioning one aspect that somehow implies them all.

The unique form of *Pippa Passes* is shaped by the idea of the organic oneness of human lives; Browning does not affirm the unity of the whole; he shows it by presenting subtly, dramatically, the "organic filaments" binding the souls of men together. And the bond between human souls is an active bond, a life, nothing imposed from without. Here is unity, not of mere event or happening, not derived from the framework of a single plot; it draws on the deep unity at the heart of things, the very variety of the experiences enhancing this depth of the bond. Through the wide diversity of apparently unconnected, scattered lives the life of the one spirit is fulfilling itself in multiform individual experiences.

IV

Browning's reluctance to acknowledge *Pauline* shows how little he saw himself in perspective against the background of the age, how little he realized the significance of his youthful experience in a transition moment. *Pauline* has, for the most part, been discussed as if it concerned Browning and his development alone. It is far more significant than that; symptomatic, great currents of deeper life were stirring in that all-receptive young heart and brain.

It was a transition period. The Georgian era had been an age of ardent vision, of vast hopes too great to realize. Wordsworth, disillusioned in regard to political and social organization, took refuge in the inner world, in the individual lives of good men, retreating more and more from the harsh actual conditions of life:

By the soul
Only, the Nations shall be great and free.

It is true that he advocated public education, but he had sadly little faith in the power of government to better conditions, and, like Coleridge, opposed measures, as in the case of the Reform Bill, whereby certain contemporaries were trying to make a dream of good for the human race become actual.

Shelley, vehement and potent in his protests against wrong, had no constructive programme, but took flight to the "intense inane," placing his martyred Prometheus in a dream cave, apart from the realities of life, entwining "buds and flowers and beams." "The World's Great Age Begins Anew" in some region of ether, far removed from the world, a region where human beings and their problems do not exist.

Keats grasped the idea of growth, evolution, and can see it working in the world of the gods, but the world of men presents a harder problem. Perhaps Apollo's tears, in *Hyperion* are due to a feeling of inability to cope with the facts, to bring "Misery and Heartbreak, Pain, Sickness, and oppression," into the world of beauty. But Keats knew, as both his letters and his verse show, that this is man's task on earth.

Then came Browning, in the dawn of a period wrestling with the difficulty of making the ideal come true in the world of fact; grappling with existent evils; working out reforms, a world of ideals striving to become actual. If *Pauline*, as Mr.

Herford says, represents "a soul compelled by quick and eager senses and vivid intelligence to recognize a host of outer realities, not itself, which it constantly strives to bring into relation with itself, as constantly baffled and thrown back by the obstinate objectivity of that outer world," it might well stand as a symbol of the attempt of the age to emerge from the world of divine dream, to wrestle with facts, to convert dream into practical reality. *Pauline* ends in failure, but failure that has within it the seed of triumph. The birth of the Victorian Era, the attempt to combine the dream, the ideal, with the hard facts, was a difficult birth; probably no other decade can show as many or as varied efforts of reform as those of the early thirties in England; no other period can show literature lending itself as generously to the uses of life as the rest of this century in England,—as the names of Carlyle, Ruskin, Dickens, Thackeray, Mrs. Browning, and others can testify.

If *Pauline* is a symbol of transition into the Victorian out of the Revolutionary Era, *Paracelsus* might well serve as a symbol of the Victorian Era itself, of the soul of young Browning and his time, both passing from the world of inner dream to the world of *Men and Women* and human deeds, carrying the energy and the imaginative vision of romanticism into a period of wrestling with fact. A youth, idealist to the core, too vigorous in mind, emotion, imagination, to tolerate any interpretation of life apart from its realities, he shows the influence of a scientific age, with its energetic grappling with observable fact, upon a mind intensely conscious of the facts of the inner life. His very temperament, tingling with vitality, physical, intellectual, spiritual, helped him in becoming, in a field all his own, interpreter of the dynamic tendencies beginning to reveal themselves in scientific and in philosophic thought. We find him in *Pauline* groping for, in *Paracelsus* reaching that faith which he was to uphold through great length of years, of the movement of all being from lower to higher phases of existence in perpetual change in which is operating divine law:

> Change, the strongest son of life,
> Here the spirit has to wife,

wrote his successor, Meredith.

The passion to know the whole slips into the passion to compass the boundless concrete variety of the whole. Browning did not register his disappointment in failing in his first aim, to grasp the infinite, by falling back for a time as did his Paracelsus, as did Faust, on sensual enjoyment, but in his youth found a healthier outcome for his energy in study of the inexhaustible variety which constitutes the whole, finding the infinite revealed in the life action of individual souls. The conception voiced by Paracelsus of the organization and upward progress of all life, through the law of growth, wherein all the changes are "tendencies to perfection," is carried out in Browning's study and creation of a long line of characters, living, developing. Recognition of the law at work in the initial stages has given him the key to the higher stages of development in man:

> All tended to mankind
> But in completed man begins anew
> A tendency to God.

In all his interpretation of human lives he is carrying further the idea of God in all creation, striving in ways yet unfulfilled to make his purposes perfect through struggling and failing human love and human endeavor. It was the idea of the possibilities of development that enabled him to face undaunted the hardest facts of life, gave him his robust faith, — the hope that lies at the heart of change. His was an energetic grappling through his long creative life with the ideal making good in the real; "This world has not escaped me, thank God," he said.

So Browning turned from the turmoil of his own inner consciousness and busied himself, through his many decades, with the attempt to fathom, in the boundless interplay of individuality, the working of the one spirit, in and through all. In all his poetic work, though he may be giving but a moment, a flash of experience, — and there are no moments in Browning without their eternal significance, — is that central conception of the One, revealing himself in the many, the infinite in the finite:

> The One in varied forms of unity expressed.

There is a philosophic poet in *Paracelsus* who never quite reached maturity. Doubtless it was well that Browning's genius was devoted to the interpretation of the growth of many individuals in many epochs, working in the concrete, as a poet should. In no other way could he have pursued so far his study of nature's purpose, revealed so fully his belief in God's purpose, in carrying development of individuality to the highest point. A poet must work in the actual stuff of personal human experience; a philosophic poet who presents his ideas in abstract terms is soon left behind and forgotten. The Deist poets of the eighteenth century may well have served as a warning of the danger of putting the purely abstract into verse. If the reader at times longs to find again in Browning the breadth, the scope, the energy of the speech of Paracelsus, the only place in which the poet presented his conception fully in theory, it must be remembered that he set for himself a harder task than he undertakes who studies only physical forces, investigating volcanic action and the rise and fall of mountain chains, or who studies man in the abstract. He was thenceforth studying man's inner life, trying to follow the working of the law of the universe in specific cases, carrying out the purpose of Paracelsus to interpret

> God's intercourse with the human mind,

the individual human mind.

He faced a more difficult problem than that of the Deist optimists, his predecessors. That sweep of pure idea, their affirmation of good apparent throughout the universe they found easier if they ignored man. The mark of development of human thought in the intervening years, of turning to the inner life is apparent here, for the rightness of the universe is worked out not primarily in the outer whole, but in the soul of man. It is indeed less difficult to follow the conception of God as love, seen in the perfect working of the visible universe, than to grasp the movement of the good in the life-experiences of many human beings, often, apparently, on the downward path. The task from which they shrank, of showing the great law of good operative in sinful man, he undertook, and fulfilled, and he did it by revealing the truth that the universe, with those who dwell therein, is not, as they had affirmed, perfected, ended. Deist assurance rested on the word "finished"; Browning's on the word "unfinished." His was not a God who had completed a flawless work, but a God still working, sharing the struggle of man in the making; to him there was no feeling, joy, passion, aspiration, no activity of life but is a part of God. And, through the saving grace of development, nothing is final; there are no end-stopped lives in Browning.

Browning was to shrink from recognition of no degradation, no sin, sure that the law of development, which is a law of good, is operative in all experience. If he inherited from Wordsworth some part of his idea of the divine working in human experience, in the impulses and the fidelities of the human heart, he kept the faith, and greatly extended the range of observation. More catholic than Wordsworth, he searched the highways and byways of human life and history, tracing the good in which his faith was fixed, becoming more and more exploratory and daring, facing with more and more defiance the problem of evil, challenging life to show him an individual consciousness in which there was not some trace of good to be found. The core of conviction to which he held in confronting stubborn fact, the faith to which he clung through all his piercing vision into sin and failure and unachieved life, is that there is no despair in a world of unceasing growth. From the first, life was to Browning spiritual striving, and he held to the end the belief that evil, necessitating that inner struggle that makes man man is, ultimately, a means of good, that Spinoza-Shaftesbury conviction of the temporary character of evil:

> All which errs
> Is but a dream which death will dissipate.

The fibre of his creed strengthened with the years from this utterance of the hero of Pauline to that of Rabbi Ben Ezra:

> Then, welcome each rebuff
> That turns earth's smoothness rough,
> Each sting that bids nor sit nor stand but go!
> Be our joys three-parts pain!
> Strive, and hold cheap the strain;
> Learn, nor account the pang; dare, never grudge the throe!

The assurance of the power manifest in the working of the universe, and in the world of the inner life, as fundamentally love; of man, on the way to God, guided by God within, with irresistible conviction of the final good, is the basis of Browning's optimism. It was a militant idealism,—faith in the illimitable possibilities of human souls, because of God within. Up and down earth's highways and byways he went, proclaiming, in the evil and in the good, the conquering divine in human experience, a strain, compelling, triumphant, as irresistible as bagpipes speeding the Black Watch in march whose every step is victory. Defeat is unthinkable to those who step to such music. One wonders if one reason for Matthew Arnold's lesser hope is not suggested in his phrase: "The enduring power, not ourselves, that makes for righteousness." — (Did he not realize that, in saying this, he was

Hebraizing, not Hellenizing?) In missing the idea that it is, in part, ourselves, he missed the deeper thought of his own period, which had its roots in his loved Greek world.

Of the best at the heart of this era Browning was the best interpreter. The new interpretation of life was an interpretation in terms of life, and Browning had a more vivid perception than have other men of the very principle of life itself. It was his own radiant vitality of mind, body, spirit that lent zest to his revelation, in *Paracelsus*, of the inner life of the universe, that gave him the power, in his manifold renderings of individual experiences, of touching the inner spring of vitality. In the case of poet, painter, musician he reveals the creative impulse, that secret inner energy from which art springs, aware less of the art product than of the living force within; in the case of a question of right or wrong, he goes back of the deed to the inner impulse. That which man would be, would do is the burden of his message:

> What I aspired to be
> And was not, comforts me:
> A brute I might have been, but would
> not sink i' the scale.

Browning's conviction of the success of failure, the promise of the incomplete, expressed in *Paracelsus* makes the poem in another aspect seem a fitting symbol of the Victorian Era. He who grasps the idea of evolution knows that growth is slow. The early twentieth century, with its tragic lack of vision, has failed to see the real nature of the Victorian effort at its best, to make the ideal come true in the real, and has dubbed it hypocrisy. At its best it was very great. The vision of the whole; the sting and stimulus of the thought of unceasing growth were working in minds perhaps hardly aware of the evolutionary idea as formulated thought, which Browning, with his whole being set to its rhythm, had accepted with exultation; which Tennyson was conscientiously rationalizing in finished rhyme; which Herbert Spencer was applying to all aspects of man's temporal existence. To poets and other interpreters the promise of endless spiritual growth seemed to follow logically the knowledge of age-long physical development. A feeling of power was abroad, of ability to compass the whole; mind, imagination, spirit leaped too swiftly to the goal. But "Behold I dream a dream of good" is not hypocrisy, nor is striving for the greatest and failing; those who point out as such the difference between dream and accomplishment make a mistake. Aspiration is not necessarily sham. Man can see farther than he can walk on a winter's day, and a glimpse of the horizon does no man harm. It is true that the thinkers of the period believed the race to be going forward more swiftly in moral and spiritual progress than was the case, but they held a conviction of continuity, of a logic of movement in the flux of human life, which no man has disproved, and which the twentieth century does ill to forget. Even if that period, like the life of Paracelsus, ended in seeming defeat, where "the graves lie thickest" in the fields of Flanders and of France, after the Great War, the belief in success through failure is a greater faith than most men hold to-day.

Browning's dynamic interpretation of life is a doctrine of becoming; character is for him always character coming to be; each person is passing from a lower to a higher phase of experience, perhaps from a higher to a lower that will eventually lead higher; man, in Browning's thought, cannot escape the law of his being. Life, in whatever phase or form, here or hereafter, is for him growth; he cannot conceive in other terms. There is no lingering in any emotion in Browning, no static emotion, no static idea in the mind of author or of character. Throughout all his work, in whatever form, there is the urge of progress, of process, thought and emotion serving their purpose in growth. He has such feeling for this idea of development as could come only from one familiar in his youth with the idea of evolution, physical as well as spiritual. Observing, his mind grew quick to catch the significance of a word, a look, a gesture; he is swift to interpret life caught in the act, that activity of being and doing that reveals character in the making. This dynamic interpretation of life dominates his imagination, colors all his thought; he sees, feels, imagines in terms of development. In all that life-long interpretation of individual experience this is not a mere idea that he is thinking about and trying to apply. It is his inmost self; in the consciousness of it he lives and breathes and has his being. It is the medium through which he sees, like light.

Browning's characteristic way of thinking sought and found its own characteristic form of expression. The steps through which he reached the form of art best fitted to express his basic way of apprehending life, the dramatic monologue, lead from the uncentered outpouring of *Pauline*, where the speaker makes a not wholly successful attempt to interpret to a shadowy listener his inner consciousness, through *Paracelsus*, which reveals a great advance in artistic skill in its graphic representation of that growth, by means of the interaction of inner and outer forces, of the wandering medical student into a seer; through *Pippa Passes*, where the living bond between human souls, later to be more subtly implied, is dramatically presented, and the swift development, in the successive scenes, of the central character, shows Browning far on the way to the fulfilment of his peculiar power to present growth of infinite significance in an instant of time, "eternity in an hour."

The long speech of Paracelsus, giving his whole spiritual history up to his discovery of the law of the universe, is a foreshadowing of the dramatic monologue, that distinctive form of Robert Browning's art, whereby, dealing with many individuals in many periods, he makes you aware in each of the inmost core of individuality, in process of growth; of the binding filaments, the interrelations with other personalities, other lives, in the dynamic adventure, life; of the interplay of character and environment, the organic relationship between man and his period, and the land in which he lives; of the infinite reach of his finite experience.

There is intense centeredness in the form, giving but a point in time and space, and an outflow from the center of personality, with its vast reach. No better form has yet been found for the interpretation of the inner world, the infinite in the finite, for revealing an instant's flash of experience that has an eternity of result. In Browning's hands the dramatic monologue is an outcome, and, in one way, a culmination of that long *inwarding* process of thought and perception down the eighteenth century, the growing interest in the inner life. It is one of the most fortunate means of expression of the change that has taken place in the focusing of attention also on the inner, not wholly on the outer working of that power which, Deist thought had affirmed,

> Dwell(s) immense within the minim shrine.

The flexibility of the form gives it great possibilities of adaptation to the artist's idea of many and varied types of individuality. At its best it is a form, sensitive, fresh, and living, shaped from within by the urge of an individual consciousness, imaginatively conceived. Browning's use of it is the outcome of his whole manner of thought, deriving from the idea he had affirmed in his youth, of man as the summit and crown of evolutionary process, — nature, or God in nature forever pressing on to the utmost development of individuality; the greater the individuality, difference, the fuller the revelation of God therein.

This living form, which pulsates with the heart beats of the individual, caught something of the rhythm of the deeper thought of the time which was the breath of Robert Browning's being. Through it he expresses his faith that the individual life moves with the life-movement of the universe; in following the underlying law of his thought in interpreting the many we find an exemplification of the idea suggested by Shaftesbury of the law of harmony in the universe shaping genius from within to fine issues in the world of art. The centered monologue or soliloquy, the self-revelation of an imagined character, is not new in dramatic literature, but here, with the same centeredness, is a new and different way of interpreting the individual and the universe, sharing a common life, one vibrating in the other. So Browning found the form best fitted to serve the need of his spirit, his peculiar insight, his special message of the sweep of the life of the universe through the individual soul, man, in his space and time relations, *sub specie aeternitatis.*

VIII

BROWNING AND MR. SANTAYANA

I

SOMETIMES a misrepresentation of a poet may be, to a mature thinker, as useful as a truer interpretation of him, throwing his salient qualities into strong relief. The discussion of Browning as a poet of barbarism by Mr. Santayana is an old one; it is, perhaps, unnecessary to recall it, except for the fact that it probably keeps many a young reader from understanding a poet who has much to offer youth in the welter of modern life. Whatever his sins as an artist, and they were many and unashamed, Browning was, and is, very great as an interpreter of life, and often very great, in a unique way, as an artist. Mr. Santayana may say what he will, from the pseudo-classic standpoint, about barbarism in form, though he misses the rare perfection of many parts of Browning's work, and the secret of its art, but Browning as a thinker was no barbarian; there is nothing primitive about his mental processes. He was an outstanding thinker of a wise, sophisticated, modern age, bringing piercing individual insight to bear upon the deeper thought of an epoch eager, original, swiftly advancing in knowledge, a great creative period. Browning's ethical idealism, based on thought, upon study of his fellows, upon experience, gives an interpretation of life that is not to be ignored.

Mr. Santayana's criticism of Browning's philosophy of life centers in disapproval of the poet's conviction of the infinite possibilities of development of the human soul, here and hereafter. "It is in spirit the direct opposite of the philosophic maxim regarding the end, of taking care to leave a finished life and a perfect character behind us. . . . A development means the unfolding of a definite nature, the gradual manifestation of a known idea." Browning's conception is of a "perpetual vagrancy." "A series of phases, like the successive leaps of a waterfall, is no development. . . . His notion is simply that the game of life, the exhilaration of action, is inexhaustible." Life is for him an adventure, not a discipline; "The exercise of energy is the absolute good, irrespective of motives or consequences." "For him the crude experience is the only end, the endless struggle the only ideal." This is "frank barbarism," full of "the lust of life, the dogged unwillingness to learn from experience, the contempt for rationality, the carelessness about perfection, the admiration for mere force."

These curious strictures would seem to have emanated from the heart of the eighteenth century rather than from the nineteenth; they are quoted because their dogmatic rationalism throws into relief the nature of Browning's ethical idealism, and its relation to the intellectual advance of his age. The nineteenth century, which admitted development as the law of life, would hardly have admitted it as the manifestation of a known idea, known, at least, to individuals. Back of Browning's study of many individuals, of varying types, in different stages of growth, lies the master-idea of his century, of the "organization and development of all life from lower to higher," following an inner law of growth, whose secret man is only beginning to discover, — a law of the universe, as of individual souls. In the last long speech of Paracelsus the cosmic theory is presented, of the formation of earth's surface, and the development of life thereon, through successive stages, up to man; thereafter Browning, who had, as he tells us, early accepted the ground idea of evolution, busied himself in studying and interpreting the complex inner forces in the growth of human souls, the key to his interpretation of spiritual growth given him, probably, in part by thought wakening in his own time, in part by that early study of Plato of which he speaks in *Pauline*. The world of thought, in science, and in the philosophy of Hegel, was passing, in Browning's day, from static to dynamic conceptions in the interpretation of the universe; he became the subtlest interpreter of the dynamic in the world of spirit. Thus interpreted, life, drawing upon potentialities only partially realized, becomes a progress toward perfection, the final defining of which would be a denial of the very process itself. Mr. Santayana's phrases would suggest that he conceives no possibility of growth beyond his present thought, the limited ideal which can be fully rationalized and stated. To him, perfection is something fully conceived, clearly marked out, attainable; it is enough for the intellect to know; to Browning, perfection is indeed always something for further search; with him the seeker for truth transcends by including the highest ideal that his mind can form at the moment; the challenge of circumstance, of present experience may waken within him insight of which he is unaware:

> Ah, but a man's reach should exceed his grasp.

The alleged "indifference to perfection" in Browning is not indifference, but the conviction within him of the infinite possibilities that lie in every human soul:

> What's come to perfection perishes.

He realizes forces at work in every human life beyond the reach of the present "known idea," posits development in which the present known idea is but a part or factor. None can foresee the end. Mr. Santayana's criticism of Browning for his disregard of the philosophic maxim to leave a finished life and a perfect character behind shows lack of understanding that, in Browning, as in life, character is still in the making; that, in the mysterious order of which we form a part, lie possibilities of individual development beyond the grasp of our present thought, though present thought serves as stimulus and goad. The term "finished life" is not in our present vocabulary, nor is the conception of leaving a perfect character behind us a part of our thought.

In opposition to the rationalistic conception that development is limited to strict adherence to a known idea, Browning recognizes the inner urge of life that runs through all being, involving the whole of the individual and his powers. Development is not a matter of the intellect alone; perhaps no thinker has shown more clearly how close emotion lies to the springs of thought. In his interpretation of human experience the individual is a unit; mind, feeling, will are involved; truth and the ways of gaining it are as many-sided as life itself. Never was an idealism more inwrought with the stuff and substance of human existence, the exercise of all the powers involved in living a single day. In all this rendering of the very life process Mr. Santayana sees only:

"The 'Soul' which he trusted . . . was a restless personal impulse, conscious of obscure depths in itself which it fancied to be infinite, and of a certain vague sympathy with wind and cloud and with universal mutation." . . . "All energies figure without their ultimate purposes." . . . Passions are aimless in their vehemence . . . their own excuse for being.

But Browning was wiser in his generation than Mr. Santayana was in his. The poet's philosophy is in accord with the newest and deepest wisdom that men of thought have wrought out in their interpretation of the stages of human experience; in racial growth feeling wakens before mind, stirs intellect; in the slow development that comes all the powers coöperate; the whole being is involved. The truth of this to the facts of racial and individual experience, none could, I think, now deny. More powers than Mr. Santayana admits are needed in the pursuit of perfection; emotion, imagination, as well as intellect; "the flash of the will that can." Attainment of virtue demands far more than a clear idea of virtue; the human soul, on its upward path, "moveth altogether if it move at all," for aspiration, longing must thrill through all present ideas, all intellectual conceptions of goodness, beauty, and the like, to make them potent. Mr. Santayana refers to ancient thought as standard in these matters, to Plato, but, in scoring Browning as one depending wholly upon emotion, does he forget the part that Eros, love of the beautiful, played in Plato's thought, in drawing the soul toward perfection?

Browning's philosophy is not only a philosophy but a faith, both instinctive and reasoned, made up of thought, feeling, observation, experience, the reaction of the whole of him to the whole of life. They are wrong who say that his work represents mere emotion; Browning was a thinker and a keen observer, living in a period given to close scrutiny of fact, and the poet was of his time, bent on investigating that which is. He watched, studied, thought, delved into his own experience, came to conclusions, and held them with resolute mind and will. Intellect and feeling met and worked in happy fusion in his idealism, and it was through the witness of his entire being that he attained and kept his faith.

Philosophy and religion, Mr. Santayana says, in his affirmation of the finalities of thought, are nothing, if not ultimate; it is their business to deal with general principles and final aims. It is true that Browning's idea of the ultimate goes beyond the present reach of human thought, but did not Plato's? Do those disciples of Socrates in the Platonic dialogues feel that they are fully in possession of known ideas, of justice, temperance, and the like, or are they summoning all their resources to come nearer and nearer truth, nearer and nearer the perfect, never reached? Socrates and the disciples of Socrates were always groping toward the truth, never wholly grasping it and caging it in a final formula. If it were otherwise, why should they discuss these questions with an eagerness in which emotion plays its stimulating part? Was not Plato himself during his whole intellectual life developing, changing, moving on from point to point, so that, from being at first a disciple of Parmenides, believing only in the immutable, he grew to recognize that not only the world of Being, but the world also of Becoming, partook of the nature of reality?[14]

Mr. Santayana has missed the deeper wisdom of his century; he has evidently no idea that the universe has come to be interpreted in terms of life. He ignores the change from a static to a dynamic conception of the world order in the late eighteenth and the early nineteenth centuries, and evidently disdains the prevailing wind of doctrine of his time in both science and the humanities. Like Peter Bell he has

> Set his face
> Against the wind and open sky.

His mind and imagination are obsessed by the idea of the stationary, the limited, as Browning's mind and imagination are obsessed by the idea of the hope lying in perpetual change and growth, which is the great contribution of the nineteenth century to thought. It was largely a Teutonic contribution; if it were not for Bruno, whose idea of development is a half-way house between ancient and modern thought, one might say, perhaps, that the Latin mind is not fitted for it, — the Latin mind, more prone to codify and lay down ultimate laws, to mark out roads that must be followed. It was more fitted to the flexible Greek mind, and it was from the Greek philosophers and the Greek scientists that the first suggestions of evolution came. Mr. Santayana is like Lucretius, in that his only idea of change is of meaningless change; the Latin mind, more set, more defined, lacks the vitality of the Greek, alert always for new intellectual experience, and far more able to interpret a living universe. How much stronger an impress has the live Greek mind left upon succeeding generations through the centuries! It has grown with our growth; in the realm of pure thought it has come with us all the way, still a living and inspiring force.

It would be a pleasing task, had one but the gift, to set forth the difference between the type of thought represented by the critic, and that of the poet whom he is discussing, by a monologue, written in Browning's fashion, presenting a Greek of the late decadence, after sleeping a thousand years or so, waking in a great Gothic cathedral, like that of Chartres or of Amiens. As he sleepily rubbed his eyes, but half awake, it would displease him, partly because of its very greatness. Failing to understand the higher type of aspiration, here represented, than that of the temples dedicated to the gods of Greece, he would dub it barbarous. These lines that soar triumphantly up toward the sky, with their fine symbolism, would be to him an instance of the disdain of perfection; lines should be horizontal, bounded. The windows of stained glass would annoy him, letting in too much light, bringing too great a play of beauty and of color. There would be too much of nature's self in the play of carven leaf and tendril; art should be geometrical, rationalistic, an expression of the formulated conclusions of man, not an imaginative interpretation of living things, and their symbolism for the human soul.

Mr. Santayana fails to find in Browning any idea of law, but it is always there, and is the center and inner core of his conception of the development of human souls. The critic evidently does not realize that Browning is a dramatic poet; that he is presenting a wide variety of characters, embodying his study of the working of human experience; that each phase of experience portrayed is not an "aimless leap of a waterfall" — (does he not know that in the leap of a waterfall there is the working of law, that it is a part of the inevitable journey of inland water out to the sea?) — but the passing of a soul from one stage of development to another, in accordance with a deep underlying law of growth, operative in the whole of humanity's experience, operative in each individual soul.

The law of development none may escape. What the critic means by saying that Browning's characters do not learn by experience is hard to fathom, for Browning's whole thought is of the "trial and error" method of finding out the law of life. Those whom he interprets are presented as passing through a phase of experience that means growth. They are all developing, Cleon, Karshish, the unhappy wife of James Lee, Luria, facing their problems intellectual or emotional; even Caliban, and Bishop Blougram, with their different ways of approaching theology; the speaker in *Fifine*, and the characters in the *Inn Album*, as well as Pompilia, Colombe, and Childe Roland. He touches in the individual the inmost center, reaches the point that is no one else. He is aware that in every human being there is something irreducible to formula. Browning's treatment, vehement, often, stormy, impetuous, from the intensity of the dynamic in him, reveals in multitudinous ways, through multitudinous cases, the law of growth, operating through the varied experiences of human souls. All his poetic life was pursuit, through the fine fibres of thought and feeling of individuals, through ideas, impulses, emotions, acts of will, of the infinite play of the law of life, a law of progression, wherein lies a tendency to perfection. He finds, not that "crude experience is the only end," but that all experience is a movement onward toward great ends, for development is the law of being and of every being; man cannot escape.

In all this, Browning is interpreter, not law-giver. If, as Mr. Santayana says, his "method is to penetrate by sympathy rather than portray by intelligence," the power to understand the processes of growth in many souls of diverse types is no small power. There is such a thing as intelligent sympathy. The affirmation reveals the limitation of the critic rather than that of the poet, and shows that the master-movement of thought in the nineteenth century means little to him, the endeavor to enter into and understand. The wisdom of these later days lies in this: not in laying down laws, but in trying to find them. We have grown away from the seventeenth century passion to dictate, and the measure of our growth is our content with the humbler attempt to comprehend. Codifying laws has given way to the less pretentious and more intelligent effort to study and interpret, — the scientific attitude. We are on the trail of deeper laws than those laid down as final by the dicta of man; if the age has given us nothing else, it has given us this.

II

The force at work in all becoming is, in Browning's thought, love. Love is the fundamental law of being, the power through which growth is made, the deepest factor in the development of the soul. This is the central thesis of the greater part of Browning's work, the burden of his deeper thought. If we may again approach through the critic it is singular that Mr. Santayana, who undertakes to discuss Browning's treatment of love, the most distinctive aspect of the work produced through his long life, from twenty to eighty-nine, should touch only poems presenting love between man and woman, ignoring the large conception through which alone the right interpretation of his treatment of that love can be made. To Browning the word love has a breadth and depth of meaning of which Mr. Santayana is not aware; love between man and woman is only one phase of that which was to him the creative force in all existence, the very well-spring and motive power of human life and achievement in its different aspects. Mr. Santayana fails to recognize the philosophical aspect of Browning's work; to him love is the ultimate reality of all life, the power from which man derives his strength, the secret of development in that passing from lower to higher phases of being which Browning believes to be the law of life in all human souls. The critic disregards the whole wide range and variety of Browning's interpretation of "the passion of love," running through the entire scale of being: love of friend for friend; of artist for his art; of patriot for his country; of the grammarian for truth; of the holy man for holiness; of mother for child; love of man for God and of God for man. In his breadth of interpretation he includes all toward which man reaches out with longing to create, all that which he wishes to attain in his own being. Love was to him God becoming manifest, revealing himself in the concrete of human life. To Hegel, life in all its aspects is the self-realization of God; to Browning, life in all its aspects is the self-realization of God through love.

Already in his first poem, *Pauline*, Browning recognizes the power to love as the central force in human life. The supreme, the inmost failure, of this young-old hero is failure to love: "I can love nothing." The creative force within him has faltered; but, characteristically for Browning, defeat turns to triumph; the power to love and to create comes back to him. Browning, already in his twentieth year, has announced himself, has made manifest the central theme of his life and thought from *Pauline* on to *Asolando*, his first work and his last. It is because *Pauline* was written when the young Browning was finding out that which was to be the controlling idea of his whole life that it is valuable; it has the blindness, the obscurity of the struggle itself, through which he found his truth, but the outcome is unmistakably clear. Love is revealed as the force which gathers all scattered hopes and aspirations into one, and touches them into power. If it is experience that is revealed here, it would seem to be experience beyond a youth of twenty; if theory, too great a conception for the mind of twenty to grasp. Already he is trying to say that the very secret of life itself in all its aspects, temporal and eternal, intellectual, spiritual, artistic no less than in the physical, lies in the power to love.

The same idea, that failure to love is utter failure, is set forth, much more objectively, in *Paracelsus*, two years later. The theme, worked out with genuine dramatic power in some of the scenes in this record of experience, is presented baldly, almost allegorically in Scene II, where the dialogue between Aprile, whose passion is love, and Paracelsus, passionate for knowledge, is but a dialogue between two aspects of man's nature, his heart and his head. Through aspiration, sin, suffering, and failure, Paracelsus in defeat reaches the moment that is victory, when to him, who had despised humanity, comes a realization of his oneness with his fellow men. So Paracelsus, through the long arduous adventure of his life, learns love, greater than love of woman, of friend for friend: love of human kind; the sum and summit of his experience is recognition, as pride, and passion for isolating individual achievement fade, of love as the central principle, the supreme force in human life. Thus Browning early affirms his conviction, here more clearly than in *Pauline*, that love is the very heart of life.

The theme of *Paracelsus* is the basic thought of Robert Browning's life and work. His deepest teaching was to the effect that the spark of love within the human breast is part of the universal love, which is God, and that man by its exercise shares the great creative power ceaselessly at work throughout the universe. Love as manifest in the making of the world had been stressed by poets who preceded him, Brooke, Thomson, and others; man, as conceived by the Deists, was the passive recipient of God's love, gratitude was all that was expected of him. To Browning, man must be able to love, to feel within himself the creative power of loving, or he perishes. Not otherwise shall he know God; hence the depth, the solemnity, the power, of Browning's treatment of love.

That earlier theory of universal love was a conception of an external power, chiefly concerned with the working of the physical universe; to Browning it is a power within. That eighteenth-century idea of God as showing love in the fashioning of a perfect universe for man's pleasure and benefit, — "proud, presumptuous man," who, because of certain evil tendencies was neither wholly within nor without the eternal perfect order, has given way to unified thought. God is in man himself, as well as in and over the outer universe: in his intuitions, his impulses, his affections, in all creative going out of himself, not only working for man, but through him. God has come inside the house of human life, and man with him. Mind has travelled a long way from those earlier to the days of Robert Browning toward a conception of unity in all life, toward the rediscovery of the inner life, toward the idea of inner development.

The Deist theory of universal love was something of a metaphysical abstraction; Browning perceived it as a fact; and he proceeded to show its working in human hearts, human experience, in concrete interpretation of individual lives in action. It would be difficult to enumerate all the ways in which Browning has flashed out the idea of love as the supreme force in human life; of power manifest in the working of the world revealing itself as love; of God, as Power, as Love, working in all the ardors, the affections, the activities of human life; of all life as striving after complete attainment of love, necessitating man's immortality. That idea of process in all life, and constant movement toward higher phases of being, set forth by Paracelsus, is carried on in study of many individuals, and the chief factor in their development is love. Love runs through the whole scale of being, from lowest to highest, the secret power whereby life becomes self-forgetful and divine, God making himself manifest. It appears as instinct, and as a factor in development in animal life, and in the lower phases or stages of human life, as well as in the later. It moves toward God; it is God within. Love is the inmost law of being.

Very beautiful down Browning's long years is the echo of Shelley's "Most vain all hope but love," to which the young poet disciple, already in his earliest work, was to give a deeper meaning than his master knew. Love as the secret of man's development, manifest in his faint aspirings, his inner struggle for truth, in overcoming evil, in quickening the upward tendency in him, that thought of God as love, which was the center of Browning's whole being, Shelley did not know. To Browning, love is the basis of all spiritual development; comparing Shelley's static Paradise at the end of *Prometheus Unbound* with Browning's conception of endless growth and struggle, one wonders whether it was in part from that ending that Browning learned the use of evil in the world. For in Shelley's childish Utopia of perpetual sunshine and flowers and idleness love would have no chance to prove itself. Here Prometheus shrinks, and Asia vanishes.

It behooves the student of Browning to try to grasp something of the breadth of his interpretation of love as working in all genuine human activities wherein man reaches out toward his good, its *modus operandi* in the concrete of human life. In making man in all his creative instincts share the life of God there is something original and deeply significant in Browning. Wordsworth revealed the divine in the human in moral life; Browning in all creative energy also, all artistic, intellectual, and patriotic activities, in which a man is actuated by a passion for what he conceives to be good. Happiest, perhaps, among his interpretations are those of painter and musician.

To Browning, love is the source of the artist's power. In interpreting art and artist, he gets far back of the achievement into the very springs of creative impulse, and finds this motive power to be love. His treatment of painter and of musician is one of the most fortunate expressions of his idea of love as the moving force in that ardor which draws man through creative activity toward his own fulfilment.

Aprile, in *Paracelsus*, states Browning's conviction that the creative power of the artist comes from love of all aspects of human life; love is the root of the passion to reproduce, to interpret every phase of man's experience:

> I would love infinitely, and be loved,
> First: I would carve in stone, or cast in brass
> The forms of earth.
> . . . .
> Every passion sprung from man, conceived by man,
> Would I express and clothe in its right form,
> . . . .
> no thought which ever stirred
> A human breast should be untold.
> Last, having thus revealed all I could love,
> Having received all love bestowed on it,
> I would die.

From ardor of central desire, which derives from the creative passion of God, his artists, musicians, draw their creative force. David, in *Saul*, exemplifies this, and voices in song Browning's idea of creative love. The rising scale of love in the world of being is presented here, typified by music, and the growth through love of man's spirit, whose logic is immortality, is symbolized. Again, in *Abt Vogler*, the creative passion, sprung from love, has within it the secret of growth, the seed of immortality, — love, the source of "the will that can."

In Andrea del Sarto, who has been passively, cravenly, not creatively selfless, the passion side of his love for a woman has choked the nobler aspect of his love for her, and has paralyzed his creative power. He speaks in a waiting pause; he has still his chance.

In *Fra Lippo Lippi* is superbly expressed the stirring of the creative instinct whereby man may lay hold on God. He has, what Aprile had not, knowledge added to love, giving the work of his hands validity; in making manifest that beauty which is truth, reality, "lending his soul out," he gets a soul so. Through exercise of his artist power this sensual man wins a right to a place in the lower corner of paradise in his great picture, in company with those who are gazing upon holy things.

The power to feel creative love for person, for country, for art, for any phase of the beautiful or the good, means insight into the infinite, the eternal, drawing man on beyond his present self. Herein he shares the divine power that is the life of the universe. Mr. Santayana's affirmation that Browning has no idea of the eternal shows that the critic fails to realize that Browning's life-long effort was to reveal the infinite in the finite, the eternal making itself manifest in the experiences of time. In all these varied types of love, friends' love, artists' love, love of truth, mother-love, love between man and woman, the finite touches the infinite.

Mr. Santayana's discussion of Browning's treatment of love between man and woman, the only phase of Browning's interpretation of love recognized by him, leaves the student of Browning bewildered as to the critic's method of reaching his conclusions. In touching this theme, presented by the poet in many different aspects, in more poems than one could readily number, the critic quotes a few brief fragments from but five of the poems, fifty-five lines in all, drawing conclusions so strange, so arbitrary, so remote from the facts that one can but wonder whether he had really read his Browning. With this brief and ill-selected list in mind, he proceeds to interpret Browning as a poet of love.

Love is depicted, he says, with truth, with vehemence, with the conviction that it is the supreme thing in life, though Mr. Santayana does not know why Browning thinks it is the supreme thing in life, unaware that it is impossible to understand the poet's interpretation of this aspect of love without having in mind the great conception which lies back of it. Love, in Browning, he affirms, has always "the quality of passion"; "it never rises into contemplation"; it always has "another person for its object or its cause." Quoting from *In a Balcony*, from *Love among the Ruins*, from *In a Gondola*, he says: "We are not allowed to regard these expressions as the cries of souls blinded by the agony of passion and lust. Browning unmistakably adopts them as expressing his own highest intuitions." "The passion he represents is lava hot from the crater, in no way moulded, smelted, or refined. He had no thought of subjugating impulses into the harmony of reason. . . . Accordingly the love he describes has no wings; it issues in nothing." "The ideal did not exist for him." He contrasts Browning with "the real masters of passion and imagination," who "began with that crude emotion with which Browning ends; they lived it down, they exalted it by thought. . . . The sudden, overwhelming self-surrender in which he rests was for them the starting point of a life of rational worship."

The most puzzling part of this criticism is that the critic does not, apparently, realize that Browning is a dramatic poet. Admiring those poets in whom "love ceased to be a passion and became the energy of contemplation," he goes on to say that emotion should be "transformed into objects agreeable to the intellect, into clear ideas and beautiful things," as this is the natural work of reason. This statement, in its connection here, leaves one wholly at sea; who is to form these concepts of what love should be, Browning, or the people he is interpreting? The mortally wounded lover in *In a Gondola*, not unnaturally asking for a last kiss, had no time left to live down his emotion, or to transform it into clear ideas at the bidding of reason. Browning is, in the greater part of his work, whether he is writing dramas, or lyrics, or dramatic monologues, trying to present phases of experience of different persons, not himself. Mr. Santayana has no more right to say that the outcry of the lover in *In a Gondola* represents Browning's highest intuition than he has to say that Shakespeare had a personal desire to smother Desdemona with a pillow. Each case is discussed by the critic as if it were Browning's personal experience of love, concerning which he had failed to rationalize, instead of an endeavor to present the working of this emotion or passion, affecting many different types in different ways. A critic should attempt to discriminate between those passages in which a dramatic poet speaks for himself, and those in which he makes others speak. A repeated statement of a philosophy of life, supplemented by interpretations of different individuals in the light of that philosophy, may well be taken as a poet's own, especially if first enunciated in youth, as was the case with Browning, before he had learned the secret of dramatic method, and had entered upon his genuinely dramatic work, but to attribute to him every impulse, every emotion of all his characters is wholly unjustifiable. He had his own point of view; so had Sophocles; so had Molière. His basic thought of life is the center from which he interprets the lives of many individuals, a thought of profound law working in endless differentiation. But herein he is not, as the critic says, merely revealing himself, but is interpreting the varied life of humanity in the light of his deepest penetration to its meaning. Man has to see with his own eyes, which is a different thing from seeing only himself.

In protesting against the expression of emotion, of sudden self-surrender to feeling, instead of the expression of rationalized ideals, in Browning's love poetry, it would seem that what Mr. Santayana really objects to is lyric poetry itself, in its most spontaneous form; and dramatic poetry, which attempts to reveal life, not dictate to it. Expression of unrationalized emotion seems to him unworthy of civilized man, yet the great masters of love poetry, whom he admires, would hardly agree with him; they expressed themselves lyrically. Among the chief treasures of our poetry are early, impulsive, unrationalized expressions of love which we could ill forego, and the Elizabethan period is as full of such song as a wood in spring time is full of the notes of birds:

> O fair! O sweet! when I do look on thee,
> In whom all joys so well agree,
> Heart and soul do sing in me.

And again:

> There is a Lady sweet and kind,
> Was never face so pleased my mind;
> I did but see her passing by,
> And yet I love her till I die.

Later poets and their readers have found moments of vivid life and feeling not unworthy of record in enduring verse. Many an impulsive utterance, flashed out under the stress of life, has become part of our lasting heritage in rendering that beauty which is truth to life.

Through freshness and intensity of feeling come Browning's happiest achievements in the matter of form. Form, in his lyrics, seems oftentimes the result of happy accident, instinctive, spontaneous, as natural an expression as a leaf or blossom on a tree. It is perhaps because he is representing the mood or thought of different speakers that he does not use the same lyric form twice if he can help it, but breaks the mould in which it is cast, going on to another, fresh, characteristic, different.

If it is the dramatic element to which Mr. Santayana objects, again he has the world of great literature against him. One Shakespeare has not been found guilty because, instead of expressing a rationalized concept of what love should be, after emotion had been lived down, he pictured it at work, in the case of two youthful lovers, who were glad to die for love without asking whether crude experience was their only end. Dramatic poetry, the result of effort to observe and understand the laws of life as manifested in individual experience, has, and will always have, its own validity, its own excuse for being. Less successful in formal drama than in dramatic monologue and dramatic lyric, Browning has, at his best, that supreme gift of dramatic genius, the power to make the reader feel that he is observing life itself in operation.

In Browning's treatment of love between man and woman, as in his treatment of love of art, or of a cause, love is not something static, attained, but an inner force, sweeping forever out and beyond. Love is dynamic, as God is dynamic power, ceaselessly at work throughout the universe. He presents it in many types, revealing its nature, sometimes in a flash of experience, an awakening leading on to new and unexpected development, sometimes giving extended study, as in the case of Colombe, of Caponsacchi. After setting forth somewhat abstractly in his first two poems the idea that salvation for the human soul comes from the power to love, Browning, in *Pippa Passes*, was far on his way to present in the concrete the growth of individual lives through love. Can the critic who affirms that love in Browning issues in nothing have read even *Pippa Passes*? The poet's deeper theory could be gathered from this one work alone; in the case of Ottima, a high type of love, creative and self sacrificing, grows out of a gross and fleshly passion; Jules, out of self-absorbed selfishness, wakens to creative love. Of the many instances that could be cited of the great issues of love as interpreted by Browning, none is more appealing than that of Caponsacchi, whom love, in all its tragedy, transforms from an unawakened worldling into a potential saint.

"He was a lover of experience; the ideal did not exist for him," says Mr. Santayana of Browning. I do not like the antithesis; of what use the ideal unless the two blend? Love, in Browning, is basically spiritual; the ultimate issues, through all the tangles of perplexity, fruition, or disappointment, are of the spirit. The ideal human love is that in which both lovers, using their chance together, find the key to the infinite, as in the case of Festus and Michal, Pompilia and Caponsacchi, the two in *By the Fireside*, who touch the eternal through the common things of daily life. *Two in the Campagna* expresses yearning for the perfect accord, missing the infinite reach of love moving through entire understanding to great fulfilment. But the poems in which love fails of its full harmony, and of this further mutual insight, as *James Lee's Wife*, *Two in the Campagna*, are equally suggestive of Browning's faith in the divine potentialities of love, are poems of the quest, only the quest is long. The note of the quest is sounded in many others, as *A Woman's Last Word*, *Love in a Life*, *Life in a Love*. One of the most significant aspects of Browning's treatment of love is that of the lover using his chance in disappointment, alone: *Evelyn Hope; Cristina; The Last Ride Together; One Way of Love; The Worst of It; Too Late*. In these, as in others, love which has no earthly fulfilment is judged a most precious experience, an experience that was not loss, for the power it has evoked in the lover sets the creative astir in him. There are those who seem to miss their chance, the Duke, in *My Last Duchess;* the Bishop, who orders his tomb; Guido, in *The Ring and the Book*, who had loved himself only. Their future growth is left in question.

The strangest aspect of Mr. Santayana's discussion is that he failed to take into account Browning's personal love poems. It is incomprehensible that he should attempt to estimate Browning as a poet of love without even mentioning those of his poems wherein he speaks most deeply, out of his own experience. There is no mention of *One Word More*; of the last lines of the prologue to *The Ring and the Book;* of *By the Fireside*, which we claim as a personal expression because of its affirmation of an ideal often enunciated by Browning. How is it possible to present a poet's interpretation of love without the poems in which he reveals not only his conception of love but his experience? The great lyrists of love whom the critic admires and holds up for contrast have written of their own experience; why should he ignore this in Browning? Can this rationalist rationally affirm that *One Word More* represents mere passion in the physical sense; that "the ideal did not exist for him"; that the love he describes "has no wings," "issues in nothing"; that we have here "passion that is hot lava from the crater"; "in no way refined"? How great a part intellect and spiritual aspiration played in Browning's experience of love is revealed here, as it is revealed in his letters. How profound, how intellectual is his grasp of the ideal! All the idealistic and creative endeavor of the two lives is folded here, at one with the great aspiration and great achievements of great artists.

In Browning's life as in his thought, expressed in many poems, dramatic and personal, love is not only an emotion, a passion, but a philosophy, as intellectual as it is emotional; and an ethic, a way of life. The love story of Robert and Elizabeth Barrett Browning is not the mere romantic tale of passion that many people suppose. Much of disinterested creative power must have gone into that "recalling to life" of the sick woman; there were many disagreeable small duties to face. The poet who, in his youth discovered that inability to love is failure, set himself to the high task of loving, in deed as in feeling; "the will as vision" is apparent here; the ideal was sought through all their life together. *By the Fireside* reveals early rapture leading to spiritual insight; the end of the prologue to *The Ring and the Book*, the soul of Elizabeth Barrett Browning leading his soul heavenward. "O winged love!"

There are two, and I think only two, poems in Browning in

which human experience is rendered as if beyond the restlessness of change, the exigencies of growth. The experience of two persons is given, one, himself, the other, the beloved disciple. In *One Word More* and in *A Death in the Desert* is inner quietude; both, in their different ways, reach through to the eternal; both reveal Browning's idea of the relation of human love to the divine. In *One Word More*, instead of transition, the swift passing from one state to another, the speaker has come to rest in something found. It would seem that the power whose working he has followed in so many groping human lives, the pursuit through fulfilment, sorrow, disappointment, hope, had been revealed to him in his own life in fuller measure, nearer perfectness. "He never rises to contemplation," Mr. Santayana says; here is quiet contemplation of the great experience, and the part that it had played in the creative life, not only of himself but of great artists and poets gone before, as if through the cumulative experience some further certainty had been gained of the presence of the divine in human love.

In *A Death in the Desert* is expressed quietness of spirit, resting in an ultimate assurance; the beloved disciple has found his way to "central peace." One can but think that the faith which Browning had held so firmly, had pursued so undauntedly in his study of many human lives, tracing in diverse experiences the power of the divine in which he had had courage to believe in spite of much evidence to the contrary, had brought reward in further insight into the soul of the beloved disciple, and through this into the perfect love, which is God.

Both are poems of fulfilment, but not of ending. In the one, love of the soul of a woman, in the other, love of Christ known in daily life, have brought eternity into the moment, the infinite into the finite.

The Pope in *The Ring and the Book* becomes Browning's spokesman for the highest ideal conception of this power which he felt working at the heart of the universe, which he divines in beast and bird, which is manifest in all the experience of human life, and is the essence of all spiritual and ethical ideals, becoming, at its highest, love creative and self-sacrificing:

> How can man love but what he yearns to help?

And the Pope may serve, perhaps, as the best commentary on Santayana's condemnation of Browning for his disregard, in his interpretation of life, of the philosophic maxim to leave a finished life and a perfect character behind; also, for the statement that development is necessarily the manifestation of a known idea. The Pope, in extreme age, confronted by a crisis that wakens undiscovered power within him, is still learning, entering upon fresh experience, gaining further insight, beyond the reach of his earlier "known ideas." That insight is deeper insight into the meaning of love in all life; the meaning of Christianity; the meaning of the divine. Whether or not his thought would have been possible in the century in which he lived, — and who can say as to this? — his survey of the world order, his interpretation of the creative power of love throughout the universe, of the relation of the human, yes, even of animal affection to the divine, gives pause for thought:

> I saw that there are first, and above all,
> The hidden forces, blind necessities,
> Named Nature, but the thing's self unconceived.

He finds there power at work mysteriously leading up to man, through whose slowly developing moral sense

> The forces and necessity grow God.

His newly-wakened paternal tenderness for Pompilia, his insight into the mother-love in her, helps him understand the great function of love throughout all life, as he had never understood it before; he finds that "Love is the fulfilling of the law" of all life:

But, brave,
Thou at first prompting of what I call God
And fools call Nature, did'st hear, comprehend,
Accept the obligation laid on thee,
Mother elect, to save the unborn child,
As brute and bird do, reptile and the fly,
Ay and, I nothing doubt, even tree, shrub, plant
And flower o' the field, all in a common pact
To worthily defend the trust of trusts,
Life from the Ever Living.

What place in Mr. Santayana's "known idea" can be found for event that brings the surprise and growth of new experience, both intellectual and emotional, as here fresh life and insight come to the Pope in age? Browning's own thought, his vital idealism, becomes evident from the way in which he has his characters face and learn from experience. The Pope at this crisis finds in Christianity a profounder meaning than he had hitherto divined. Christianity appealed to Robert Browning, and also, perhaps anachronistically, to his Pope, not from historical evidence alone, but because he saw that it was an answer to the deepest need of life, the fullest revelation of what he felt was the fundamental fact in all life. Far from failing "to achieve a recognition even of the traditional ideal . . . of religion," as his critic alleges, he has not only perceived this ideal but has added a valuable word of interpretation. The Pope, scrutinizing the outer order of nature with reference to the needs and the possibilities of the inner nature of man, completes the philosophy of growth set forth by Browning in the final speech of Paracelsus, carrying further the interpretation of the developing spiritual in human life. The charge of barbarous irrationality brought against the poet might well be refuted by the power of thought brought to bear upon the Pope, in making him interpreter of Christianity, the supreme expression of a love which he felt working at the heart of the universe; this tale, "of love without a limit," in which he finds, if not the fulfilment, the promise, the hope of fulfilment, of the beauty and harmony of the universe, the "perfection fit for God."

Evil, in the Pope's interpretation, is "a power giving love a chance to prove itself"; sin and sorrow help evolve the moral qualities of man:

> To make him love in turn and be beloved,
> Creative and self-sacrificing too,
> And thus eventually God-like.

This is in accord with many utterances of Browning throughout his life concerning evil, and many interpretations of its working finally toward the good. Its ultimate nature he does not know, but its service in increasing the strength and vitality of the good through struggle he does know. He recognized the existence of evil, but did not recognize it as alive, as real. It is precisely because love is a life, an activity, a positive force that evil, which is a negative thing, will not prevail. The good, drawing its power from love, has within it the reality of life, energy, primal force. There is for him a centralizing power in love, drawing the whole nature to one central potency, life, strong to prevail over the scattered temporary forces, obstacles, that come to be known as evil.

In this conception of the sweep of love throughout the universe, culminating in the Christian ideal, is a profoundly felt interpretation of God, a profoundly felt interpretation of love, working through the whole scale of being. Love was to Browning God becoming manifest, revealing himself in the concrete of human life. As the microcosm of the mind reflects the macrocosm, God and the mind of man, in the words of the Pope, meeting in truth, so God and the soul of man meet in love. Though Browning is one of the world's great interpreters of the personal experience of love between man and woman, as holding within it a key to the divine, the highest type is surely that exemplified by the Pope, a great compassion, the nearest approach in human experience to the love of God for man:

How can man love but what he yearns to help?

Browning's "vague religion," says Mr. Santayana, "has far more affinity to the worship of Thor or of Odin than to the religion of the Cross."

Whence this philosophy of spiritual evolution, of illimitable growth through the power of love came to Browning no one can say. Deeply original as he is, and close as his theory of life lies to the heart of his own experience, he doubtless owes much to the creative touch of earlier thought upon his ardent mind. The idea of spiritual evolution, with its infinite reach, has a long tradition. Already in Plato we find the conception of the development of individual souls toward the perfect through Eros, or love, drawing toward the beautiful, the good, the true. From the time that Plotinus, the first psychologist spoke, the conception of human souls as part of the enfolding soul, emanating from the divine, has never wholly departed from the mind of man, and the idea of the return activity of the individual soul in mystical longing for utter union with the divine from which it sprang has been vastly influential in later thought of progress through the desire of the soul Godward. None, perhaps, could give a full history of the growth of the idea through the centuries, appearing in gleam, intuition here and there, but quotation or brief statement in regard to some who have contributed to it may give suggestion of its growing power.

Browning's theory has the sanction of those idealisms, pagan or Christian, that deal with the fall or with the ascent of the soul of man: Plato, Plotinus, Boehme all suggest fall from the divine, a groping back, up toward it through longing for the perfect. In Boehme the One, or God, who is pure power and love, expresses himself in the many, whose will and desire turn in earthly experience toward their source. Bruno gives significant utterance:

"The first step in the desire for the infinitely beautiful is but the beginning of an endless series; the heart goes out on an endless quest, while the intellect can but follow. The will cannot be satisfied with a finite good, but, if there is other good beyond, desires and seeks it."

Probably the earliest influence upon Browning was the deepest; the certainty of knowledge of the beloved disciple that "God is love" blended with the teaching, given in his childhood, that in the beginning God created the heaven and the earth, and said "Let there be light in the firmament of Heaven." From Dante, with his idea of love as a cosmic force, moving "the sun and other stars" may have come suggestion which set early astir in Browning's mind the idea of Love as the central power in the universe. His predecessors, the Deist poets, had been fond of stressing the idea of Love shown in the creating and the shaping of the world. There was ample material to draw upon in his father's library and elsewhere, and Browning had always an eager, burrowing mind. From how many sources, besides his own powerful intellect and imagination, Browning's thought drew its rich content we can only conjecture; the influence of past thinkers is hard to trace in him, for he has so much original, creative energy that he transmutes, transforms outer influence; to whatever he received he imparted his own peculiar individuality. But it is evident that far-reaching thought of past ages, including that of the deep diviner of the ancient world, Plato, and the profoundest utterances of the Christian gospels are, in his thought, fused, and brought face to face with modern knowledge regarding the universe, and modern method of approach. In him the energy of modern thought gives force and validity to the aspiration of the mystic; belonging to a later age, he knows man more a part of the physical forces of the earth than did his idealist predecessors though not less a part of the divine spirit immanent therein. Experience and observation taught him more than did poet and philosopher. Child of the past and of the present, he has forged ahead, giving the kind of authentic interpretation of life that can come only through individual imaginative insight, and experience, trying it out. Love was his working hypothesis; in his own life and in his interpretation of the lives of others he tried it and found it good. Love was to him the creative force in all life not only in the physical but in the spiritual world, moving in every creature, impelling upward, or downward in order to go upward. It is the power by which the individual, through attainment, failure, sin, great achievement, moves toward perfectness. The truth which he discovered in his youthful days when he was writing *Pauline* and *Paracelsus* he carried with him to the end, trying through a lifetime to express it in his interpretation of the lives of many individuals:

> For life, with all it yields of joy and woe
> And hope and fear. . . .
> Is just our chance o' the prize of learning love.

NOTES

NOTES

1 (*23*). See Kuno Francke's *History of German Literature*, pp. 318–328.

2 (*34*). For interesting discussion of influences touching Shaftesbury's thought, see L. Stephen's *History of English Thought in the Eighteenth Century*, and J. M. Robertson's *Introduction* to his edition of *Characteristics*.

3 (*41*). "Shaftesbury, in his reaction to the prevailing utilitarianism, went back . . . to Plotinus, for his mystic principle of formation, according to which a work of art develops in obedience to the rhythm of its peculiar form." L. A. Willoughby: *The Romantic Movement in Germany*, pp. 157–158.

"The ancient conception of life, in accordance with which morality coincides with the undisturbed unfolding of man's true and natural essence . . . became the living basis of his thought. . . . Morality consists for him, not in the control of general maxims, . . . but in the rich and *full living out of an entire individuality*." Windelband: *History of Philosophy*, p. 508.

4 (*50*). From *The Evolution of the Bird*, by D. M. S. Watson, in *Creation by Evolution*, ed. by F. Mason.

5 (*63*). *Studies in Philology*. Vol. XIV. July, 1917.

6 (*114*). This study of Herder is based on his *Philosophy of History*, and those early works in which the central idea of his life-long thought is most vividly presented. There is no attempt to cope with the vast volume of his theological and other writings. My work has been done partly in German, partly in English translations. I have often preferred to quote a good translation already made rather than to make a new one.

7 and 8 (*129*). See *Die Idee der Entwicklung bei Herder*, by F. M. Bruntsch.

9 (*224*). *The Poems of John Keats*, by E. de Selincourt, p. 428. Notes.

10 (*286*) and 11 (*294*). Quoted from Berdoe's *Browning Cyclopaedia*.

12 (*296*). *Die Idee der Entwicklung bei Herder*.

13 (*296*). *The Life of Robert Browning*, by Griffin and Minchin, p. 295.

14 (*328*). *The Theory of Imagination in Classical and Mediaeval Thought*, by M. W. Bundy.

BIBLIOGRAPHY

BIBLIOGRAPHY

I

Histories of Philosophy

A course in philosophy with Josiah Royce, centering in study of Kant's Critique of Pure Reason.

Fraser, Sir James George. The Golden Bough. New York. Macmillan. 1923.

Mason, Frances, ed. Creation by Evolution. New York. Macmillan. 1928.

Mitchell, P. C. Evolution. Encyclopaedia Britannica. 11th edition.

Osborn, Henry Fairfield. From the Greeks to Darwin. New York. Scribner. 1929.

Royce, Josiah. The Spirit of Modern Philosophy. Boston. Houghton, Mifflin. 1892.

Schwegler, Albert. A Handbook of the History of Philosophy, trans. by J. H. Stirling. Edinburgh. 1867.

Stephen, Leslie. A History of English Thought in the Eighteenth Century. London. Smith Elder. 1876.

Thilly, Frank. A History of Philosophy. New York. Holt. 1914.

Whittaker, Thomas. The Neo-Platonists. Cambridge Univ. Press. 1928.

Windelband, W. A History of Philosophy, trans. by James H. Tufts. New York. 1931.

II

Histories of Literature

Francke, Kuno. A History of German Literature as Determined by Social Forces. New York. Holt. 1901.

Herford, C. H. The Age of Wordsworth. London. Bell. 1909.

Hillebrand, Karl. Six Lectures on the History of German Thought. London. Longmans Green. 1880.

Moore, C. A. The Return to Nature in English Poetry of the Eighteenth Century. Studies in Philology. Vol. xiv, No. 3, July, 1917.

Scherer, W. A History of German Literature, trans. by Mrs. F. C. Conybeare. Oxford. Clarendon Press. 1886.

Willoughby, L. A. The Romantic Movement in Germany. Oxford University Press. 1930.

III

Individual Authors

Akenside, Mark. The Pleasures of Imagination. A poem in three books. 1744. In Select Works of the British Poets, ed. by Dr. Aiken. Philadelphia. 1841.

Berdoe, Edward. The Browning Cyclopaedia. New York. Macmillan. 1891.

Brooke, Henry. Universal Beauty. Printed in Works of the English Poets from Chaucer to Cowper, ed. by Alexander Chalmers. London. 1810.

Browning, Robert. The Poetic and Dramatic Works in six volumes. Boston. Houghton Mifflin. 1888.

Bruntsch, Friedrich Max. Die Idee der Entwicklung bei Herder. Dissertation. Leipzig. 1904.

Bundy, M. W. The Theory of the Imagination in Classical and Mediaeval Thought. Univ. of Illinois Studies in Language and Literature. May, August, 1927.

Carlyle, Thomas. History of Frederick the Great. (n. d.)
Critical and Miscellaneous Essays. Boston. Aldine. (n. d.)

Colvin, Sidney. John Keats. New York. Scribner. 1917.

Cooke, G. W. A Guide Book to the Poetic and Dramatic Works of Robert Browning. Boston. Houghton Mifflin. 1891.

Goethe, J. Wolfgang von. Dichtung und Wahrheit, trans. by John Oxenford. Boston. Aldine. 1910.

Herder, Johann Gottfried. Sämmtliche Werke. Berlin. 1877.
Fragmente über die neuere deutsche Literatur.
Treatise upon the Origin of Language, trans. by L. G. von Herder. London. 1827.
Von deutscher Art und Kunst.
The Spirit of Hebrew Poetry, trans. by James Marsh. 1833.
Volkslieder.
Ideen zur Philosophie der Geschichte der Menschheit.
Outlines of a Philosophy of the History of Man, trans. by T. Churchill. London. J. Johnson. 1800.

Griffin, W. H. and Minchin, H. C. The Life of Robert Browning. New York. Macmillan. 1910.

Inge, Wm. Ralph. The Philosophy of Plotinus. London. Longmans. 1918.

Jones, H. Browning as a Philosophical and Religious Teacher. Glasgow. Maclehose. 1912.

Keats, John. The Poetical Works, ed. by H. B. Forman. Oxford University Press. London. 1910.

The Poems of John Keats, ed. by E. de Sélincourt. London. Methuen. 1926.

Letters, ed. by S. Colvin. London. Macmillan. 1928.

LESSING, G. E. Dramatic Notes (Hamburgische Dramaturgie) in Selected Prose Work of G. E. Lessing, trans. by E. C. Beasley and H. Zimmern. London. Bohn. 1889.

LOWELL, J. R. Lessing. Vol. II. Literary Essays. Boston. Houghton Mifflin. 1910.

MCINTYRE, J. L. Giordano Bruno. London. Macmillan. 1903.

NEVINSON, HENRY. A Sketch of Herder and his Times. London. Chapman and Hall. 1884. Used freely.

OWEN, MRS. F. M. John Keats: a Study. London. Kegan Paul. 1880.

PLATO. The Dialogues, trans. by B. Jowett. Timaeus. Phaedrus. Symposium. New York. Scribner. 1902.

PLOTINUS. Works, trans. from the Greek by Stephen Mackenna. London. Medici Press. 1917–1930.

Select Works of Plotinus. Thomas Taylor's Translation, ed. by G. R. S. Mead. London. Bell. 1914.

POPE, A. The Poetical Works, ed. by A. W. Ward. New York. Crowell. 1896.

ROBINSON, H. CRABB. Diary. Boston. Fields, Osgood. 1870.

SANTAYANA, G. Interpretations of Poetry and Religion. New York. Scribner. 1911.

SHAFTESBURY, ANTHONY ASHLEY COOPER, EARL OF. Characteristics, ed. by J. M. Robertson. London. Grant Richards. 1900.

SPINOZA, BENEDICT. Short Trestise on God, Man, and his Well Being, trans. and ed. by A. Wolff. Black. 1910.

THOMSON, JAMES. The Seasons, ed. with life of author by Patrick Murdoch. New York. Harper. 1842.

THORPE, C. D. The Mind of John Keats. Oxford Univ. Press. New York. 1926.

WORDSWORTH, W. The Poetical Works. Oxford Univ. Press. London. 1910.

The Prelude, ed. from the Mss. by E. de Sélincourt. Oxford. Clarendon Press. 1926.

Prefaces, ed. by A. J. George. Boston. Heath. 1892.

YOUNG, EDWARD. Night Thoughts on Life, Death, and Immortality, ed. by J. R. Boyd. Barnes. New York and Chicago. (n. d.)

Conjectures on Original Composition, in English Critical Essays, ed. by G. D. Jones. Oxford Univ. Press. 1922–24.

NOTE. — This bibliography gives only those authorities from whom statement of fact, direct quotation, or expression of opinion has been taken, not the wide range of reading necessary for background work in the courses mentioned in the foreword.

INDEX

INDEX